To my children, my grandchildren, and our future generations—
This book is dedicated to you.

May the stories of grace in our rich history reveal
the indescribable love God has for you!

And may His goodness and mercy pursue
you all the days of your life.

*"We will tell the next generation the praiseworthy deeds
of the LORD, His power, and the wonders He has done...
He commanded our ancestors to teach their children,
so the next generation would know them, even the children
yet to be born, and they in turn would tell their children.
Then they would put their trust in God and would not
forget His deeds but would keep His commands."*
~Psalm 78:4-7 (NIV)

In Loving Memory of
Summer Sunshine,
whose smile lit up the room,
whose laughter brought so much joy, and
whose life blessed everyone who knew her.

Summer Elisabeth Beddingfield McCall
November 1, 1980 - January 3, 2025

"Absent from the body...present with the Lord."
~2 Corinthians 5:8 (KJV)

"In Your presence there is FULLNESS OF JOY..."
~Psalm 16:11 (ESV)

Table of Contents

Introduction 11
Prologue 15

Part One - Looking Back
Seeing God's Grace in My Heritage 21

- *One* - **The Preacher's Family** 25
- *Two* - **Humble Beginnings** 33
- *Three* - **The Sweet Early Years** 49

Part Two - Looking Around
Seeing God's Grace in Our Home 63

- *Four* - **A Preacher and a Prodigal** 67
- *Five* - **Transitions** 79
- *Six* - **Living in the Mountains** 91
- *Seven* - **The End of the Road** 107

Part Three - Looking Up
Seeing God's Grace in the Highlands 115

- *Eight* - **Rolling into the 80's** 119
- *Nine* - **Off to College** 129
- *Ten* - **Wife and Mommy** 139

Part Four - Looking Through
Seeing God's Grace in the Heartaches 147

    Eleven - **The Unraveling** 151
    Twelve - **From Bad to Worse** 161
    Thirteen - **Layer Upon Layer** 169
    Fourteen - **Though I Walk Through the Valley** 177
    Fifteen - **A Different Kind of Death** 187
    Sixteen - **Let's Do This!** 203

Part Five - Looking Ahead
Seeing God's Grace in Our Healing 217

    Seventeen - **Let the Healing Begin** 221
    Eighteen - **Unexpected Gifts** 231
    Nineteen - **Beauty from Ashes** 237
    Twenty - **The Birth of a Ministry** 245
    Twenty-One - **Tsunami of 2016** 251
    Twenty-Two - **Sawubona** 259
    Twenty-Three - **When Cancer Brings Healing** 267
    Twenty-Four - **Layers of Healing** 275
    Twenty-Five - **Last, but Definitely Not Least** 295

Epilogue 317
Acknowledgements 321
Notes 325
About the Author 329

Everywhere I look

Seeing God's grace in your story

Charity Margaret Rice

Everywhere I Look —Copyright ©2025 by Charity Margaret Rice
Published by UNITED HOUSE Publishing

All rights reserved. No portion of this book may be reproduced or shared in any form—electronic, printed, photocopied, recording, or by any information storage and retrieval system, without prior written permission from the publisher. The use of short quotations is permitted.

Scripture quotations marked (KJV) are from The Authorized (King James) Version. Rights in the Authorized Version in the United Kingdom are vested in the Crown. Reproduced by permission of the Crown's patentee, Cambridge University Press.

Scripture quotations marked (ESV) are from the ESV® Bible (The Holy Bible, English Standard Version®), © 2001 by Crossway, a publishing ministry of Good News Publishers. ESV Text Edition: 2025. The ESV text may not be quoted in any publication made available to the public by a Creative Commons license. The ESV may not be translated in whole or in part into any other language. Used by permission. All rights reserved.

Scripture quotations marked (NLT) are taken from the Holy Bible, New Living Translation, copyright ©1996, 2004, 2015 by Tyndale House Foundation. Used by permission of Tyndale House Publishers, Carol Stream, Illinois 60188. All rights reserved.

Scripture quotations marked (NASB) are taken from the (NASB®) New American Standard Bible®, Copyright © 1960, 1971, 1977, 1995, 2020 by The Lockman Foundation. Used by permission. All rights reserved. lockman.org.

Scripture quotations marked (NIV) are taken from the Holy Bible, New International Version®, NIV®. Copyright © 1973, 1978, 1984, 2011 by Biblica, Inc.™ Used by permission of Zondervan. All rights reserved worldwide. www.zondervan.com The "NIV" and "New International Version" are trademarks registered in the United States Patent and Trademark Office by Biblica, Inc.™

Scripture quotations marked (MSG) are taken from The Message, copyright © 1993, 2002, 2018 by Eugene H. Peterson. Used by permission of NavPress. All rights reserved. Represented by Tyndale House Publishers.

ISBN: 978-1-952840-82-1

UNITED HOUSE Publishing
Waterford, Michigan
info@unitedhousepublishing.com
www.unitedhousepublishing.com

Cover and Author Photography:
Savannah Marie Photography, savannahmariephotography.com

Interior Layout and Design:
Matt Russell, In The Light Creative, matt@inthelightcreative.com

Printed in the United States of America
2025—First Edition

SPECIAL SALES
Most UNITED HOUSE books are available at special quantity discounts when purchased in bulk by corporations, organizations, and special-interest groups. For information, please e-mail orders@unitedhousepublishing.com

Introduction

"My ears had heard of You, but now my eyes have seen You."
Job 42:5 (NIV)

"Why on earth can't I ever SEE these things?" These were pretty much my exact words, every time I strained to see a stereogram. Do you know what that is? That's the fancy name for those pictures with hidden images. You know, those 3D images hidden within a million little 2D images? In order to view the 3D image, you have to stare at the picture until it starts to take shape. I literally tried to see the hidden images in stereograms for years before I was able to do it. And honestly, the first time an image came into view it was so mind-blowing it almost scared me. It was just freaky . . . and kind of other-worldly.

Learning to 'see' God has been a similar journey for me. At times, when I was straining to see Him, I couldn't. At other times He was the last One on my mind, and I was actually sort of covering my eyes and doing my best NOT to see Him. But somewhere along the way, He began to come into focus. The experience has been similar to discovering that hidden image and equally mind-blowing, and yes, sometimes a little freaky. Over the course of my life, I've had a gradual awakening to the 3D image of God, even as I was staring at the little 2D images. Because what I could see very clearly, the entire time, were the people around me, specifically my family. Their lives were like the 2D images of a stereogram which are easy to see. And God used their lives and their stories to reveal a 3D image of Himself to me.

Throughout my life, I've been surrounded by family and friends who loved God deeply. I felt the warmth of His love through theirs, and it planted seeds of desire in my heart to know Him. Some of my loved ones struggled like I did in their journey to know Him. Through their struggles, a gracious God was drawing them, pursuing them, refusing to give up on them. I was watching all of this carefully . . . and what I didn't know then, is that God was revealing His grace to me through their lives— those who knew Him deeply, and those He was still pursuing.

As we go through this journey together, you will see the 2D images of people who surrounded me, and a few 2D images of my own making. (Remember these are the ones which are EASY to see.) But my biggest desire is for you to see the 3D image (the one less easily recognized) of God's grace.

Everywhere I look I can trace this grace to the hand and heart of God. When God's love for me came clearly into focus, I realized it wasn't just for everyone else. It was for ME! I'm praying these stories will help you see Him too, and that you will have an equally mind-blowing revelation of His grace.

Building Bridges

Throughout this book, I am hoping and praying that together we can "build bridges" from my life to yours. I'm borrowing this concept from the Feuerstein Institute's program which I use in my work with students and adults (I'll explain more about this later). Simply put, a bridge is a connection between two things, a link which leads from one point to another. I want you to make connections as you read, from my experiences to your own, and see how my story relates to yours. So I'll pause occasionally to give you time to build those bridges.

Ask the Spirit of God to reveal to you the areas where He has been at work in your life, surrounding you with the same beautiful grace I'm describing. And take a minute to thank Him for what He's been up to. I promise you, my experience is not unique. I'm just putting mine down on paper, but yours is equally amazing.

The same God who has pursued me all the days of my life, is pursuing you as well. Ask Him to give you eyes to see, and He will be faithful to do it!

Prologue

*"Dear Little Charity,
Surely goodness and mercy shall follow you
all the days of your life . . . "
~Aunt Charity
August 1967*

Childhood home

Memories flood my mind as I sit here in front of my childhood home in Travelers Rest, South Carolina. My life has come full circle, and now I only live five minutes from this beautiful old house. I love to come here, where I am instantly transported back in time. It's surreal, and strangely therapeutic.

No one lives here now. So I like to walk around, peek in windows, and visualize where everything used to be. I walk up onto the big covered front porch, and I can peer through the windows into the front bedroom where my brother, Charley, gave his life to God. I walk slowly over to the other side of the porch and look into the front window and see the spot where our piano was nestled against the wall on the left. It's where I used to sit, practicing my lessons and dreaming of one day being a missionary in the African jungles. I wanted to play the piano for the little kids and teach them songs about Jesus, but I wasn't sure how I'd get my piano to Africa. Across from the piano was our couch, and at one end of it sat the big container my grandpa had built for my brothers' pet boa constrictors. One time the biggest one escaped, and we searched everywhere for it. My brother, Rusty, finally discovered it, up inside the coils of the couch! That crazy snake was wrapped so tightly around the coils we couldn't get it out. So it stayed there for a couple weeks until it grew hungry enough to come out. Meanwhile, when people came to our house, my parents would remind my little six year old self to keep my mouth shut, because people might freak out if they knew a snake was inside the couch they were sitting on.

Through the doorway into the dining room I can see the far wall where Mom's oak buffet stood. It used to be her mother's, and one time when my grandma was suffering from Alzheimer's, she stood by the buffet crying, because she thought my mom had stolen it from her. I can still see my grandpa and my mom standing there beside her, trying to calm her down and remind her of how she had given it to us.

I walk around to the back, and look out over the four acres of lush, green pasture surrounding the house. The driveway winds around to the back of the house where our horse, Sparky, got spooked once while my sister was riding him. He bucked and threw her off backwards. She hit her head hard, and we were afraid she'd have a concussion, but thankfully, she just had a big bump and a new hatred for that stupid horse. On the other side of the driveway is the area where we came home one day from school to find the ground blanketed with feathers and spotted with a couple of duck bills and feet. Probably wasn't a good idea to have pet ducks when you also have two German shepherds! Out there in the pasture, I can see my grandpa leading me around on my little pony. Her name was Lynny. Not Lenny, but Lynny. No idea where I came up with that one. As he led us around, I was trying to be brave, but it felt scary, especially since our big horse had thrown my sister. My sweet grandpa patiently reassured me and helped me have courage. He was such a good grandpa.

The sidewalk in front of this house runs all the way down the street to the area where a trailer park used to be. There's an apartment complex there now, and it made me sad when they built it over that spot, abruptly erasing part of my history. My grandma and grandpa's trailer was in that trailer park, and I loved to ride my bike down there to see them. If you keep following this road out to downtown Travelers Rest, you can see Brown's Feed and Seed on the right where I used to go with my grandpa to get the food for all of our animals, and sometimes we'd bring some fuzzy baby chicks home with us.

I walk over and peek inside the metal barn which is still standing behind the house. It's really more like a big garage, but we considered it a barn. Under the huge, gorgeous oak tree in the backyard, I used to sit with my orange record player and play my 45 speed vinyls, singing along with John Denver's "Sunshine On My Shoulders" and Karen Carpenter's "Top of the World."

It's been fifty years since we moved into this house, but I can close my eyes and be a little girl again, with all the hopes and dreams and burning curiosity about how my life would turn out. Would I get married? Would I have kids? Would I ever be able to sing like Karen Carpenter? Would I ever get to be a missionary?

What I really wish I could do is go over and sit down with that little innocent girl and tell her a thing or two. Maybe warn her about some rough spots. Maybe tell her she has a big tangled up mixture of good and bad ahead of her. I'd be sure to tell her to keep the faith that's already starting to grow in her heart, because it will be what carries her through all the good and the bad, the happy and the horrible.

And I would also tell her to pay attention and keep her eyes wide open, because the goodness and grace of God will surround her on every side, every step of the way. It will follow her all the days of her life, just like the verse says, which her Great-Aunt Charity prophetically wrote inside the little, engraved Bible that was given to her at birth.

It may be a while before her vision is clear enough to see the grace, but eventually it will be everywhere she looks.

Building Bridges

What about you? Can you relate to these thoughts and memories? Is there a place where you could go that carries a precious piece of your past? Imagine those days from back then and see yourself there.

What would you tell your younger self? Would you have any tips for the journey ahead? If you're like me, perhaps God wasn't always obvious to you, but when you peel back the curtains and remember the stories of your life, you just might see Him everywhere you look too.

Part One

Looking Back

Seeing God's Grace in My Heritage

"I will remember the deeds of the LORD; yes, I will remember your miracles of long ago. I will consider all your works and meditate on all Your mighty deeds."
~Psalm 77:11-12 (NIV)

"You have given me the heritage of those who fear Your Name."
~Psalm 61:5 (ESV)

What in the world was going on? He stood, gripping the pew in front of him so hard his knuckles were turning white. His heart was pounding, and he knew something crazy was happening inside of him. Why did he feel such a strong reaction to what the speaker was saying? What did this even mean?

He didn't come here with any intention of actually listening to, much less acting on, what this man was saying. He wished he'd never made the stupid promise in the first place. His friend wouldn't leave him alone about coming to church, so he finally agreed, just to get her off his back. When the day finally arrived, he debated about whether he'd actually keep the promise.

But he was a man of his word. So he had to do it. He wouldn't be able to live with himself if he made up some excuse and skipped out. He knew she'd just keep bugging him. Might as well get it over with. It was a Sunday night so he'd have to face her tomorrow morning if he didn't keep his word, and he knew what she would say. So he went. And he hoped it would be over quickly.

But the man who was speaking was reading his mind! He was extending an invitation to the congregation. He was pleading with them to give their lives to God, and some kind of weird telepathic argument was taking place.

The man asked, "If you die tomorrow, do you know where you would go?"

I don't . . . I really should take care of this. Maybe I'll come back next Sunday and do that.

But then the man said, "How do you know you'll be alive next week?"

This was weird. It was like this guy knew his thoughts.

That's true. I better take care of this tonight when I get home.

And then the man argued, "You may not even make it home. You could die in a car wreck on your way back home."

How did this preacher know what he was thinking? The pressure was unmistakable, and almost tangible. He felt himself standing at a crossroads, and he knew deep in his heart this decision could change the course of his life.

Chapter One
The Preacher's Family

When was the first time you stepped through the doors of a church? I wish I could remember when that was for me, but in reality, I'm trusting the memory of someone else because they say I was less than a week old.

I've heard the story my whole life—how my mom bundled me up, on a frigid February night, and off to church we went, because that's just what you do when your dad is the pastor. In many ways, it became the story of my life. I'm the girl who was raised in church. The preacher's daughter, totally and completely. To be honest, though, I've had a pretty confusing mix of emotions surrounding this identity.

I was the fourth child born to Russell and Beverly Rice, and the six of us made up a sweet little pastor's family. At the time, we lived near the breezy, beautiful Outer Banks of North Carolina, and my dad pastored a small independent Baptist church. When I entered this world, our family lived in the parsonage beside the church so my earliest memories are from those two buildings. Back and forth we went, between those two places, all the time. It's not an exaggeration to say the church was my whole world during those first five years of my life. Flannelgraph stories, bedtime prayers, and children's songs about Jesus made up my early introductions to God. On Sunday mornings and Sunday nights and Wednesday nights, I sat on the pew beside my mom while my dad preached. There was no such thing as "children's church." We did have Sunday School, but during all the services, the kids sat with their parents and tried to occupy themselves with crayons and toys.

Everywhere I Look

Quiet toys, that is. If I made too much noise even with the crayons, they went back in my mom's purse. And if my sister and I dared to talk during the service, we were interrupted by a quick, tiny yank on a little strand of our hair by our mom. But if I got sleepy, I could put my head in my momma's lap, and she would gently twirl my hair behind my ear until I drifted off to sleep.

Besides the church and our house, the other place in my vague, earliest memories is the mobile home where my grandparents lived, which was behind the church. I could walk just a few steps from my house over to theirs, and then over to the church. It was a sweet little triangle of security. Our church had a kindergarten, and my mom was the teacher. While she was teaching every morning over at the church, my maternal grandparents took care of me. I remember running over to the church sometimes to see my mom when she was teaching those "big kids," the kindergarteners. I couldn't wait to be big enough to go to school like them. But meanwhile, I got to spend mornings with my Grandma and Grandpa Clingerman, some of the finest people this world has ever seen. I felt like I had two sets of parents during those years, since they were always there, and so involved in my life. It was an incredibly secure and loving environment, and this solid foundation would serve me well in life.

Rice Family in Edenton

The Preacher's Family

All of this is a foggy part of my memory, though, almost like a dream. But when I close my eyes and go back in time, I can still recall how those places made me feel. Everywhere I looked there was love and safety. It was a pretty charmed childhood.

But I was oblivious to the spiritual storm brewing in my little world.

No pastor has a perfect family, and our family was definitely no exception. Looking back, and knowing now what I didn't know then, I can see my dad had an incredibly powerful calling on his life and the enemy of God was not happy about it. As the enemy often does, he targeted the pastor's kids. That's not to say we didn't each bear the weight of our own choices—we did. But we all definitely took spiritual hits. Preachers' kids often get a bad reputation, and there are many reasons for this, but the overarching reason is there are unseen principalities and powers at work in the world. Our fight is not against flesh and blood. And if the enemy can't take out the pastor, he will do his best to destroy his family. The goal, of course, is to push the pastor deep into the pit of discouragement and silence him. And unfortunately, it's a pretty successful strategy. Many pastors are deeply wounded by it, and some ministries are even destroyed in the process.

So our family was targeted, and the war was on. As I was enjoying my perfect little life, my oldest brother, Rusty, was becoming a teenager. He started hanging out with a group of kids who were spending their days skipping school and getting high. My other brother, Charley, looked up to Rusty, and followed closely in his footsteps. Although we didn't know the extent of what they were doing, we did know they were getting in trouble . . . a lot! At school and sometimes with the law. As the war waged on, our parents felt we needed to relocate.

That's when my dad accepted the role of lead pastor in a church in Winston-Salem, NC. But things only got worse. My brothers spiraled out of control in that town. Some of the issues were minor, but others were not. They were Beatles-loving hippies, and one of the frequent fights I remember them having with my dad was over the length of their hair. But the bigger argument was over how they always reeked of pot or alcohol. My dad had an incredible sense of smell, and he could detect both of those a mile away. My brothers were always denying it, but Daddy knew better. And again, they were getting in trouble with the law. It was a disaster.

The intensity of the spiritual war drove us to relocate again. My dad's sister, Joy, lived in Michigan, and as a family rehab of sorts, my brother went to live with her. The rest of us moved to Greenville, SC, and Daddy temporarily stepped out of the ministry. I didn't know why until much later. Many church cultures do not look favorably on pastors whose kids are out of control. I could explain to you how they justify this biblically, but there's a right way and a wrong way to handle these sensitive issues. Entire books have been written by well-meaning people, trying to discern the right steps in these confusing situations. Sadly, having wayward sons silenced my dad and took him, for a season, away from his calling. I would agree it may be too stressful to parent a prodigal while also pastoring an entire congregation. But I shudder at the memory of the shame he carried. How could he have been loved and supported well through that difficult season? I'm not sure, but I feel like there should've been a better way.

Thankfully, it didn't silence him forever. Two years later, we moved to Candler, North Carolina, near Asheville, and Daddy started pastoring again. It was at this church where I first started understanding my position as the "preacher's daughter." But this really only affected me at church, not at school. My parents prioritized a Christian education, so my mom traveled an hour each day to take us to school. Most kids there didn't even know I was a preacher's kid, and those who did, didn't attach that identity to me.

The years in North Carolina were the ones which really formed me. We lived on fourteen acres of land, nestled at the bottom of Mount Pisgah, in the beautiful Blue Ridge Mountains. Our house was on the top of a hill, surrounded by rolling pastures, and at the bottom of our

The Preacher's Family

land was a bubbling creek. We had cows, chickens, sometimes a goat or some sheep, and always more dogs and cats than I can remember. I spent those years roaming our land, fishing in our creek, and swinging on the tire swing my grandpa hung for me in a huge oak tree. Yep, you guessed it, my grandparents lived beside us. That mobile home they lived in just followed us wherever we went. And those sweet people continued to shower me with love and security.

During those years, though, my grandma was suffering from Alzheimer's disease. We didn't call it that then—it was commonly referred to as "hardening of the arteries" and we knew it was passed down from her father who had also suffered from this horrible disease. I never knew him, but I heard stories about how my grandma took care of him when he got "really bad." And now it was our turn to take care of her. For seven years my grandpa lived to care for her every need. He didn't really do much else. He couldn't. But I watched him love her, as she gradually became more and more like a child, and then like an infant. He carried her from her bed out to her rocking chair each morning. And he carried her back each night. He bathed her, dressed her, fed her, and made her comfortable. And he never, ever complained. Not once did I hear him say one unkind word about her or the situation which they could not escape. We all tried to pitch in to help him, but he bore the brunt of it.

Even as a child, I could recognize the tangible love of God being poured through my grandpa. There's a supernatural grace given in hard circumstances, and it was on display during those years. God was coming into focus. Have you ever been a caregiver for a season or have you seen someone do it? Did they seem to have an unusual gift to help and serve selflessly during a difficult time? That is God!

During that season, I'm pretty sure we were all quietly fearing that my own mother would inherit that awful disease. We could see the genetic potential, so it was a reasonable concern, but we didn't dare talk about it. And we all had no idea it would be my dad, rather than my mom, who would eventually be diagnosed first with the dreaded disease.

As a child, I loved being a preacher's daughter, because it's an honor to be part of the "first family" of the church. Humans are funny creatures. We tend to idolize each other, and this happens frequently in churches. Many people want to be close to the pastor and his family. And many people want their kids to be friends with the preacher's kids. Well, at least until they turn into teenagers. Then things change. But during my childhood, I felt like people loved me because they loved my dad. And that was okay. I was honored to be his daughter, and to have everyone treat us with special favor. I mean, who wouldn't enjoy that?

We had an unusual youth group at Good News Baptist where my dad pastored when we lived in the mountains. I was barely old enough to be in it, but the group had a profound effect on me. We were like a big family. We had a youth choir which traveled and sang in other churches. We constantly found things to do so we could be together, and sometimes those things included crazy outings. Like the time we decided to go down Sliding Rock in the snow. That's a big waterfall that splashes down a huge boulder on the side of a mountain. And we were the only ones dumb enough to risk the ice cold waters in freezing temperatures, while it was actually snowing. We also liked to hike Mt. Pisgah, but during the daylight hours wasn't crazy enough for us. It was more fun at night after church. Fumbling our way up the side of the mountain on a moonless night was just the adventure we were looking for. I'm not sure where our parents were during all of this, but I'm glad they didn't stop us. We survived, and we lived to tell our tales.

The Preacher's Family

Good News Baptist Youth Group

When I was fourteen we moved to South Carolina. My dad started pastoring a larger church which also had a Christian school affiliated with it. So now I was known as the preacher's daughter at church *and* at school. Suddenly every aspect of my life was affected by this identity. I felt things shifting—inside me and all around me. I didn't necessarily love being the preacher's daughter anymore. All the adults still showed me special favor, but my peers were a different story. I started feeling like some of them felt afraid to be around me. Like they thought I might go tell my dad what they were doing. I don't know . . . maybe this was just my imagination. But I began to feel like I had to prove I wouldn't. If I just dared to be a little edgy myself, then all the kids at church and school would feel comfortable doing whatever they wanted to do. And that's when the storm inside of me started to swirl. It was the same angst my siblings had felt when they each went through the same shift. I don't remember any of us discussing this phenomenon at the time, but we've since made some interesting connections. At the time, though, each of us went through this rite of passage on our own.

As I look back now on some of our family's hardest seasons, I can understand more clearly now how strong the pressure was on us as preacher's kids. What I can't imagine is how strong the pressure must have been for my parents, and how deep their heartache must have been when we made bad choices which not only affected our family, but also an entire church. I can see vivid images in my mind of my mom and dad on their knees beside their bed, holding hands, praying, crying out to God for their kids. It was just another day in my life. A normal scene.

It really wasn't normal, though. Most people don't have a clue how to fight an unseen enemy. And not everyone is privileged to literally watch their parents wage the war.

By the grace of God, I had a front row seat.

Building Bridges

Let me pause here for a second and ask you something. Who do you run to for help? If you have kids, who (or what) do they see you running to when life comes crashing down all around you? Are you prepared to fight an unseen enemy? He is certainly prepared to fight you. And it makes me sad to think of the unfair advantage he has if you aren't even aware he's trying to destroy you.

Life has thrown me a few curveballs, and I've sometimes felt paralyzed by pain. But when I stop to remember the examples I've seen, I know deep down inside where I will find help. I saw my parents live this out right in front of my very eyes.

That kind of faith doesn't just happen. It is cultivated and developed over the course of a lifetime. It takes a special kind of person to kneel with his wife and cry out loud to God for help. Not many people know how to do that. But thankfully, my daddy did.

Chapter Two
Humble Beginnings

He was only seven years old when he became the man of the family. Russell, my father, had a big sister named Joy, and a little sister named Roberta. And there was a fourth baby on the way. His mom, Sarah, was expecting his baby sister, Bethie, when his dad left their family. As a little second grader, my dad had to grow up overnight and start protecting all those girls.

Their drafty log cabin in Hazel Park, Michigan had no indoor plumbing. A garbage dump was at the end of the street, and the big dump trucks would bring all kinds of interesting things to the dump each week. The kids would wait and watch, then dig through all of it, searching for buried treasures. Behind their cabin, a mentally ill man was kept in chains by his family, and sometimes his wailing frightened them all. Eventually, Sarah had to make the decision to take her little ones and move in with her mother.

Russell as a boy

Everywhere I Look

Now Russell was the only boy surrounded by five women—three sisters, a mom, and a grandma, which might seem unfortunate at first glance. But actually, this situation ended up shaping him in many beautiful ways. He learned from an early age how to understand women, how to be sensitive to their needs, and how to deal with their emotional ups and downs. Those were probably survival skills in his world at the time, but they became invaluable when he had a family of his own and later when he was in ministry.

Living in Clawson, Michigan, at 217 East Baker Street, Russell was happy to have another boy nearby. His best friend, Jamie Seefeld, was a kid who lived down the street. They did what little boys did in the 1940's—they wandered around the neighborhood, exploring and learning about life. In his grandma's house, there were only two bedrooms—one for his mom and grandma, and one for his sisters. So he got the couch. They didn't have a washing machine, so the laundry man came every two weeks, and the milkman came every other day. The Mills man delivered bread on Mondays, Wednesdays, and Fridays. As soon as Russell was old enough, he got himself a job delivering newspapers. Each morning before the sun came up, he roused himself from sleep and rode his bike around Clawson in the dark, tossing papers to his neighbors and earning a little money to help his mom. She was a hard-working single mom, who found secretarial jobs to support her little family. The kids also pitched in and did their part.

They weren't a religious family during his early years. They weren't church goers, and they didn't claim to be Christians. But somewhere along the way, his big sister, Joy, started to feel a deep desire to know God. When she was ten years old, she decided to try to figure out how. One Sunday morning, she got ready by herself and walked to a church a mile and a half from their home. She found out that day in church there was a God, but she realized she didn't know Him personally, and she really wanted to. They didn't really tell her how, though. So for the next several years, she was on a mission to figure this out.

Humble Beginnings

There were a lot of churches within walking distance, so each Sunday, she visited a new one. Sometimes, she'd go to Sunday School at one, and the service at another. She would listen to the pastor intently, and try to figure out how to know this God he was talking about. She would walk in there wondering about this, and would leave still not sure of the answer.

Until one day, when she went to a church and heard the pastor explain how God loved her so much He sent His Son to die on a cross, to pay for all the wrongs she had ever done. She realized how important she was to this God. Joy knew she needed to pray and ask Him to forgive her for all the wrong things she had done, and as she prayed, she immediately felt His presence deep inside her and a wave of peace washed over her. Someone gave her a little Bible, and reading page after page, she learned more of God's great love for her and for the whole world.

After that, it became her mission to share this love with her family. She began to take her little brother and sisters to church with her. They all went, because Joy made them! But it took a while for them to understand what all of this was about. Sometimes the church gave out delicious treats, like cookies or doughnuts, so it wasn't all bad. Russ usually took his comic books with him to keep him occupied while the preacher talked on and on.

Although no one was fully aware of the seismic change that was underway, God was molding and shaping our family through all of this, and He was using that little girl to be a chain breaker for generations to come. Through my Aunt Joy's decision to pursue a relationship with God, an entire family legacy was transformed. That is the power of one person's obedience and influence. Never underestimate what God can do through your life. You may be just one person. But one person can change the course of history. My Aunt Joy did that! She's one of the 2D images I had growing up, and as I trace God's grace through the pages of my life, it's incredible to think about how He was faithfully pursuing our family long before I was ever born.

During his teen years, Russ was active in the youth group, but he never actually had a true relationship with God. Most people would've assumed he did, though, especially since he was a leader in the youth group, and also spoke at events and preached in prisons. But deep down he knew differently.

Talking was always easy for him. He loved to tell stories and people thoroughly enjoyed hearing them. One of his favorite things to do was jump on his bike and ride for miles and miles out to his Aunt Charity's house in the country. Charity was his mom's sister, and she was like a second mother to him. She had five daughters and one son, and Russ soaked up every minute with his cousins. When he pedaled his bike out to their home, he liked to make a pit stop at the schoolhouse his cousins attended. The teacher thought he was fabulous and was amazed at his ability to captivate her students with his tales, so he stopped by the little school frequently and shared interesting stories with the class. This was the first sign of a storytelling gift God would continue to develop throughout his life.

But his home life had never been easy, and the older he got, the more challenging it became. His mom struggled through two more destructive marriages, and experienced abuse in both of them. Those stepfathers made things difficult for Russ. He hated the way his mom was being treated, and he wasn't about to tolerate it. Fiercely protective of her and his sisters, he often came to the rescue by intercepting the abuse. He could also see what the emotional turmoil was doing to his mom, and how she struggled with an addiction to alcohol in response to her pain. It wasn't until 1960, after he was out of the home, that she finally gave her life to Jesus and was truly rescued from her turmoil.

When he was in high school Russ started going to youth camp with the church he attended. They would travel to Beulah Beach, a beautifully wooded retreat center tucked away on the coast of Lake Erie in the state of Ohio. One of his favorite speakers at camp was a preacher

Humble Beginnings

named A.W. Tozer, who would later become his hero of the faith.

In the summer of 1951, as a fourteen year old boy on his first trip to Beulah Beach, he saw a pretty girl walk out onto a balcony with her friends. Instantly his heart skipped a beat, and he said to himself, "That's what I've always wanted." It was love at first sight!

Beverly Clingerman had come to camp with her church's youth group, as well. That boy from Michigan mustered up the courage to introduce himself to her and later that night, they sat together during the service. Afterwards, he sneaked over to the window of the room where she and her friends were staying. The other girls in the room told her someone was at the window to see her. So she walked over curiously to the window, knelt down beside it, and rested her arms on the windowsill. The two of them started talking, and at some point in the conversation, his hand touched her hand. They both felt a spark of electricity! The magic was unmistakable and for the rest of the week, they were a couple.

Building Bridges

It's incredible to see the hand of God in all of this, orchestrating events which would determine the future. Their future, and mine. Have you ever looked back at your parents' story and marveled at the seemingly simple steps being taken which would eventually lead to your entrance into this world? Take a minute to let your mind go back there. It may have been beautiful circumstances, or it may have actually been horrible circumstances. But either way, it was no accident. God had you in mind.

And it was no accident those two very young teenagers met and fell in love at Beulah Beach. It was a divine appointment.

Miracle Baby

She was the baby that was never supposed to be born. Twenty-seven years earlier, long before she came into this world, Beverly's father had stood quietly by the grave of his first wife, processing the overwhelming events of the previous year.

It wasn't supposed to be this way. They had made their mistakes, yes. And they had lived with the humiliating consequences. She had even been disowned by her family because of the scandalous situation. But Charlie and Emma had bravely faced up to their responsibilities, had gotten married, and had been looking forward to the arrival of their sweet baby.

But then it all went terribly wrong. There were unexpected complications. Both mom and baby were in distress. And then suddenly, they were gone. Just like that. In a matter of hours, his whole life got flipped upside down. Now he stood in this dismal little cemetery, with no wife, and no baby, wondering how to pick up the pieces of his life.

My grandfather, Charlie Clingerman

One county over, in another small town, Eva was also trying to pick up her own pieces of a shattered life. Her first miserable marriage had been a total disaster. Earl was an alcoholic and a chronic gambler, and she had been pretty sure he was cheating on her. Friends kept warning

Humble Beginnings

her about how he had been seen with other women, so she got up her courage and confronted him. But he was also a liar. For a while, she struggled with her nagging suspicions, but then something happened which confirmed them once and for all.

After encountering some strange and painful physical issues, she made her way to the doctor's office, hoping to get answers. The doctor examined her and then had the unfortunate job of breaking the awful news to her. She was suffering from a sexually transmitted disease, and it had caused extensive damage. In one life-changing blow, he told her she would never be able to conceive a baby.

That did it. She finally decided to pay a visit to the bar Earl frequented. And sure enough, there he was with another woman, and that was all it took for her to make up her mind. She felt the door of her heart slam shut, and she went straight home, packed her bags, and never looked back.

My grandmother, Eva Clingerman

Life for Eva had never been easy. At eight years old, her mother died suddenly of appendicitis. Her heartbroken father tried his best to raise his two little girls, but couldn't quite handle them and his grief simultaneously. So her little sister went to live with an aunt, and she was left with a grieving father. From that point on, Eva had to fend for herself. When she was old enough to get a job, she moved out and got married, hoping to build a happier life for herself. But the awful marriage left her feeling like she would never marry again.

Charlie had also come to the same conclusion since he never wanted to open up his heart again to someone and risk losing them like he had lost Emma and their baby boy. But God had other plans. He often does!

Eva had been living in a duplex, and Lydia Clingerman, the sweet girl who lived on the other side of it, had a brother she wanted Eva to meet. So she decided to set them up, and wouldn't you know it? They hit it off. In those initial getting-to-know-you conversations, Eva wanted to be up front and honest, so she let Charlie in on her personal secrets, and disclosed the most heartbreaking part—she would never be able to have children.

But hey—this was just fine with him. A relief, actually. Now he could put those fears behind him of ever losing another wife in childbirth. The two started seeing each other, and then on the seventeenth day of April, in 1927, Charlie and Eva said their marriage vows to each other and started a life together. For almost ten years, it was just the two of them. They got along beautifully and built a blissful marriage filled with stability and joy. They had both given their lives to God before they met, so their relationship had a strong foundation, and they felt like they could weather any storm.

But then a very unexpected storm did hit. Eva found out the doctor had been wrong, or maybe God had miraculously healed her. But one thing was clear. She was pregnant! That startling news didn't come as the joyous surprise it is for most couples, though. The pregnancy, which should've been a wonderful season of expectation, became a terrifying season of difficulty in their marriage. For one thing, Eva was now in her late thirties, well past the age of what was considered at that time to be healthy childbearing years. In a desperate attempt to guard his heart, Charlie unintentionally broke her heart. He gradually pulled away emotionally, blocking her and the pregnancy out of his mind. Eva thought she was losing him. In his own mind, he was sure he would

Humble Beginnings

lose her. The pregnancy was a time of fearful uneasiness, with both of them tormented by all the unknowns.

And then on the day before her thirty-seventh birthday, Eva gave birth to a beautiful, blonde-haired, blue-eyed baby girl. The delivery was smooth and uneventful, and the baby was perfectly healthy. Together they breathed a huge sigh of relief and named their miracle baby Beverly Jo. My mother would be the only biological child Charlie and Eva would ever have. God opened my grandmother's womb for one little girl to enter this world.

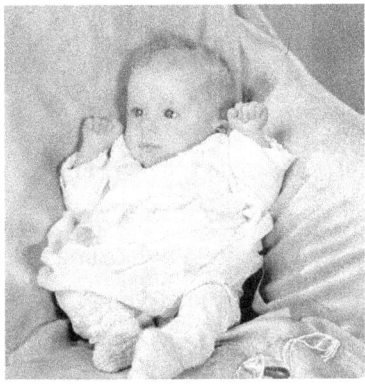

Beverly as a baby

Bev was brought up in a home much different from the one Russ had known. Her parents faithfully took her to church from the time she was a little girl. They taught her about Jesus, and said bedtime prayers with her each night as they tucked her in bed. As a twelve year old girl, Beverly gave her life to the Lord, and she never looked back.

She grew up in the small town in Ohio where she had been born, and she lived in the same house for the first eighteen years of her life. It was a very peaceful, secure childhood, filled with ballet lessons, roller skating with friends, and pony rides in the country. Each day she walked to school (yep, even in the snow) and whenever she wanted to, she wandered all around the charming little town and never worried for one minute about strangers. The Clingermans had a wonderful, large extended family, so even though she was an only child, Beverly had a million cousins and they became the siblings she never had.

As a teenager, she loved her youth group at church, and when she finished up her freshman year of high school, she was excited to be able to go with them to camp.

And that's when she met the boy from Michigan.

Young Love

The two young teenagers were inseparable that week at camp, and when they parted ways, they promised to write each other letters. Russ went back to Michigan, and Beverly went back to her hometown of Kenton, Ohio.

They did write letters during their sophomore year of high school, but they had also agreed to date other people too. Beverly's mother, Eva, had a friend whose son was interested in Beverly. Of course the two moms loved this, and they both encouraged the relationship. So Beverly started dating a boy named Gordon during her tenth grade year. She told Russ about this in a letter, and he stopped writing to her after that.

By the time camp rolled around after their sophomore year, Beverly and Gordon were "going steady." She went off to Beulah Beach again with her youth group, and saw Russ, but she had a boyfriend so they just noticed each other from a distance the second year.

That fall, during their junior year, Bev and Gordon stopped dating. Gordon didn't really show much interest in spiritual things, and that bothered Bev. She had been impressed with the way Russ had loved God, or at least seemed to, so Gordon's lack of interest made her wonder if she should consider Russ again instead. She was pondering all of this when she packed up and headed to camp for the third year.

But there was a complication. That summer when they got to camp, he was the one who was "taken." Russ had started dating Shirley Wells during their sophomore year, and when they all arrived at Beulah

Humble Beginnings

Beach, Beverly realized Russ was no longer available.

One day that week Beverly was in the bath house, and she heard a group of girls come in. They were chattering away. One of them was Shirley, and Beverly recognized her Michigan accent. She sounded just like Russ, and not only because of the accent, but also because she was talkative and outgoing like him. Shirley reminded Bev so much of Russ, she quickly came to the conclusion those two must be perfect for each other. They had similar personalities, where he and Bev had been opposites. They made a great couple, so she flipped a switch in her mind, and decided Shirley must be the girl he should be with, and not her.

Shirley actually knew Russ and Bev had been an item at one point, and that made her a little curious about this Beverly girl. During the week of camp, she decided to make some attempts to get to know her. Maybe it was curiosity, or maybe a little jealousy, but she struck up a friendship with Bev, and the two girls even exchanged addresses so they could keep in touch after camp.

One evening toward the end of the week at camp, Russ and Bev bumped into each other when Shirley wasn't around. Immediately they could both tell the old spark was still there. This presented a dilemma for him. He felt torn and wasn't sure what to do, but at that moment, he thought he would need to break up with Shirley, because he clearly hadn't gotten over Beverly. Later, when they were all back home, he couldn't bring himself to hurt Shirley's feelings. Beverly waited for a letter from him, but after a month of not hearing anything, she had to accept he had changed his mind. She was heartbroken this time, but she decided not to dwell on it. Like she had first thought, he was probably better off with Shirley.

Meanwhile, Shirley did keep in touch with Beverly like she had promised. The two girls exchanged letters during their senior year of high school, and after graduation, they sent each other their senior pictures. Shirley put Bev's picture in her scrapbook, and one night when

Everywhere I Look

she and Russ were looking at the book, a strange thing happened. Another divine appointment!

Before he had gone over to Shirley's house that evening, he had been playing baseball with some friends. Standing in the outfield, for some crazy reason, Beverly Clingerman had popped into his mind. This happened every once in a while. He never could quite get over that girl, no matter how hard he tried. He stood there thinking of her, wondering what she was doing, wondering if they should've ended up together.

Russell's senior photo

After the game, he stopped by Shirley's house. They sat on the couch, catching up and talking about their day. Suddenly, Shirley jumped up and went to get her scrapbook. She opened it up and started showing him the pictures she had collected. He was only half interested, but he tried to be polite as she talked and rhythmically turned the pages. Until she turned the page, and there in front of him was Bev's senior picture! Before he even realized what he was doing, his hand went down to stop her from turning the page. Immediately, they both realized what had happened. Shirley stopped and looked at him. She saw the way he looked at that picture. And she knew . . . she just knew. She asked him if he ever thought about Beverly Clingerman, and he had to admit sometimes he did. Well, this did present a bit of a problem. She told

Humble Beginnings

him he needed to take a trip to Ohio and figure this out once and for all.

Beverly's senior photo

And so he did. It was the summer of 1954, and Beverly was preparing to go to college down in South Carolina, to a place called Bob Jones University. Her best friend had already been there a year, and she couldn't wait to join her. And then, out of the blue, Russ Rice called her! He wanted to come to Ohio to see her, and this was a strange and perplexing turn of events. Wasn't he still with Shirley? Well, that's what he wanted to talk to her about. So she agreed to let him see her, and he didn't waste any time. As soon as he could, he jumped on a bus to Ohio and hoped this would clear things up. And boy, did it! When they saw each other, they both knew without a doubt this was what they wanted. They spent a few days together, and by the time he headed back to Michigan they were both certain of their feelings for each other. Before he

Russ and Bev at Beulah Beach

left, he gave her his class ring, and promised to give her a diamond at Christmas.

Like she had planned, Beverly started college in the fall, and Russ started working at Goodyear back in Michigan. And just like he had planned, he gave her a diamond ring for Christmas. During that semester, while they were apart, they did manage to see each other a couple times. She came home for a visit, and he made one trip down with her parents and his mom. That was his first exposure to Bob Jones University, and he was not impressed. Mainly because he wasn't even allowed to hold her hand on the campus. But also because the whole place just seemed way too strict. At one point they had their first argument, and it was about this college. She hoped someday their children would be able to go there, and his response was, "Never! Over my dead body!"

Did you know God has a great sense of humor? I like to think He was amused by this little discussion, knowing someday Russ would get his degree from the crazy strict school, and a couple of their kids would too. Bev would get her wish.

Building Bridges

We think we know what's best, don't we? We think we've got it all figured out. But God is looking ahead, and sometimes He's preparing us for things we never would have imagined. Have you ever been determined to follow your own plan, only to have God completely rearrange that plan? I know I have.

I can remember so many times where I didn't understand why things weren't working out like I wanted them to. But God was at work, and He was ordering my steps in ways I never could have. Why do I get so set on my expectations, when I have no clue what even tomorrow

Humble Beginnings

holds? It's a good thing I can rest safely in the arms of the God who does.

Lord, would You help us surrender our plans to You? Remind us You are ordering our steps, and You alone know the path ahead of us. Thank You for the peace that comes from resting safely in Your plan for our lives.

Chapter Three
The Sweet Early Years

Back to South Carolina? Long distance relationship? This doesn't feel right. Russ was not happy at all with Bev going back to college in South Carolina and being so far away from him. But he certainly wasn't interested in going to the strict school himself. After wrestling with the thought of a long separation and considering their options, they decided to attend college together at a different school. They made a plan to go to Nyack College in New York in the fall. But as the summer went on, they decided to just get married and postpone college altogether. Getting married became the top priority.

So on September 10, 1955, at the Christian and Missionary Alliance Church of Clawson, Michigan, Beverly put on her white satin wedding gown, and Charlie Clingerman proudly escorted his little girl down the aisle. Russ couldn't take his eyes off of his beautiful bride as she came and faced him at the altar of the quaint little church. Bev's cousin, JoAnn Jones, sang the beautifully prophetic words of the song "Savior, Like a Shepherd Lead Us," and the Reverend Salvadore Farinel officiated the ceremony. After a simple reception, the newlyweds headed off to enjoy a romantic week-long hon-

Russ & Bev's wedding

Everywhere I Look

eymoon on magnificent Mackinac Island.

When they returned, Russ and Bev moved into a shoe box of an apartment in Royal Oak, Michigan. It was actually only one side of the upstairs of the landlord's house, and their small room was a combination bedroom and kitchenette. They shared a hallway bathroom with another couple who lived on the other side of the upstairs. That first year, their free entertainment was listening to the other couple fight. The sound of raised voices and broken dishes seeped through the thin walls of the old house while the newlyweds eavesdropped.

While he was still working at Goodyear, Russ was quickly promoted to Budget Manager and Bev soon found out she was expecting. In less than a year, they saved up and purchased their first home in Ferndale. A month later Russell William Rice, Jr. came into this world. He was an adorable little baby with brown hair and big blue eyes just like his momma's. Russ had always wanted a "junior" and now his wish was coming true. They called him "Rusty."

During this time, Bev was finding out Russ wasn't the committed Christian she thought he was. In fact, on their honeymoon she heard him swear for the first time, and it actually made her cry. It was surprising to her, but also very disappointing. She made more discoveries that first year. He really didn't have any interest in going to church, so she decided to go without him. And he liked to drink. Especially with his buddies. They would get together and play cards, and they liked to get drunk. One weekend while she was visiting her parents down in Ohio, he had a bunch of guys over, and they all had too much to drink. The next morning, while he was cleaning up the mess and mopping up their vomit, he swore off drinking forever. He was afraid she might find out about their drinking party, and he knew how much it would hurt her.

Church was still something he was not interested in at all until his buddy's wife made him promise to go. Dave Anderson was a good friend to Russ, and his wife, Mary, worked downtown near Goodyear. One day when they were all together, Mary was complaining about

The Sweet Early Years

her bus ride home, and out of kindness, Russ offered to give her a ride. That was when she started encouraging him to go to church. He finally agreed, but immediately wished he hadn't.

The weekend came, and Sunday morning he decided to put it off, thinking he'd just go that night to the evening service. He had no interest whatsoever, but the promise was hanging over him like a dark cloud. He knew he just needed to get it over with. Right before it was time to go, the doorbell rang. His sister, Roberta, and her husband, Gordy, had stopped by to see them. This was perfect. Now he had an out. But he couldn't actually bring himself to go through with using this as an excuse. His whole life he had prided himself on being a man of his word, and he had made a promise to Mary, even if he did resent and regret it. So he told them he had to leave, and he and Bev drove to the Clawson Christian and Missionary Alliance Church, where they had gotten married.

It was 1957, and Reverend Farinel was still the pastor. Russ had always admired and respected him deeply, but this was the night of the strange altar call, and it seemed like Reverend Farinel was reading his mind. Before he could argue anymore, he slipped out of the pew and went down to the altar. And there in that little church, on a cold November night, he gave his life to God. His friends, Dave and Mary, and of course his sweet Beverly, were all there beside him when he prayed.

Immediately, everything changed. He didn't feel the same at work, and the dirty jokes his co-workers liked to tell weren't funny anymore. He found himself thinking differently, talking differently, even acting differently. And his feelings about church changed too. He wanted to be there every time the doors were open. They started going three times a week, and before long, he started feeling like maybe he was supposed to become a preacher. And most surprisingly of all, he sensed the Spirit of God leading him to go study for the ministry at none other than Bob Jones University in South Carolina!

Everywhere I Look

Building Bridges

Can you trace God's hand to a moment in time when everything shifted in your life? Priorities, passions, even direction. What were you feeling? It can be overwhelming when the ground beneath you feels like it suddenly turns to jello. I've been there a few times, and I know how unsettling it feels. But it's so comforting to remember in times of uncertainty, God knows the path He has carved out for us. He is our True North, our constant stability in an ever-changing world.

Isaiah 33:6 tells us God will be "the stability of our times." If you are in the middle of chaotic or confusing circumstances, cling to this beautiful truth. There is a Rock you can stand on.

Studying for the Ministry

Providing for a family while going to college? Whew, that's not exactly how they would've planned to start out, but they knew they had heard the call of God, and they trusted God to provide. By now their second child was on the way, which added a new level of pressure and responsibility. They had to make the decision to step out in faith, and when they did, God came through. Bev's parents offered to help them by sending them $100 a month to survive. They would have to make it work. To cover tuition, Bev and Russ decided to work during the summers and save money to take care of those costs. So with this plan in place, they started making arrangements to move.

Randy Charles Rice was born on January 5, 1958, while they were still living in Michigan. He also had those blue eyes like his momma's, but his hair was blonde instead of brown. They liked the name "Randy" and it sounded cute when they paired it with the name "Rusty." The name "Charles" was in honor of Beverly's father, Charlie. They called

The Sweet Early Years

him Randy when he was little, but he loved his Grandpa Charlie so much he wanted to be called by that name instead. So it actually ended up being "Rusty and Charley" instead of "Rusty and Randy."

Rusty & Charley

In August, Bev's father loaded up all of their worldly goods onto the back of his pick-up truck and covered it with a tarp. With two little boys in tow, they all made their way to Greenville, SC. The couple moved into an apartment at Woodland Homes Apartments. It was a two bedroom apartment, so Russ and Bev took one bedroom and gave Rusty the other. Charley was a baby, so they turned one of the closets into a cozy, little nursery where his crib fit perfectly in the space. Soon Russ started school, and Bev stayed home and took care of the boys. After the first school year, they decided to go back up north for the summer, so Russ could work and Bev could take some college classes herself. This was the routine they established for those early years. He would take classes during the school year, and she would take them in the summer.

One summer when they arrived back in Ohio, they had a surprise for everyone. It was May of 1961, and Bev was seven months pregnant. Russ had had to stay back in South Carolina for a little while, so she and the boys rode the train to Ohio. They had managed to keep the pregnancy a secret until that moment. When she stepped off the train, with her big pregnant belly in all of its glory, her parents were in for a fun surprise.

In August, they welcomed a sweet baby girl into their little family. Sara Elizabeth Rice was born. In keeping with their tradition of using family names, they named their little girl after both of their mothers—Sarah, after his mom, and Elizabeth, using Eva's middle name. And they called her "Sara Beth." Russ's baby sister was named Beth, so she was also named after her Aunt Beth. A beautiful little brown-haired baby with brown eyes like her daddy, Sara Beth quickly stole the hearts of the entire family.

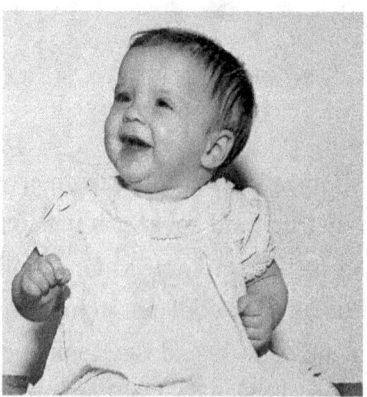

Sara as a baby

At Woodland Homes, they became great friends with another young couple, Rod and Lenore Bell. Russ and Rod had met in school at Bob Jones, and the two hit it off immediately. Rod was attending Tabernacle Baptist, a local church pastored by a dynamic preacher named Harold Sightler. It wasn't a pentecostal church, but if you walked into a service during those years, you could have easily mistaken it for one. Lots of energy filled the air, and the congregation freely raised their hands and offered up loud praise and frequent "amen's." Some were even known to walk or run around the sanctuary if the Spirit really started to move. Rod invited Russ and Bev to visit Tabernacle, and they decided to give it a try. But all the noise and activity was so distracting. They both felt uncomfortable, but Rod kept inviting them, so they kept trying it.

One night during a particularly loud service, a line of the song they were singing caught Russ' attention. They were singing about going to Heaven some day, and it finally dawned on him why they were all being so loud. The idea of seeing Jesus face to face was making them so excited they couldn't contain themselves. Suddenly, it all started making sense, and after that, it was just a matter of time before he was joining them and shouting "Hallelujah" himself!

Building Bridges

Can you relate at all to his experience? Have you had a time when you thought, "That's weird!" or "I'll never do that," but then God changed your mind? I've actually been in a season of change for the last few years (more on this later) and God just keeps revealing areas of my thinking which were never fully surrendered to Him.

Sometimes God has to break down our barricades, brick by brick, until we can see the full revelation of what He wants to teach us. And if we will submit to this process, He will be faithful to give us new glimpses of His glory.

Teaching and Preaching

I can't believe they are asking me to do this!

Russ was thrilled at the idea of getting his first opportunity to preach and pastor. It was the summer of 1962, and the Alliance church in Bev's hometown of Kenton, Ohio was in need of an interim pastor. Russ had just graduated with a degree in ministry from Bob Jones University that spring, so they asked him to step into this role in their church for

Everywhere I Look

those summer months. After all of the studying and learning, he was so excited to finally get a taste of actually pastoring, and that summer experience was exciting and fulfilling. In the fall, they returned to South Carolina, and he and Bev both started teaching at Tabernacle Christian School, which was affiliated with the church they'd been attending.

During the school year, their pastor, Dr. Sightler, helped Russ get several opportunities to preach in various churches in the area. Each time his mind would race with excitement and nervousness. Would he know what to say? Would it make sense? Would it actually help anyone? With each opportunity, when he stepped behind the pulpit, and opened his Bible, the Spirit of God took over. He gave him the words. He guided his thoughts. People were moved by the Spirit and lives were changed. Russ was constantly humbled and amazed God would use him like this.

The next fall, in their second year of teaching at Tabernacle, he got another invitation. Pleasant View Welcome, a little church in Travelers Rest, SC, asked him to be their interim pastor, and they offered to pay him a whopping $5 a service. Filthy rich! It started out as a week-to-week opportunity, but they loved him and eventually voted him in as their new pastor. The little family moved into the parsonage across from the church during the Christmas holidays of 1963.

The ministry at the little church in Travelers Rest was a wonderful experience. It was a charming Mayberry-esque town where everyone knew everyone, and most people had never lived anywhere else. Russ was definitely in his element, meeting people everywhere he went, and inviting them to church. He would walk into a gas station or a store and strike up a conversation with the workers or the owner, and before long they would all be best of friends. Then he would go back again and again, and after a while, he'd convince them to come visit the church. Russ also went door to door, talking to people, getting to know them, and just showing them kindness. He loved driving up and down the back roads of the town, and if he saw someone working in

The Sweet Early Years

their yard, he'd stop and find some way to connect with them. He always eventually invited them to church, but his first goal was to show them God's love, and he was really good at that. God blessed my dad with the ability to make friends with everyone he met, and people were drawn to his good humor and friendly nature. People in the town were soon talking about the new preacher at the church up the road. More and more people were coming to visit, and before long, the church membership had doubled. They were actually running out of room, so they made the decision to build a bigger building. They worked hard to raise the funds, and the men in the church all pitched in to help build a beautiful colonial brick church, complete with porch columns and a white steeple.

Another significant event took place in 1963. Dr. Sightler, the pastor at Tabernacle, had envisioned a Bible college for young men who wanted to enter the ministry. He asked Russ and Rod Bell and Jim Smith, another friend of theirs, to head this up. They all brainstormed and discussed their ideas for weeks. What they really wanted was a night school, so guys who were called into the ministry could still work during the day, and then attend classes at night. So in the fall of 1963, God allowed them to make this vision a reality. Tabernacle Baptist Bible College was birthed, and off and on over the next 30 years, Russ would teach there. He would train and mentor countless young people over the course of those years, and through that opportunity, he would have a profound influence for the Kingdom of God.

Three years later, another opportunity presented itself. A church which was located near the Outer Banks of North Carolina needed a pastor. Russ' old friend, Rod Bell, connected them with Russ, and in the fall of 1966 Russ agreed to be their pastor.

For Thanksgiving that year, the little family made another trip to Ohio. Beverly was six months pregnant with their fourth child, and a whole host of relatives showed up to see them. The relatives were also there to say goodbye to Charlie and Eva (Bev's parents), who had recently retired and had decided to move down to North Carolina to live near their only child and grandchildren. They were especially excited to be able to help with the new baby that was on the way. Such a sweet time for all of them. Life was looking good, and everything seemed to be falling into place for the young preacher and his little family.

Building Bridges

As I look back now on all of this, I'm amazed at all the details God orchestrated. His sovereign grace is all over this story. He didn't just single them out for service, but He divinely guided their steps and opened doors of opportunity. I'm also pretty amazed at the courage of my parents. It couldn't have been an easy decision to leave their families, and the places they had always called home, to step out into unknown territory. But I heard their reasons all my life. It was about the call God had placed on them. They stepped out in faith and in obedience to that call, and they trusted God with the unseen.

Stop and ponder this with me for a minute. Where can you see the hand of God in the path you're taking in life? Can you recognize His hand? Looking back we can see so much we may not have recognized at the moment. When I think about the events of my own path, the 3D image starts coming into focus again. He goes before us. He comes beside us, and His strong arms are holding us each step of the way.

Edenton

The church in Edenton was meeting in a small, cramped building, and they were growing. So, just like his previous church, they also needed a new building. Russ had successfully led his first church through a building program, so this was familiar territory. He jumped

The Sweet Early Years

right in and helped them with this project and got busy getting to know the families in his new church.

According to plan, Charlie and Eva moved South. They rented a lovely little farmhouse out in the country, and the boys enjoyed having a couple of horses there. A few months after they all arrived in town, in February of 1967, I was born. And again they followed tradition with the family names. I was named after my dad's Aunt Charity and my mom's Aunt Margaret. Because my dad's mom was named Sarah and her sister was named Charity, my sister and I weren't the first sister set named "Sarah and Charity." In fact, we were actually the third set of sisters with these names in our family. I don't think my parents even knew this, but we later found out my great-great grandmother, named Charity, had a sister named Sarah. Funny little tradition we have going here.

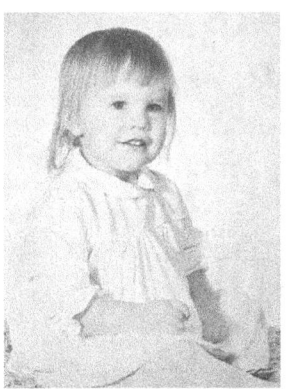

My baby photo

Grandma Sara & Aunt Charity

Russ and Bev now had two boys and two girls, and their growing little family was happy and healthy. The boys didn't waste any time making plenty of friends in Edenton. One family in particular welcomed them warmly, and the kids all hit it off. Orval and Ruby Williams had several kids, and their two boys, Gary and Neal, were close in age to Rusty and Charley. The four boys were immediately good friends, and have remained friends for years. Rusty was the more outgoing one of my two brothers, and he soon became a ring leader with a group of kids who liked his sense of adventure. They ran around town, having fun and occasionally doing things they shouldn't, but it was all pretty tame. At first.

After two and a half years, construction of the new church building was complete, and the congregation started meeting in the new sanctuary. Our family moved into the parsonage beside the church in the summer of 1969. By now, Rusty was getting into more serious trouble. We had a few law enforcement officers in our church, and they started coming to my dad with bad reports and discussions of how to turn things around. My parents tried everything they could think of to keep him out of trouble, but nothing seemed to work. Rusty had a mind of his own, and he didn't really care about the consequences of his actions. Things were getting ready to go from bad to worse.

Rusty & me

Now after reading this first part of the story, you might only see the minor struggles of newlyweds and the normal ups and downs of preparing to fulfill the call to ministry, and you might assume everything was pretty close to perfect in our home. A few challenges here and there, but so far things were going in the right direction.

The Sweet Early Years

But nothing could've prepared our little preacher's family for the treacherous storms ahead. Only God could help us navigate those deep waters.

Part Two

Looking Around

Seeing God's Grace in Our Home

"Friends love through all kinds of weather, and families stick together in all kinds of trouble."
~Proverbs 17:17 (The Message)

"Above all, keep loving one another earnestly, since love covers a multitude of sins."
~1 Peter 4:8 (ESV)

He woke up in the middle of the night and tried to get up, but for some reason he couldn't move. It felt like someone was on top of him, holding him down.

He couldn't figure out how anyone could have gotten in there. The bedroom he was sleeping in was down in the basement, and the bedroom door was locked. How could someone have gotten in? But he didn't have time to think about it. Somehow they had, and now they were pinning him down to the bed.

It was pitch black, and he couldn't even see his hand in front of his face. But he could feel the heavy weight of whoever this was, and he was absolutely terrified. He was young and strong, but he was no match for this. He couldn't move at all.

Suddenly he remembered to pray. Not that God would care to listen to him. He was pretty sure God was sick and tired of his craziness. But out of complete desperation he started praying in his mind.

"God, help me! Please! In Jesus' Name!"

At first nothing changed. Maybe it wasn't going to work. Maybe God was too mad at him. He tried to move, but still felt something heavy holding him down. The fear was overwhelming and panic was rising up inside of him like a volcano. He tried to mumble the name of Jesus. But the weight was so heavy he could barely make a sound come out of his mouth. And still, he couldn't move his body.

Again and again he tried with all of his strength, and finally he managed to force the words out.

"Get away from me! In Jesus' Name . . . In Jesus' Name!"

Immediately, he was released! Just like that the crushing weight was suddenly off of him. He jumped up and ran over to the wall to turn on the light, so he could see who had been holding him down.

But when the light came on, he looked around. No one else was in the room. Coughing, sputtering, gasping for air . . . he realized he was all alone in the room. Whatever had pinned him down had literally disappeared.

Chapter Four
A Preacher and a Prodigal

My oldest brother was a force to be reckoned with from day one. My mom told us all stories of how Rusty did everything early. He pulled up onto his elbows the day after he was born, when they were still in the hospital. He rolled over when he was only six days old, and he took off running when he was ten months old. He didn't walk first, he ran. And he climbed . . . everything! There is a picture somewhere of him as a little guy, around two years old, on top of the refrigerator, which was one of his favorite things to climb.

Back when they were still living in Michigan and Rusty was only two years old, Bev's dad, now known as Grandpa Clingerman, decided to help Russ build a fence for their backyard. Back behind the house was a busy road, and they were all afraid Rusty might get in the road and get hurt. So the two men bought all the materials and spent an entire day building a good, strong fence. That evening, when it was finished they brought him out to play in his newly fenced-in backyard. But the little rascal ran straight over to the fence, and climbed right over it. The boy was not going to be contained.

He wasn't just energetic. He was also very strong-willed. "No" meant nothing to him. It actually just made him want to do it even more. This did not go over well when he started school. He actually enjoyed kindergarten and was already reading by the time he entered first grade. But this just meant he was bored out of his mind when the first grade teacher was teaching the others who hadn't caught on as quickly as he had. So he did what most bored students do—he found ways to entertain himself and everyone else in the process. First grade was pretty fun for the class clown, but in second grade things changed.

At first he really liked his second grade teacher. But then she left on maternity leave, and the new teacher was a different story. This lady was not amused in the least at Rusty's antics. She tried to teach him a lesson by bringing him to the front of the class, pulling his hand back, and popping his palm with a ruler. This did not go over well with Rusty. The more she did that, the more angry he became, so the more he misbehaved. He grew to hate her, and by the end of the year, he hated school too.

By third grade he had checked out completely. School was dumb and a waste of time, and he had no desire whatsoever to be there. By fifth grade, when they moved to Edenton, he was finding ways to skip school. And over the next few years, between the ages of ten and fourteen, he started down a path which would have serious repercussions for the rest of his life.

He and his new friend, Chip, and a few other guys started sneaking away from school and going to "the woods," a nearby forest, to just hang out. Occasionally they would bring some wine that one of them had stolen or managed to somehow get their hands on. They tried pot a few times, but it was expensive and more difficult to get. One day Chip told him about something he'd read in a magazine. There was a way to use common ingredients they could easily find, mix them together, and smoke them to get high. They tried it, and sure enough, it worked. So they started keeping their homemade concoction on hand in little ziplock bags and they skipped school regularly to run off to the woods and get high.

The teachers and principals were frequently contacting my parents now about Rusty skipping school. No one knew about the drugs. He would get in trouble for skipping, but to him, it was all worth it. He'd much rather take the punishment than sit in school. By this point, he despised sitting in a classroom.

A Preacher and a Prodigal

This really became how he made his decisions. He often knew what he was doing would get him in trouble, but he would weigh that against the alternatives, and most of the time he'd rather take the chance and deal with the punishment. He loved living on the edge, trying not to get caught, and doing what he wanted. It was a constant adrenaline buzz.

When our parents decided to move to Winston-Salem, it was an attempt to remove Rusty from the situation he had created in Edenton, and to surround him with new people. Rusty didn't waste any time finding new friends. He was a charismatic leader, so it was always easy to find followers. People were drawn to his daredevil courage. But unfortunately the new friends he found were troublemakers like the others had been. In Winston-Salem, he was introduced to acid, and that led him down a whole new path. He started getting in trouble with the law, and he became more and more calloused toward any and all authority figures.

Rusty, popping a wheelie!

My dad started encouraging my brothers and their friends to just hang out at our house, hoping this would keep them from running around town, breaking the law. My parents suspected they were sneaking around and using drugs, but they weren't sure what to do about it, so my mom actually took a college class on teenage drug use, to try to

Everywhere I Look

figure out how to help her boys.

The church my dad pastored in Winston-Salem was Cedar Forest Baptist Church, and we lived in a parsonage across the street from the church, like we had in Edenton. The church also had a kindergarten, and when we arrived in October of 1971, I was four years old. The following fall, I was thrilled to finally be old enough to go to school and attend the church's kindergarten. In spite of the chaos invading our home, I have sweet childhood memories of riding on my daddy's shoulders each morning as he took me across the street to kindergarten. These are powerful core memories which molded me and gave me a secure foundation. I felt so safe and confident up there on his shoulders. I can still close my eyes and tap into that feeling to this day. The older I've gotten, the more I can see the correlation between the security he gave me, and the security God continues to give me. My daddy's love was the first taste of God's love I had, and even as a child, it was shaping me. God's sweet grace was already chasing me down, through the love of my daddy.

Timmy

My dad's sisters, Joy and Roberta, still lived in Michigan, but his baby sister, Beth, had moved South. I loved all of my cousins so much. Our trips to Michigan always included staying at my Aunt Roberta's house and my Aunt Joy's house, with cousins everywhere. At Aunt Roberta's, there were six kids: Gordy, Sheryl, Robin, Mark, Matt, and Roger. At Aunt Joy's, there were also six kids: Laurie, Bonnie, Julie, Allen, Nellie, and Melanie . . . plus a few foster kids, who I also claimed as my cousins. My Aunt Beth lived in North Carolina, so we saw her more often, especially during the years when we lived in Winston-Salem.

At the time, Aunt Beth had two little boys, Timmy and Todd, and later she would also have Jennifer, Cady and Sheryl. Her oldest, Timmy, was just a couple years older than me, and at this point Todd was

A Preacher and a Prodigal

a baby. For as long as I could remember, Timmy had been fighting cancer. Once when they came to visit us, my dad wanted to take him to get ice cream. He was very fragile, but my brothers and my dad and grandpa came up with a plan to give him a comfortable ride. They took out the back seat of my grandpa's van to make room for the lazy boy Timmy was sitting in. I remember them lifting the big chair into the back of the van, as they all cheered for the king on his throne, and I can still see the smile on Timmy's face.

Timmy Spain

Timmy passed away on September 25, 1972. I still find it difficult to imagine the devastating pain my sweet Aunt Beth had to go through. He was only seven years old. It was my first experience with losing someone close to my age, and even though I knew he was with Jesus, my heart was so sad.

For a while after this, I remember thinking about death and Heaven, and pondering it all. Sometime during this particular season, another impactful event took place. My mom and sister and I were at church during a Wednesday night service. Toward the end of the service, during the prayer time, my sister leaned over and whispered a question to me. She asked if I'd ever asked Jesus to be my Savior. This was something I had heard about my whole short life, but I had never personally taken a step of faith. I knew exactly what she was talking about, and I told her I never had. She encouraged me to kneel right there beside the pew and give my heart to Jesus. And so I did. Even as a five-year-old I had a clear understanding of my sin and my need for a Savior. It would be years before I would fully surrender my life to the Lord, but that was the beginning of my personal relationship with God.

Childlike faith . . . that's all it takes.

Difficult Decisions

We had an unfinished basement in the parsonage, and my brothers set up a make-shift bedroom down there with cardboard walls. Having them in the house did keep them off the streets and out of jail, but now all the turmoil was right under our roof. I wasn't allowed to go downstairs. At the time I didn't know why, and I don't remember ever caring. I already hated my brothers' actual bedrooms, which were across the hall from the bedroom I shared with my sister. Their rooms had blacklights that gave off a strange glow which gave their weird velvet posters a purple tint. It smelled weird in their rooms too, since they were always burning incense. Their music was also strange, and the combination of all those things made my little five-year-old self feel scared of that scene. I was never afraid of them personally. My big brothers were both always loving and protective of me, but the atmosphere they lived in was a little creepy. So when my parents told me to stay out of the basement, I didn't argue.

I've thought a lot about my parents' decision to let my brothers and their friends hang out in our basement. I have mixed emotions about it all. As a parent now myself, I can't imagine having all those hoodlums under my roof. My tendency would be to run down and monitor everything. I'd want to put my foot down, and shut down any stupidity. But when I try to get in my dad's head and understand what he was doing, I realize he was operating from a very different premise.

First, he knew better than to try to put his foot down. He had tried

A Preacher and a Prodigal

that since two-year-old Rusty first climbed over the fence he and Grandpa Clingerman spent a whole day building. Rusty was going to do what Rusty was going to do. Whether Dad put his foot down or not. And by this point, Rusty didn't respond well to heavy-handed authority. So my dad knew he had to tread carefully if he had any chance of helping this boy of his.

But even more importantly, my dad was hoping if those crazy rebels stayed there under his roof, then maybe he could at least try to influence them and protect them. So he prayed over them, engaged them in conversations, and decided to love them well, in hopes of helping them stay alive and maybe out of jail.

There are many characteristics of God I saw consistently in my dad through this experience. I don't know if I recognized them then, but as I've looked back through the years, I can see them all very clearly. Two which stand out strongly are God's love and God's mercy. My father's love always resembled the love of the prodigal son's father, who waited patiently with arms wide open for the return of his son. In spite of their rebellion, my brothers were always, always loved. Their friends were loved too, and they all loved my dad in return. Some of them stayed in touch with our family all through the years, and I heard them talking about how much they loved and respected my parents, particularly my dad. Would they have felt that way if he had refused to let them in his house? What would Jesus have done in that situation? It's an interesting thing to ponder.

The other characteristic I saw is mercy. My dad showed them so much mercy. From Scripture we know God delights in showing mercy (Micah 7:18) and mercy triumphs over judgment (James 2:13). So even with all of the craziness going on, the heart of God was constantly on display through my parents. And even though Rusty's choices continued to bring chaos into his own life, one thing remained constant—his relationship with my parents. It was never broken or destroyed . . . and honestly, that is a miracle.

Everywhere I Look

Often we judge situations as an outsider looking in without knowing all the facts and the heart behind the decisions which were made. How my parents treated Rusty in this season taught me important lessons about withholding judgment. Although I haven't always done this perfectly, the Spirit of God frequently reminds me of the godly example my parents consistently were in my life. Sometimes when I'm tempted to pass judgment unfairly, I literally feel the conviction of the Spirit reminding me of my parents and how they lived and loved so beautifully. I've heard God speak these words to my heart many times: "That's not what they showed you. And that's not what I've taught you. Walk in love."

I do want to point out that each situation is different, and there is no "one size fits all" play book for these heartbreaking situations. The specifics of how my parents handled their situation does not set some kind of standard for everyone to follow. There are so many variables, and individual family dynamics are all different. This is where the Spirit of God needs to be called upon for supernatural wisdom and guidance. Only God knows the steps each family needs to take. Sometimes love must be tough, and lines must be drawn. Eventually, my parents had to draw their own lines. But through it all, the love of God was on display for all to see.

Building Bridges

What is your knee-jerk reaction in situations where you feel judgmental and maybe even arrogant toward those you don't understand or agree with? What kind of example are you setting for those around you?

As God reveals the judgmental tendencies of our hearts, I pray we

A Preacher and a Prodigal

will tear down our pride and let God's love and mercy be demonstrated through us. We may never even realize the ripple effects of that obedience. Possibly even generational ripple effects.

Out of Control

Somewhere along the way, Rusty realized selling drugs was a lucrative business. He started selling pot to people at school—to the students who could afford it, and eventually to some of the teachers, believe it or not. He skipped school more than he actually attended, but the ironic part was that his punishment for skipping school was suspension.

At one point when he was in the 11th grade, he was suspended for five days. But this created a dilemma for Rusty, since he had some customers at school who were expecting him. So he went up to the school to do some business, and this turned out to be a disastrous mistake.

He wasn't allowed on school property during a suspension, but he sneaked inside anyway. As he stepped into the hallway, he saw the assistant principal coming toward him. He yelled Rusty's name, and Rusty darted quickly into the closest bathroom. The principal followed him and was continuing to yell and scream at him, which always triggered worse behavior in Rusty. He grabbed the first thing he could find and started breaking everything in sight–the sinks, the mirrors, the urinals. Then he raced out of the bathroom and back into the hallway.

By now other faculty members were chasing him and yelling at him too. The anger was exploding inside his mind, and he was like a wild animal. Years of hatred for authority erupted like a volcano. He had a lighter in his pocket, so he pulled it out. Grabbing some papers from a nearby trash can, he lit them on fire, in a desperate attempt to keep the teachers all away. He tossed the papers back into the can, which set the whole thing on fire. Immediately, everyone pursuing him stopped dead in their tracks. What in the world was this kid doing?! This was crazy!

I'm sure they wondered if he had truly lost his mind, but I'm convinced now there was a demonic influence on him. He has since described to me the demonic effects of any mind-altering substance, like alcohol or drugs. He would warn you today that when you mess around with anything which alters your thinking, you are opening yourself up to that influence and putting yourself in a vulnerable position. When you look at this chaotic and irrational response to authority, it literally seems like the enemy is having a heyday with this kid. After lighting the fire, Rusty turned quickly and sprinted out of the school as fast as he could.

And that was the last time he ever stepped foot in the school building. After the incident, the state of North Carolina banned him from every public school in the entire state. They'd had enough of Rusty Rice. He and my parents actually had to appear in court to accept the charges and the decision. But of course it didn't break his heart to hear he was never allowed to go to school again. That was exactly what he wanted. He had no real understanding of the severity of this situation until many years later.

My parents, however, were devastated by all of this, and they were totally out of ideas. Since he couldn't go to school now, his only option was to enter the workforce without a high school diploma. They decided Rusty needed a complete change of scenery and new voices speaking into his life. But where should he go and what should he do?

In a sheer act of love and compassion, my Aunt Joy and Uncle Al offered to let Rusty come stay with them in Michigan, and get a job up there. After much discussion and prayer, they all decided this would be a good idea. It would give Rusty a fresh start again, and it would create a separation between Rusty and Charley. Because by this point, Charley had firmly established himself on his own unique path of destruction, and they needed to deal with that separately from Rusty's rebellion. So this seemed like a good solution, all the way around.

Michigan did give Rusty a fresh start. And my Aunt Joy and Uncle Al were both so good to him. Their kindness was another 2D image helping to bring the full picture of God into view. But just like he had done in Winston-Salem, he soon surrounded himself with new rebels like himself, and he found new ways to get into trouble. In fact, trouble just seemed to follow Rusty wherever he went.

Or maybe he followed it . . . I'm not sure which.

Building Bridges

As you can see, our family went through years of intense difficulties, and it was the gracious hand of God which inspired other family members to become involved and to help be a part of the solution. God used Aunt Joy again (remember, she is the one who first brought faith to our family) to be a beacon of hope.

We need our tribe. We need people we can trust and be vulnerable with, who can lend a hand or offer wisdom and prayers when needed to help us get through hard times. Community is so important. Do you have people like this in your life? Or have others stepped in to be a rock for you when things were shaking?

Even though this provided some relief for my family, this isn't where the story ends.

Chapter Five
Transitions

The decision for Rusty to move to Michigan didn't just affect him. My dad decided he needed to step away from the ministry for a season, so now we were all moving. I was so young. It didn't make a lot of sense to me. I just knew my brothers were causing a lot of trouble, so my dad wasn't going to be a pastor for a while. My parents explained we would be moving to a new place and I'd be going to first grade at a school in South Carolina. My family was familiar with this place, but it was brand new to me.

Tabernacle was kind of like a home base for my parents. When they decided to go back to Greenville, Tabernacle felt like a good place to land. They could both teach there again, and the kids could be in the Christian school. By now my parents were solid fans of Christian education. Rusty and Charley had both been exposed to drugs in a public school, so that's the last place they wanted us to be.

At the end of the school year, we packed up all of our belongings and took them from Winston-Salem to South Carolina. My parents had found a house in Travelers Rest, the sweet little town where Daddy had first pastored . . . back when pastoring was easy and fun. But the house wasn't going to be available for us to move into it until right before school started. So we put everything in storage, and headed to Michigan.

Summer of '73
Spend the summer on a quaint little lake in beautiful Michigan?

Everywhere I Look

Sounded like a great plan, so off we went to Aunt Joy and Uncle Al's even though they already had a houseful. My aunt and uncle were unusually big-hearted people. They had had three biological daughters, and adopted a son and two more daughters. And because their hearts were so incredibly huge, they still had room to love and care for foster children. But not just any foster children, mind you. My Aunt Joy accepted placements of severely disabled children into her care. One child had cerebral palsy and was wheelchair-bound. Another was severely autistic and blind. Two others had multiple diagnoses of severe mental and physical disabilities. Although there were many others through the years, those particular four children were long term placements. She didn't just have them temporarily; she cared for them until they "aged out" of the system. Their home was overflowing, and yet they found room for all of us for a whole entire summer, and were graciously willing to let my trouble-making brother live there for as long as necessary. God's kindness and love on display, everywhere I look!

Aunt Joy's Family

Going to Michigan was a very familiar trip for our family. Every summer and every Christmas of my life we made the trek up North. We would always stop in Ohio at my mom's hometown, to visit my mom's

Transitions

cousins, the Woodards. I loved playing on Don and Marcella Woodard's farm with my Woodard cousins— Amy, Bonnie, and Danny.

The farm was out in the country, in the middle of an Amish community. As a child, it always fascinated me to watch the horse-drawn carriages ride by. It was like a scene from a different era, and it felt a little like stepping back in time. That farm was another place where God's love permeated the atmosphere. My mom's family loved Jesus, and their hearts and homes were always open to us.

Charley and me at the Woodard's Farm

After visiting all of the Woodards, we would head to Michigan and visit my dad's family. We would see my Grandma Sarah, and my Aunt Charity, and all of my dad's cousins. We usually split the visit, and stayed a while with Aunt Roberta and her family, and then a few days with Aunt Joy and her big gang. Cousins literally everywhere. I didn't realize as a child how much love and security God was giving me by surrounding me with such a beautiful extended family.

Everywhere I Look

Roberta, Joy, Russ, Beth, and Grandma Sarah

Aunt Joy and Uncle Al lived on Tipsico Lake in Holly, Michigan, and those hot, summer days were filled with breezy pontoon rides, swimming in the lake, and water skiing every day. Well, actually, let's be honest. For me, there were a few failed attempts at water skiing, but my siblings and cousins were all great at it, so we were on the lake constantly. My cousin, Nellie, and I were the same age, so the two of us were inseparable. We ran around the neighborhood, playing with all the kids on the street, making lemonade stands, and doing silly things like painting rocks. Sweet, beautiful, carefree days.

Aunt Joy had a giant bedroom for all of her girls, and whenever we visited, she piled a heap of blankets and pillows all over the floor to create a big bed for any kids who didn't have one. The house was filled with love and activity and the noise of kids, adults, and a few dogs. This is another scene which amazes me when I go back in my mind. It was such a normal atmosphere to me then, but the older I get, the more I realize how unique her home was. My exposure to this beautiful atmosphere, and the friendships I had with my mentally and physically challenged "foster cousins" actually shaped the direction of my life. When I studied education in college, I decided to work with students who struggle. I majored in special education, and I still teach struggling

Transitions

students to this day.

In the fall, through a teary embrace, we said our goodbyes. Rusty stayed there, and the rest of our family made the long journey down to our new home in South Carolina.

We all started school together that fall of 1973 at Tabernacle Christian School. Daddy was the principal, Mom taught second grade, and I was starting first grade. Sara was going into seventh, and since she had decided to drop "Beth" we just called her "Sara" now. Charley was going into tenth grade, and he was still kind of a mess. Winton-Salem had done a number on him.

But things were about to change.

Charley Rice

He was Randy for a while, but when he went to school, he started writing "Charley" on all of his papers. His teacher and the other students started calling him that, and soon my parents found out Charley wanted to have the same name as the grandpa he loved so much. The spelling was slightly different from Charlie Clingerman, though, to make a distinction between the two.

Charley had been born in Michigan, and spent his very early years at the apartment in Woodland Homes in Greenville, SC. As a baby, he was the extreme opposite of his big brother. Where Rusty was constantly escaping and crossing every possible boundary given to him, Charley was perfectly content to play in one place and occupy himself for hours. This was actually a huge gift for Beverly, who was very grateful on those days when she had to leave Charley in the playpen for a few minutes to go wandering around the apartment complex searching for Rusty, who didn't know how to sit still. Charley was a calm, happy little guy, with a personality much like his momma's.

In 1960, my parents bought a house near Tabernacle, and their two little boys both went to the church's Christian school. Charley also attended second grade at Tabernacle, and after that, the family moved to

Everywhere I Look

Edenton, where he spent third through eighth grade.

In Edenton, while Rusty was getting into all kinds of trouble, Charley was mostly an observer. He looked up to his big brother with admiration, which wasn't necessarily a good thing. Sometimes he tried to join in, but Rusty usually pushed him away. After all, he was the little brother, and it's not always the coolest thing to have a younger brother tagging along. Charley and his friends did manage to steal wine occasionally, and take it out to the woods to hide and drink it. But that was about as bad as it got for him in Edenton. School was always easy for him, and he actually enjoyed it. Skipping school wasn't something he was interested in, because Charley didn't mind being in a classroom. He loved to read, and he loved to learn.

But things shifted dramatically for Charley when we moved to Winston-Salem. He was going into ninth grade, just starting high school, and he was beginning to find his own ways of getting high. He experimented with smoking pot, drinking alcohol, and sniffing glue.

The most damaging experience, though, had to do with a group of kids he met who were involved in witchcraft and the occult. Not long after we settled into our new life in Winston-Salem, he began a descent into this dark world. He soon realized there was a supernatural power available to him through this, and he began to dive deeper and deeper into it.

As strange as it sounds to those with limited knowledge of this dark spiritual realm, there are demonic entities which exist, and Charley learned to communicate with them. Eventually, they released power and knowledge into his life that was unexplainable in the natural realm. Rusty had always had the ability to gain followers, so for all of Charley's life, Rusty had held the "power card" with their friends. Suddenly, that began to change. Now Charley had strange new abilities (more explanation is coming) to make things happen, and Rusty and all of his friends became very curious about it.

One day, Rusty's gang of friends were wanting to get their hands

Transitions

on some money for more drugs, and they decided to test out Charley's new ability. When they asked him about how to get money, he directed them to a place where there were rows of cars. He told them to find a specific row, then look for a specific car in that row. He said that on the back seat floorboard they would find what they needed. They didn't exactly believe him, but they headed to the spot anyway. They searched where he told them to look, found the car, and looked in the back seat. And sure enough, sitting on the floorboard of the back seat, they saw a bag. They quickly grabbed it and opened it up, and to their complete astonishment, it was filled with cash. From that point on, they had a new admiration for Rusty's little brother. Charley was the new go-to guy if they needed anything.

Rusty himself had a hard time believing Charley was really tapping into some kind of magical power, and he made fun of him about it. He wasn't sure how it was all happening, so one day he asked for proof. Charley described a series of steps he could take which would give him the proof he was asking for. It was actually a satanic ritual designed to communicate with demons. Rusty decided to take him up on it, not really believing anything would actually happen. But he wanted to put this nonsense to rest once and for all, so he followed the steps Charley gave him.

Charley had been very clear—it had to happen exactly as he said. So Rusty followed the directions, and when he did, he encountered a demonic creature which scared him so badly he didn't talk about it for years. It was an experience that shook him to his core and he never forgot it, but neither of them ever discussed it with anyone else. I was an adult before I learned any of this. My brothers were both very protective of me and my sister, and they didn't want us to have this knowledge. I'm very grateful for that. But Rusty never made fun of Charley's abilities again. The experience made him a believer. He didn't have any desire to mess with those terrifying creatures himself. But now he knew it was all very real.

Everywhere I Look

In The Screwtape Letters, C.S. Lewis warns, "There are two equal and opposite errors into which our race can fall about the devils. One is to disbelieve in their existence, and the other is to feel an excessive and unhealthy interest in them."[1] Charley definitely fell into the "excessive and unhealthy interest" category. Most people in our current culture would probably fall into the "disbelieve" category. Even Christians, who can read clearly about them in Scripture, tend to live as if evil spirits no longer exist. It's taboo to discuss them, even in Christian circles. I'm guessing most people don't want to be labeled "crazy," or lumped in with the few Christians who seem to have an unhealthy interest in them.

There's also another dynamic fueling the confusion surrounding this topic. In our culture today, every possible issue we struggle with as humans has a new medical label attached to it. We are obsessed with our attempts to explain everything in the natural, and we avoid the spiritual realm like the plague. Christians are as guilty as everyone else of sticking their heads in the sand about all this. It's so much easier to call it all "mental illness" and explain it away with a diagnosis, than it is to accept there might be underlying or correlating spiritual forces involved. We wouldn't know what to do with that, so we tend to give it a label and throw medication at it, treating only the natural, while ignoring the spiritual. Now don't get me wrong. I fully understand and have had up-close, personal experience with situations which involved very real chemical imbalances that needed medical intervention. Modern medicine and natural practices are God-given means of addressing the physiological dynamics involved. But if there are also spiritual forces of darkness tormenting a person, this will often never be addressed or even acknowledged.

C.S. Lewis' warning goes on to say the devils themselves are "equally pleased by both errors." They love it when we stick our heads in the sand. What they really fear is a Christian who knows and walks in his or her authority, who comes against their activity and releases the

Transitions

power of God into it. Since we don't talk about it very much, our current culture is overrun by demonic influence, and unfortunately, for the most part, the church just stands by watching, powerless to do anything about it. And sadly, many Christians will probably read this and roll their eyes. But that very ignorance is what's perpetuating this problem.

We were only in Winston-Salem for two years, but Charley's life was changed forever during that short time. Some portals are not meant to be opened, and the opening of this one proved to be difficult to close. Even though Charley's story would soon take a monumental turn, he had entered a level of warfare in which there was no return. The spiritual opposition we all experienced as a pastor's family never came close to the warfare he personally experienced for the rest of his life. It was on a completely different level.

Moving to the Winning Team

Remember the creepy vibe I talked about when we lived in Winston-Salem? Charley's room felt the same way in Travelers Rest. But only for the first few months. After that, things changed dramatically.

This three bedroom house we moved into is the one I described at the beginning of this book. It's the house I still love to visit. My parents shared the master bedroom, my sister and I shared the middle room, and Charley had his own bedroom at the front of the house. He had a dog named Pepper, a sweet-natured mutt with black and gray speckles, and the two of them stayed in his front bedroom most of the time.

After Charley started tenth grade at Tabernacle, he became

Our family during this season

Everywhere I Look

fascinated with the last book in the Bible, the Revelation. He would sit there in his classroom, reading about the apocalyptic events and fantasizing about the battles. He actually enjoyed envisioning himself fighting for the enemy's side, since he had clearly made the choice already back in Winston-Salem. Charley was well aware the Bible depicted this as the losing team, but even if this were to come true, he liked to picture his team going out with a dramatic, explosive bang. For some crazy reason, it all seemed wildly exciting and worth it to him.

But one night in his bedroom, he was reading the book of Revelation again, and he came to chapter twenty, verse ten.

"Then the devil who had deceived them, was thrown into the fiery lake of burning sulfur, joining the beast and false prophet. There they will be tormented day and night forever and ever."

Suddenly a question came into his mind: "What then?"

He tried to shove the thought away, and his first response to the question was they would all just party for eternity. But was that true? Then he heard it again: "What then?"

The voice grew stronger, and the same question kept coming. He began to recognize it as the Spirit of God. He couldn't answer the question, and as he wrestled with all of this, he started to come out from under the cloud of delusion. Clarity was taking over, and he became aware of a choice he had to make: live with uncertainty, or turn to God and forsake this darkness forever.

He weighed this decision carefully. It was a battle for his soul, and his mind kept going back and forth. Slipping out of his bed, he knelt down on the hardwood floor. The decision was made. There was no turning back. Asking God to forgive him, he chose to position himself on the winning team.

It was an immediate and drastic transformation. The light overcame the darkness, and he was forever changed. That night, his life literally moved from one path to a completely different one.

What he didn't realize until much later, was that the enemy does not

Transitions

deal kindly with traitors.

Chapter Six
Living in the Mountains

Was this door really opening? Was God actually paving the way for him to pastor again? After being out of the ministry for two challenging years, my dad was thrilled when things started to come together for him to return to what he was most passionate about.

By this time, Charley had given his life to God and had experienced a radical transformation. Unfortunately, Rusty was still on a destructive path, but since he lived in Michigan and was an adult now, my dad felt released to get back to what God had originally called him to do. Good News Baptist Church was a small, independent Baptist church in Western North Carolina, just outside of Asheville, and they asked my dad to be their pastor in 1975.

With plans to build a house, my parents searched for some acreage near the church. They found a beautiful piece of land about ten minutes away, with rolling hills and green pastures. At the bottom of the fourteen acres, was a wide creek. And at the top of the tallest hill, with mountain views in every direction, they built the home of their dreams.

Being at the church in Western North Carolina was a really sweet experience. We all fell in love with the people there, and my dad enjoyed seven years of ministry at Good News Baptist. It was only an hour's drive back to Greenville, so every Thursday and Friday evening he drove down the winding highway through the mountains to teach at Tabernacle Bible College, the school he had helped establish back in the sixties. He taught classes on the books of Daniel, Romans, and Hebrews, as well as pastoral classes in hermeneutics, homiletics, and more. His students usually went on to become pastors, and through the years he was frequently invited to speak at their churches. So another avenue of ministry was born: preaching "revival meetings." My dad preached in churches and camp meetings all over the Southeast and beyond. He was eventually invited to speak in other countries too—in churches where his students had gone on to serve on the foreign mission field.

I loved going with my dad when he preached these revival meetings. During the summers when school was out, I would go with him whenever I could. There was a different atmosphere in those services, especially if they were "camp meetings." Those were held outdoors, under a pavilion, with dirt floors usually covered with sawdust. Some of my earliest memories include playing in the sawdust and carving out little streets for my Matchbox cars.

For some reason, the spiritual atmosphere at those revival meetings and camp meetings would often come alive and people would worship with freedom and excitement. The music would welcome the presence of the Holy Spirit, and by the time my dad started preaching, the presence of God was already tangible. His preaching was anointed and full of the Spirit's fire. He especially loved the Old Testament stories, and he could tell them better than anyone else I've ever heard.

There were several sermons which were my favorites. Since he was preaching at many different places, and to many different congregations, the Spirit would lead him to preach certain messages again and again. One of these, which was my absolute favorite, was from the list of David's mighty men in 2 Samuel 23. He picked out three stories and told them in detail with each story representing a godly characteristic he wanted to highlight. Being a good Baptist preacher, Daddy also loved alliteration, so most of the points of his sermons were alliterated to help people remember. And let me tell you, that works. I still remember these points, to this day. The three points in this sermon all started with the letter "D"— Determination, Devotion, and Denial (of self).

Living in the Mountains

The first story came from 2 Samuel 23:11-12, and it was this story which made me call this sermon the "Shammah and the Bean Patch" message. In these verses, we learn that Shammah, all by himself, defended a piece of ground full of lentils from an attack by the Philistines, and he was victorious. My dad used his imagination to create details and when he told this story, he described Shammah planting himself in the middle of the bean patch and swinging wildly at every Philistine who came near him. Shammah represented "determination," and he was a superhero in my mind. I wanted to be as strong and brave as that guy.

The second story came from verses 13-17, and they described an act of devotion by three of the mighty men. Those guys overheard David longing for a drink of water from the well in Bethlehem, and they decided to go get him some. I loved watching my dad act this one out, as he described those three breaking through the garrison to grab some water and take it back to David, only to have him pour it out to the Lord. He wouldn't drink what he considered to be equal to the blood of the men who risked their lives to get it. That story represented "devotion."

And the third story was from verse 39, where you have to look elsewhere in Scripture to read the entire story. Uriah the Hittite was called from battle to come home and sleep with his wife, Bathsheba. It was all an attempted cover-up for David's sin, so this story was so sad to me. Uriah was such a great guy, though, and he refused to spend an evening with his wife when his fellow soldiers were on the battlefield. He denied himself, and his great act of sacrifice messed up David's plan, but demonstrated a remarkable character. His story represented "denial."

That sermon might not have been my dad's most theologically deep message, but I loved it because of the incredible excitement Daddy had for these stories, and the beautiful way he told them. That storytelling gift he had had even as a boy was now being used by God to bring the Bible to life. Everyone would be on the edge of their seats, hanging on every word. And at the end of the night, inevitably the altar would be filled with people, moved by the Holy Spirit to dedicate their lives to serve God with the same kind of passion.

It's a pretty amazing thing for a kid to witness on a regular basis. God's presence being felt, and His Spirit being poured out. There was that grace again . . . everywhere I looked.

Building Bridges

Are you seeing grace yet in your own story? What glimpses of God can you identify? We're told in the first chapter of the book of Romans that God's invisible traits are revealed to us through the visible things all around us. He's there, and always has been. The question is, do we have "eyes to see?"

If you look back on your life, and aren't sure where God was, I would love to invite you to ask Him. Sit with Jesus for a while, and ask Him to give you eyes to see where He was working, and what He was thinking and feeling during that time in your life. You may be surprised at what He shows you.

Jesus, I speak a prayer of blessing over my readers right now. Would You give us all eyes to see Your amazing grace at work in our lives? Reveal Yourself to us, more and more, Lord. We want to see You!

Life in Candler

The music director at our church owned a travel agency, and one year he invited my father to Israel to lead a tour in the Holy Land. They took a group which included some of the church members, and toured the famous places my dad had preached about for years. At each stop, the local tour guide would describe the geography, history, and culture

Living in the Mountains

of the area. Then my dad would lead the devotions and explain the Biblical significance of the site. That first trip sparked a passion inside of my dad for Israel, and he went on to lead trips to that area every year. He took many of his friends, family, and church members to Israel over the years– actually anyone he could convince to go. He wanted everyone to see for themselves what a life-changing experience it is.

Sidenote worth mentioning . . . when I was sixteen, I had the amazing privilege of going on one of those trips, and it truly was life-changing. I finally understood why my dad was so crazy about going to Israel. For my entire life, the Biblical stories had seemed real to me, but they took on a whole new meaning when I could actually put my foot in the Jordan River and take a ride in a boat on the Sea of Galilee. The air even felt different. It was so dry and dusty and hot. Being in that place, and seeing it all with my own eyes gave me a completely different perspective. Everything moved from flannelgraph to real life, from black and white to brilliant color. If you ever have a chance to go, I highly recommend it!

With my parents in the Holy Land

After we moved to North Carolina, my parents immediately started searching for a Christian school for us to attend. The closest one was Faith Christian School in Hendersonville, NC, but it was almost an hour's drive from our home. This didn't matter to them one bit. To give us an education with a Christian worldview, the drive was 100% worth it. My mother started teaching at the school to help with the bills and to ease the load of tuition for their three kids who would be attending. Eventually many other families in our church decided to send their kids to Faith, so my mom ended up driving a van full of students every day.

When we started going to Faith, Charley was heading into his senior year, Sara was going into high school, and I was in third grade. We all settled into our new life, and the next spring, Charley finished high school. After graduation, he made the decision to go to college at our dad's alma mater, Bob Jones University. My mom's wish had come true, and my dad had to eat his words from their first argument. God works in funny ways.

By that point, Sara was in tenth grade, and she had fallen madly in love with a senior named Sam Beddingfield. Sam's little sister was in my class, and we thought it was great that our siblings were dating. We had no idea we would all become family.

"Bara Seth"

She was a daddy's girl, through and through, but she wasn't always crazy about being a preacher's daughter. He affectionately nicknamed her "Bara Seth," and it was their own little joke. Their relationship was sweet, but early on, Sara Beth found the rules and expectations for preacher's kids to be a little overwhelming. To be sure, there were a few perks to being in the pastor's family. When guest speakers came to our church, for instance, it was kind of nice to have them treat her with special favor. But overall, in her mind, the disadvantages outweigh the advantages. It would take her a lifetime to untangle some of the confusion all of this caused in her mind and heart.

Living in the Mountains

"Sara Beth"

Back in Edenton, her earliest memories of her brothers were of them always getting into trouble. Sara tried to mind her own business during those years and fly under the radar. But there were a few things about being the preacher's daughter that just didn't quite sit well with her.

During the early years, I was too young to fully understand what was happening in our family, and my brothers didn't care one bit about Dad's ministry, or how they might affect it. But Sara felt the full weight of being a preacher's kid. The most frustrating part to her was how we were held to a higher standard than most kids, and our family in particular was on display for all to see. We, of all people, had to have good "convictions" about godly behavior and appearance. In the church culture we were a part of, there was a pretty strong emphasis on outward appearance—men wore their hair short, women dressed modestly, which usually meant dresses only, and in general, we stayed away from movie theaters and any place that could possibly "hurt our testimony."

But here's where it got confusing. Different churches have slightly different "convictions" or standards for Christian living, so when our family moved to a new church, our convictions might get slightly looser or tighter, depending on that particular group of people and how they interpreted Scripture on these things. My dad personally didn't have a problem with women wearing pants, except at church. Dresses only for church. But in any other setting, he didn't care, as long as they were modest (another area which was up for debate). However, if all the people in the church felt strongly about it, he didn't mind conforming to their standards, in order to avoid offending them. I don't think he felt like any of these extra-Biblical rules were important enough to make an issue over or cause division. As an individual, he made a personal decision which sounds a lot like Romans 14 Christian living to me, now that I'm old enough to understand it. But at the time, I didn't fully understand it, and neither did Sara. It was just confusing, and she eventually grew to resent it.

When we lived in Edenton, for example, we girls weren't allowed to wear pants, but when we moved to Winston-Salem, we could. Then when we moved to Travelers Rest, and were going to Tabernacle, it was back to "no pants" again. Then we moved to the mountains, and we could wear pants again. Back and forth we went.

In Edenton, boys and girls never swam together at pools or the beach. (Anybody else remember the "no mixed bathing" rule? I always thought it was weird to call it "bathing" when it was actually referring to swimming.) When we moved to Winston-Salem, Sara was allowed to go to the neighborhood pool with her friends, even though boys were there. But then at Tabernacle, that was out. Again, it just depended on how strict the church culture was, and we had to conform to it.

There was another setting where the rules changed. Every summer and Christmas our family went to Ohio and Michigan to visit all of our relatives. My Aunt Joy lived on a lake, so in the summer, everybody ran around in their swimsuits all day long. We were allowed to do that too, as long as we wore a "one piece" and not a bikini. No matter which church we were at, when we went to Michigan, we pretty much followed their rules instead of the ones we had back home. I honestly only have vague memories about all of the rule-changing, but it was

Living in the Mountains

an ongoing cause of frustration and confusion for Sara. As a teenage girl who was being told one thing at one place and another thing in a different place, she found it very frustrating to live by rules she didn't understand or agree with. And through it all, a confusion was setting in that the enemy continued to use against her for years.

It's so easy for us, as humans, to slip into performance based religion. And as preacher's kids, I think we all felt like we needed to perform. I mean, honestly, I'm sure there were times my parents felt like they were performing too. Who hasn't had to overcome that? But for each of us kids, over the course of our lifetimes, there was a gradual awakening to the difference between rule-based religion and grace-based relationship. God so faithfully and gently guided each of us in our individual understanding.

For Sara, the confusion had become a tangled mess by the time she met Sam. Getting married was her way of escaping all of it. She and Sam married when she was just sixteen years old. She wanted to be on her own, making her own decisions, and putting distance between herself and all those rules. But of course, sixteen is so very young to go out into the world on your own. It led her down a complicated path, with many ups and downs.

She kept trying to "find God," but He seemed so elusive. Did He expect her to keep all those rules? Which ones? Were they always the same rules or did they change, depending on who you were with at the moment? She found herself trying to perform her way into a relationship with God, and it never worked. She wanted to live for God, but felt like she couldn't quite keep it up. She didn't realize it, but she was constantly getting sucked back into Old Covenant thinking.

Under the Old Covenant, having a relationship with God involved a long list of rules and regulations. Under the New Covenant, we have a relationship with God based on our faith in His Son, Jesus, who perfectly kept every single rule. No other human has ever been able to do that. Our right standing with God will never happen if it depends on us.

Everywhere I Look

We just can't do it. But by coming into relationship with God through the work of Jesus, we can be made right with God. This is the beauty of the New Covenant which Jesus established through His death and resurrection.

Every other religion in the world is based on behavior and performance. It's just so easy for us to think we need to "do" something to earn God's favor. I think this is because we all know we fall short. We know we mess up, and if we're honest, we know we could never stand in the presence of Almighty God, whose holiness is on a whole different level from the very best of us. So we try harder, and we do more, and we strive like crazy to make up for all of our faults and failures. But we can never do enough. The discrepancy is just too great. That's why we need Jesus!

In a lot of Christian circles, there's still an emphasis on behavior and outward appearance. Our pride pushes us into self-righteous thinking, and we easily slip into caring more about what people think than what God thinks. So differentiating between what's for God and what's for people can be an incredibly confusing journey.

This is especially true if you've grown up the way we did, with a strong awareness of how we were being perceived, and how it constantly reflected on our parents and the ministry. My siblings and I had to make sense of each of these pieces to make distinctions between the performative aspects of religion and our own relationship with God.

Even as an adult, Sara found that being the daughter of the pastor was still just as overwhelming as it had been as a child. As Barnabas Piper, son of well-known pastor John Piper explains, "On a purely lifestyle level, one of the greatest challenges PKs (pastor's kids) face is scrutiny. It feels perpetual, and persistent, even invasive." He goes on to describe how people in the church have what he calls "hyper-awareness" of the pastor's kids. And believe me, we know it. We can sense it, and even see it, and we definitely hear about it. He says, "Watched is what the PKs so often do feel, all the time, in everything. It is life in

Living in the Mountains

a fishbowl, exposed, on display."[2]

It's enough to cause many pastor's kids to slide into perpetual bitterness, especially if all those watching eyes also seem to be casting judgments. That can make it feel like there are only a couple of options: bolt and run far away from all the oppressive judgment, or stay on and learn to wear a mask. I mean, people are watching, and they are expecting you to be the model Christian kid. We all know we can't keep up, so until God's transforming grace catches up with us, we either jump ship or try to fake it. My siblings all chose to bolt, in one way or another. I chose to wear a mask. But more on this later.

Eventually Sara realized she needed to get away from all of it, and fully separate herself from my dad's ministry. She moved to Florida, and established a whole new life for herself. And this was finally the step which enabled her to make the distinctions. Without having to consider how her decisions would affect my parents and the ministry, she was able to toss out the Old Covenant, works-based mindset for good. She found a church where she could focus on her relationship with God instead of her performance for God, and she was finally able to lean into a sweet relationship with Him.

Another beautiful story of grace! I'm telling you, it's literally everywhere I look.

Sara and me

Everywhere I Look

Building Bridges

So what about you? Can you relate to the struggle Sara had? Have you spent a lot of time trying to impress God or people? I know I have, and it's an ongoing area of growth for me. I need God's Spirit to reveal it to me when I'm starting down this path. I can't even see it half the time, until I'm in too deep. I'll start recognizing my heart is feeling weighed down, and I'm starting to slip into discouragement. Then, if I stop and ask God what's going on, He will often reveal to me that I've gotten my eyes off of Him, and onto my performance, or onto my concern over the opinions of people. But this is not His will for us. He wants us to rest in the finished work of Jesus. The price was too high for us to live as if what Jesus did was not enough.

God, give us discernment and a quick recognition of when this is happening. Help us to realign our thinking with Your heart and mind. Free us from performance-based bondage, and empower us to live in the light of Your freedom and grace!

Rusty's Continued Craziness

Get a job and go to church. These were the only two rules Aunt Joy and my dad had established for Rusty while he lived with my aunt and uncle in Michigan. But Rusty wasn't great at following rules. He did get a job at a restaurant and managed to do pretty well the first year. But during the second year, he was getting a little stir crazy and decided to hitchhike back to Winston Salem, North Carolina to see his old buddies. He and one of those friends stole a tent from someone's backyard, and he lived in that tent in the woods for the better part of a year.

When I interviewed him for this book, I learned a lot about his crazy life that I had never known before. And in all of our discussions, I

Living in the Mountains

came to realize sometimes people actually want to be homeless. He really loved living in a tent, with no one to answer to and no responsibilities. He stole food when he needed to eat, and he had his buddies around to help him out whenever he needed it. But eventually it got too cold, so he came to visit our family. He occasionally popped in like that to see us for a few days. It was always such a happy time for me. I missed him so much when he was gone, and I loved it when he came to visit. He was always so much fun to be around, and we all genuinely loved having him in the house. It was during this visit, right after his tent-dwelling homeless phase, that he was introduced to another area of crime: stealing safes.

One day some of his friends called him up and asked him to help them open a safe they had just stolen from a local fast food joint where they worked. The little group of amateur criminals all worked together and figured out how to get into it, and they split the money they found inside. But somehow the police found out who did it, and they began searching for all of them. As soon as Rusty realized they were looking for him, he took off to Michigan. But this only made things worse. Law enforcement officers eventually contacted my parents. It took a while for my dad to get in touch with Rusty, but when he did, he begged him to come back and turn himself in. Rusty was now wanted for grand larceny and safecracking, and the FBI was actually looking for him because he had crossed state lines.

By some crazy miracle, my dad convinced Rusty to come back and turn himself in. My dad had a friend who knew the sheriff, and that friend offered to go with them when Rusty turned himself in. So the three of them drove over to the sheriff's office and went in and explained the situation. The sheriff leaned back in his chair, listening intently as Rusty apologized and begged for mercy. After the apology, the sheriff looked Rusty in the eye, and said, "Here's what we're gonna do. I'm gonna put you on my First Time Offenders Diversion Program." Then he took his lighter, lit the paper where the charges were listed, and threw it on the ground. He told Rusty to pay back his share of the money they had stolen and get out of there. And so he did!

At this point in the story, I would love to tell you that being offered mercy in that situation made Rusty turn his life around. But honestly, I think it only served to embolden him and make him feel unstoppable. So the criminal behavior only intensified. Now that he knew how to crack a safe, he found other friends to help him with this new way to get money.

They started breaking into pharmacies, where they could get a safe plus a bonus stash of drugs to sell.

One day, he and one of his buddies broke into a pharmacy, and this time they ran into some trouble. Back then, the alarm systems were all along the floors of businesses, so they would break in through the roof and use a rope ladder to come down into the pharmacy, but not all the way to the floor. Rusty had mastered this technique, but his buddy was a little too 'high' that day, and he lost his mind when he saw all the drugs. He jumped off the ladder and started running around the store like a maniac, grabbing everything in sight. And of course, it immediately set off the alarm. Rusty knew it wouldn't be long before the police arrived, so he started yelling for his buddy to come back up and get out of there. But the guy wasn't listening, and pretty soon the sirens could be heard coming their way. Rusty waited as long as he could, but the sirens were getting closer. He yelled one last time, then climbed up as fast as he could and got out of there. He took off running toward a church next door, and he hid in the graveyard to watch. Pretty soon the police arrived and quickly surrounded the place. He was sure his buddy would be arrested, but strangely, he never saw him come out. The police searched the entire place for a long time, then gave up and eventually they all left. As soon as the coast was clear, Rusty walked to a nearby gas station and called my grandpa, who came and picked him up. Grandpa knew nothing of what had happened, but the next day when he was at our house, Rusty heard him talking about how he had gone to pick up my grandma's medicine, and they didn't have it. He said someone had broken into the pharmacy and stolen it all.

That did make Rusty feel terrible, but again, it wasn't enough to stop him. He found out his buddy had actually gotten out in time too, so no one was arrested. He had thought for sure there wasn't any way he could've gotten out before the police arrived, but his buddy had grabbed a huge, metal stamp machine standing by the front door, slammed it through the glass, and had barely escaped in time.

Close calls, but not close enough. Rusty was starting to feel invincible.

Building Bridges

Are you starting to see the amazing grace which was all over Rusty's life? He kept running, but God kept working. Sometimes in small ways, like letting Rusty hear about my grandma's medicine. God just dropped those words right down into Rusty's heart, where He knew they would affect him. To this day, Rusty hasn't forgotten how that felt.

Do you have someone you're praying for who's running from God? I want you to hear me now . . . rest assured, God is working. He never stops working. Even when we don't see the effects just yet, we can be sure of this fact: He leaves the ninety-nine to chase the one who is lost.

That's right—chase! In the twenty-third psalm, most Bible translations use the English word "follow" for the Hebrew word "radaph" in the phrase "Surely goodness and mercy will follow me all the days of my life." But this is unfortunate, because "radaph" does not mean to calmly walk behind someone. It actually means to chase, to pursue, and to hunt down. It's the same word used in Scripture to describe what the armies of Israel did to their enemies. They didn't just follow them around like a puppy dog. They pursued them and chased them down. And that's a better picture of what God does to us. His goodness and mercy aren't just following us around. They are chasing us and pursuing us all the days of our lives. It's a beautiful, comforting thought. Not just for us, but for those we love who are still on the run. His faithful love is chasing after them, all the days of their lives.

Chapter Seven
The End of the Road

There's a time to run, and there's a time to stop running. Although he didn't realize it, Rusty's time of running from God was coming to an end. He had gone back and forth from Michigan to North Carolina more times than he could count, but as he was nearing the end of the 70's, he was also nearing the end of this season.

He had had several run-ins with the law by now. One time he even had to sit in jail for a week. That little fiasco happened when he and some buddies decided to hitch-hike to Florida. One of the drivers who picked them up stopped for gas and decided not to pay, but instead just drove away. The police quickly caught up with them and the whole gang was arrested. They sat in jail for a week, but for some reason, when the higher powers realized they all had Michigan driver's licenses, they decided it would be too much trouble to deal with them. So they let them go, and again, Rusty laughed in the face of mercy, and walked out of there feeling a little more confident.

But one of the craziest stories of unbelievable mercy happened when Rusty was back up in Holly, Michigan, staying again at my Aunt Joy's house on Tipsico Lake. It started when he and a friend went to steal a safe from a convenience store down the road. Inside the store, the safe was up on a platform, and his buddy scooted it to the edge to push it off to Rusty. But he pushed too hard, and the safe weighed a ton. It fell through Rusty's arms and landed on his foot, squashing it like an orange. His entire foot and ankle were completely crushed, but he still had to get out of there. It was snowing outside, and he had to jump from the roof of the building to escape and hobble away on his badly broken foot. His buddy took him back to Aunt Joy's house, where they made up a story about having a flat tire, and the car sliding off the jack onto Rusty's foot. (Side note: I actually believed this story my whole life—we all did—and I was always terrified of changing a tire. It was just a few years ago that he told me the real story.)

Uncle Al rushed him to the hospital, where he ended up in surgery to try to save his foot. They weren't sure if he would ever walk correctly again, and it took an entire year to heal, but he did recover. However, the experience made him finally give up safe-cracking. Thankfully!

During that year, when he was laid up at my aunt and uncle's house, he slept on the couch in their living room. One night after everyone was in bed, he heard a knock at the door. Another buddy of his had been driving in the snow and had slidden off the road into the woods. His buddy had walked to the closest house and had found a nice car with keys in it, and had decided to steal it. Then he had stopped by to get Rusty so they could go for a ride in his "new car." Rusty limped out to the car with his big cast on his foot, and they took off for what ended up being a three day joy-ride.

While it snowed heavily, those hoodlums drove all the way to Detroit, hitting mailboxes and stop signs and even a few cars along the way. They stopped at a few strip bars, stole a lot of beer, and stayed drunk the whole time. It's a miracle they didn't kill somebody! Or themselves, for that matter. At one point they stole new tires for the car, and at another point they got in a huge fight in a bar and ran out and drove their car into a bunch of Corvettes in the parking lot just to get even. How the police never caught up with them during this insane escapade, I'll never know. But they finally got tired and decided to head back to Holly.

Because Rusty's foot was so messed up, he couldn't drive, so his buddy was doing all the driving. As they were heading back, Rusty had been dozing off when the car suddenly started shaking. It jolted

The End of the Road

him back to reality, and he looked over and saw his friend sound asleep at the wheel, with the gas pedal pushed hard to the floor. They were speeding straight toward a tractor trailer. He yelled out to his friend a split second before the impact. Their car crashed violently into the back of the semi, and the hood of the car was torn off as the car became wedged up under the back of the truck!

Bouncing along like a basketball, they went over a bridge, where somehow the bumps dislodged the car. It went sliding in the snow, turned a few circles, and landed in a ditch. Up ahead, the truck driver had pulled over and was slowly backing up to get to them. After all that chaos, they were miraculously unharmed. The two of them got out of the car and ran to the truck. As they did, Rusty's buddy told him to let him do the talking. And when they got to the cab of the truck, Rusty's friend started in.

"My dad's gonna kill you! You ran me off the road! Did you even see what you did?! You just changed lanes right in front of me, and ran smack into my new car! My dad's gonna KILL you!"

The poor, terrified truck driver probably thought he might lose his job. He started apologizing profusely, then pulled out his wallet, which was full of cash, and handed them enough to cover the cost of the car! He even offered to drive them back to Holly if they'd just keep quiet and never tell anyone what happened.

And they decided to let him. They jumped up into his cab, and he drove them back and dropped them off at Rusty's buddy's house. Not only did those two never have to pay for what they did, they actually walked away with a big wad of cash. It's one of the most bizarre stories I've ever heard. But I do think it had an effect on Rusty because not long after this, he actually started to settle down. As crazy as that experience was, I think even he was starting to realize he was living on borrowed time.

Everywhere I Look

Sweet Surrender

Rusty knew he couldn't keep up this pace forever. Occasionally, he would decide he was going to settle down. The squashed foot disaster got his attention for a little while, but he kept sliding back into danger. The adrenaline rush was just so addictive.

In an attempt to somewhat slow down, he moved into the basement of a friend's house, and started working for the guy's father. It was a plumbing company, and for a while he was working consistently and trying to actually start living responsibly. He and his buddy were both starting to feel a sense of heaviness about the life they'd been living, and what they didn't want to admit was the Spirit of God was convicting them.

At one point during this time, Rusty made a trip down to see us. We didn't know he was coming, and we were all at church. It was a Wednesday night, and this meant we were at "prayer meeting," the mid-week service where my dad would teach a short devotional, and then everyone would share prayer requests. Afterwards we'd all go down and kneel together at the altar to take our requests to God. Kids could share prayer requests too, and although I don't remember this, I apparently raised my hand and asked everyone to pray for my big brother who was far from God. What I didn't know was that when Rusty had gotten into town and had realized where we were, he had slipped into the back of the auditorium. He saw me raise my hand, and he heard my prayer request for him. It pierced his heart and brought tears to his eyes.

There was that conviction again! It was starting to show up a lot, and it was feeling stronger and stronger. Undeniable now.

On an earlier occasion when he had visited us, Charley had actually confronted him. It was right after Charley had gotten right with God, and he was experiencing the peace and freedom Jesus brings, and he was burdened for Rusty. He stopped Rusty one day in our living room, looked him straight in the eyes and asked, "When are you gonna get

The End of the Road

saved?"

Rusty beat around the bush and tried to avoid the question, but Charley shot it straight. "You need to get saved, Rusty."

That must have taken a huge amount of courage, and Rusty couldn't get over the confrontation. It had been eating at him ever since, and now, here he was in the back of this church, hearing his baby sister ask everyone to pray for him. It was all starting to pile up like layers of snow, and he could feel the avalanche coming.

Not long after this, he was back in Michigan, still feeling like the Holy Spirit was on his heels. He and his friend were having conversations about it all the time now, and they both knew what they needed to do. It was time to stop running from God, but they both still had something holding them back.

One night after work, Rusty headed down to his basement bedroom to go to sleep, and that's when the forces of Hell came against him with such fierce aggression he was terrified he was going to die. Something was literally holding him down, just like he had been feeling like something had been spiritually holding him back. It was time for a show-down, and in his own strength, he was completely powerless. This thing was trying to kill him. There was no amount of pushing that could shove it off of him.

Mustering up his very last breath, he cried out to God and in an instant he was free! When he spoke the Name of Jesus into the atmosphere, the enemy had no choice but to flee.

By the grace and mercy of God, he had been rescued. And immediately he fell to his knees in humility and repentance. Right then and there, he surrendered his life to Jesus.

Beautiful, incredible, amazing GRACE!

Everywhere I look.

Building Bridges

If you don't have a relationship with God through His Son, Jesus, I'm going to shoot it to you straight, just like Charley did. When are you going to decide to follow Jesus? What are you waiting for?

The conviction of God's Spirit is such a beautiful gift. It's an invitation to stop running and start resting. We aren't promised tomorrow, and God's Word says that today is the day of salvation. So it's time to go for it. There is literally nothing in the world worth missing this. What a tragedy it would be to gain the whole world and lose your own soul.

God's love for us is beyond our comprehension, and He's continually inviting us "further up and further in," as CS Lewis puts it. So what are you waiting for? Come on in!

Spirit of God, would You pour out the gift of Your loving conviction on anyone reading this now who may be running from You? Your love is better than life, and I ask for Your love to be evident right now to every person reading these words. Release the captives, Lord! Recover sight to the spiritually blind! Set the oppressed free, in Jesus' Name!

Part Three

Looking Up

Seeing God's Grace in the Highlands

"The LORD alone guided them . . . He let them ride over the highlands and feast on the crops of the fields. He nourished them with honey from the rock . . . "
Deuteronomy 32:12-13 (NLT)

"He has given me a new song to sing, a hymn of praise to our God. Many will see what he has done and be amazed. They will put their trust in the LORD . . . May all who search for You be filled with joy and gladness in You."
~Psalm 40:2-3, 16 (NLT)

If we could just get her back to her dorm, get her into bed, let her sleep it off . . . maybe, just maybe, we could actually get away with this!

None of us meant to get into this big, giant mess. We weren't exactly angels, but all we wanted to do was go off campus and feel normal again. The strict Christian college we went to had a million rules, and all three of us were preacher's daughters. We knew better, but we were also sick and tired of rules. This school we chose to come to had more rules than all of our preacher's families put together.

So we had gravitated toward a fun-loving, rule-breaking girl who had a friend that lived off campus. When we all went out one weekend, we stopped by the girl's apartment. But we had no idea our fun-loving college friend would pull out a bottle of Jack Daniels and start playing Quarters. I didn't even know what the game was, but I quickly found out it was a really fast way to get completely smashed. My PK friends and I were immediately terrified. We weren't interested in drinking alcohol, but we knew that just being with someone who was drinking would be enough to get us into a whole lot of trouble with the school.

In no time at all, our college friend was so drunk she could barely walk, and we had a serious situation on our hands. We drove her back to school and carefully snuck her into her dorm. So far, so good. Helping her into bed, and pulling up the covers, we gave her strict orders to stay put. Then we headed over to the dining hall for supper, which couldn't be skipped or we'd be breaking another rule.

As we stood around on the terrace waiting for the dining hall doors to open, I tried to get my anxiety under control. *Just breathe, Charity. Inhale, exhale. Deep breaths. You can do this. You're good at acting like everything's okay.*

But then I saw her . . . staggering across the parking lot, like Otis Campbell coming into the Mayberry jail. Oh my gosh! What in the world?!

I immediately knew this was not going to end well for any of us.

Chapter Eight
Rolling into the 80's

Who was this guy? I almost didn't recognize my brother when he moved back home. It was 1979, and at the age of 23, Rusty had just experienced a radical transformation. He actually changed outwardly as much as he did inwardly. He cut his hair, changed how he dressed, went to church every time the doors were open, and sat around the house reading his Bible. It was completely amazing.

The end of the 70's brought the end of one season and the beginning of a new one for my family. Everything was changing. Sara had gotten married in 1977, and for the first time in my life I had a bedroom all to myself. My sister and I had always fought like cats and dogs. With five and a half years between us, I was too young to ever really fit into her world. I loved annoying her, and she loved picking on me. We were like oil and water.

But something changed when she got married and moved out. I actually missed her, and I think she must have missed me too, because suddenly we started getting along. I loved going over to her house and learning all about what married life was like. I couldn't wait to get married too. Adulthood looked so fun to me. Especially after Sara had her baby girl, Summer Elisabeth in November of 1980. That sweet baby girl became the light of our lives, and I loved taking care of her.

Charley had graduated from high school in 1976, and had gone to Bob Jones University to major in theology and minor in Greek. Both Rusty and Charley eventually answered the call of God to enter the ministry. Rusty completed his GED and started studying at Tabernacle

Bible College, where Dad was still teaching. Both boys were now on a spiritually healthy track.

In May of 1981, after struggling with Alzheimer's disease for seven horrible years, my sweet Grandma Eva passed away. My grandparents had lived right next door to us, so our whole family had both the pleasure of having them near, and the heartache of watching her decline and eventually leave us. My grandma had been like my second mother, and this was my first experience in losing someone so close and so dear to me.

That spring semester of 1981 was my last semester at Faith Christian School. I was in eighth grade, and in those last few months of the school year, I had a boyfriend. He and I had known each other since I first came to Faith in third grade. My mom had taught him in fourth grade, and had also taught his younger brother. He played on the junior varsity basketball team, and I was a JV cheerleader. We went to the Athletic Banquet together that spring, and there's an awkward photo to prove it. We were only a "thing" for a short time, but it was a sweet thing while it lasted. Nothing serious, but we did go on what I considered my "first date." Since we were too young to drive, our moms dropped us both off at the Asheville Mall, and we walked around holding hands and trying to be all grown up.

Soon after my grandma's death, my dad was asked to be a pastoral candidate at a church in South Carolina. In the summer of '81, he accepted the position, and in the fall we moved to Anderson. I actually don't even remember telling my boyfriend I wouldn't be coming back to school in the fall, but I'm sure I did at some point. That was the end of our little relationship. We never kept in touch, and I don't remember if I even thought about him again. I had no idea 35 years later he would come back into my life.

Rolling into the 80's

Oakwood

Pastoring Oakwood Baptist Church was a huge career shift for my dad. Not only was there a church to pastor, but now there was also a Christian school to oversee. Administration became a big part of his life, and this was much more stressful than just pastoring. He still enjoyed it all, and he adjusted well to the new responsibilities. My dad was a natural born leader. It was just in his DNA. One of the things I loved most about him was that he was a servant-leader. He served and loved people so well, even as he was leading them.

Anderson is only 30 minutes from Greenville, so he continued to teach Bible college classes at Tabernacle. He also continued to preach revival meetings for all the students and friends who invited him. Eventually he needed to limit the number of trips he could take out of town for those meetings, though. Although he loved going to them, the folks in his congregation weren't always happy about him being away, and he struggled to find a balance.

My mom was able to teach kindergarten in the church's Christian school, which was perfect because she loved teaching kindergarten the most. My dad filled his days with hospital visits, counseling sessions, school board meetings, church board meetings, and personal study for his classes and sermons. It was an intense schedule, but he seemed to thrive on the intensity of it all.

Just as my parents were experiencing shifts in their life, I was starting to feel the effects of being the "preacher's daughter" in every area of mine. Sometimes I liked it, and sometimes I wanted a different identity altogether. I was definitely trying to "find" myself. But in the process, I kept getting lost.

I'll never forget our first Sunday at Oakwood. While my dad preached, Mom and I sat together in the center of the auditorium. Surrounding the floor level was a balcony which stretched around the auditorium in a semicircle. As I sat there in the middle, looking up and all around, the church felt gigantic. And I felt like all eyes were on us.

Everywhere I Look

It was incredibly intimidating, and I immediately felt like I was in a fishbowl, with people watching my every move.

My first day of school wasn't much better. Most of the kids in my class had been there for years, and it seemed like they were all friends. I felt like I was standing outside, peering in at them through a glass window. I didn't realize until much later that since I was the new pastor's daughter, they were as intimidated as I was. But in a few short weeks all of my discomfort disappeared. I fell madly in love with a boy who was a senior, and my whole world started to revolve around that relationship.

Fourteen is way too young to be in a serious relationship, but my parents had met at fourteen, so no one was too concerned. The world was a different place in the eighties though, than it had been when my parents met in the fifties. And people were getting married much later now than eighteen, so fourteen was pretty young to start thinking about marriage.

But my boyfriend was eighteen, and we both had marriage on our minds, as crazy as it sounds. That relationship was intense and sometimes scary. It was my first exposure to someone who was controlling and jealous, and frequently angry. It made me feel afraid, but I didn't let anyone know how volatile the relationship was. After two years, though, it was getting out of hand and my parents started seeing the destructive nature of it. They decided to intervene, and they made us break up. Even though it was painful to separate myself from him, I actually felt a sense of relief. I trusted their judgment, and knew they were right, so I didn't resist their intervention. Turns out, trusting their authority in that situation was a foreshadowing of things to come in my life.

Not long after this, I was in another serious relationship. That one wasn't really destructive, but an unhealthy pattern was forming in my life. I was finding my identity and my happiness in having a boyfriend and in getting the attention of guys. And the inappropriate nature of

Rolling into the 80's

these relationships often felt like an addiction and was more damaging to me spiritually than I realized. During this time, I had no interest in a relationship with God. In the back of my mind, I figured someday I would settle down and start being a serious Christian. But that didn't look very fun. So I pushed it off for later in life.

Meanwhile, I pretended to be a good little Christian girl. It was a mask I wore well, and I talked myself into believing I had everyone fooled. It was extremely important to me to play the part and to avoid bringing shame or heartache to my parents. They had already been through so much. I had seen their tears firsthand, and I didn't want to be another wayward child bringing them more pain. But I didn't exactly want to be a good little Christian girl. So I learned how to be a good liar, and I lived a double life all through high school.

Parts of my high school years were just carefree and fun. I wasn't always sneaking around being an idiot. I was kind of a chameleon during those years, blending in with whatever group I happened to be with. My best friend was Cinnamon Ashley, who was (and still is) a genuinely wonderful person. We regularly heard the question "Are those your real names?" when we introduced ourselves. I guess it's not everyday you meet two girls whose names are Charity and Cinnamon. We both loved plain cheeseburgers and 80's music, and we were both cheerleaders, so we hung out a lot. But even 80's music and MTV was "sneaking around" for me, because my parents would not have approved. Sneaking around was gradually becoming my way of life.

Cinnamon and me

Everywhere I Look

As graduation approached, I started investigating colleges to decide where to go. My parents were only willing to pay for a Christian college, and there were really only a few they liked. So I picked the one near a beach, naturally!

The college I chose is located in beautiful, sunny Florida, in an area that is famous for its stunning white sand beaches. Hanging out at the beach and soaking in the sun sounded like a great way to spend my weekends. And being seven hours from home was another perk which was very appealing to me. By now, I was getting really tired of the mask, and it seemed like a great idea to get far enough away so I wouldn't have to wear it anymore.

I didn't realize I was walking into a land mine of rules like I never could have imagined. Demerits were given out like candy, for any and every possible offense. And when all those rules collided with my rebellious heart, it created the perfect storm. I was actually heading into a tornado.

And sneaking around would continue to be my norm.

New Sisters in the Family

Is it possible to be addicted to higher education? If it is, then I'm pretty sure Charley was. After he graduated from Bob Jones University in 1982 with his Bachelor's degree, he went on to receive a Master of Arts degree and a Master of Divinity, and he still wasn't done. He eventually took all of the courses for a Doctorate in Divinity, and if he had been able to complete his dissertation, he would've earned a PhD.

In the fall of '82, Charley started teaching at Tabernacle Christian, where we had all attended school. While he was there, he also attended the church, and pretty soon he began to notice a beautiful girl we had actually known years before. Phyllis Hall had been friends with my sister, Sara, in junior high school, but now she was all grown up, and Charley decided to ask her out. The Saturday after Valentine's Day 1983, they went on their first date, and they immediately fell in love! In

Rolling into the 80's

June, he proposed, and seven weeks later they were married on August 6 in the sanctuary of Tabernacle Baptist Church.

Charley and Phyllis' wedding

It was a beautiful ceremony, and we were all thrilled for them. Phyllis was so quiet, compared to our loud and crazy family. But she fit in beautifully, especially since she and Sara were already friends. And Charley was absolutely crazy about her.

In 1984, Rusty followed suit. While he was taking ministry classes at Tabernacle, Sharon Rush was studying education there at the college. Sharon had been in our youth group in the mountains at Good News Baptist, and we all knew her and loved her. So when she and Rusty started dating, she also fit in beautifully with our family. They were married in June of 1984, and now I had two new sisters.

Charley and Phyllis had their first baby the year I graduated from high school. Nathan Charles was born in August of 1985, on my dad's birthday. We were all completely over the moon, and two years later they welcomed James Russell into their little family. In 1993, their baby girl, Julia Grace, was born, and their little family was now complete.

Charley started pastoring a small church the same year their first baby was born. Bethel Baptist was in a little town right outside of Anderson, and he pastored there for the next 20 years. Being an introvert,

Charley had no desire to pastor a large church like my dad's. He loved pastoring his small church of 50-75 people, and considered this his unique calling.

During this time, he also taught classes at Tabernacle Bible College, and eventually became a dean there. With incredible intellect, and a gift for teaching God's Word, Charley became the resident Greek scholar of our family. Anytime we had a theological question or wanted to know what the Greek wording was for a passage, we would call Charley. In fact, everyone he knew did too. His friends, his students, and the people he was pastoring and mentoring all considered him an expert in Biblical knowledge. He was a walking encyclopedia of all things theological.

Rusty graduated from Tabernacle in 1984, and that same weekend he and Sharon were married. Right after the wedding, he started working full time as the youth pastor at our former church, Good News Baptist. They actually lived in our old house, since my parents still owned it. This made it really fun to visit them, because it was my old home filled with childhood memories.

Having both boys in the ministry was a dream come true for my parents. Who would've imagined this just a few short years before? I was now surrounded by preachers!

Building Bridges

Is it hard for you to imagine someone you love being completely transformed by grace? Unless you've witnessed such a drastic change up close, it may seem impossible. I honestly never could have imagined the huge turn-around we saw in both of my brothers. They literally turned into completely different people.

Rolling into the 80's

In second Corinthians 5:17(NLT), Paul describes it this way:
"Anyone who belongs to Christ has become a new person. The old life is gone; a new life has begun!"

If you are praying for this transformation in someone you love, I want to encourage you to keep praying. I watched my parents persist in prayer for their boys for many long and painful years. I saw them weep and grieve for those boys. And then I saw them weep for joy when those boys turned to the Lord.

God is working in your waiting!

Chapter Nine
Off to College

Beautiful, sunny Florida. I could not wait to get there. Moving far away sounded so exciting to me, until I actually finished unpacking everything, and had to imagine my parents leaving. It started to hit me that I would be all alone there, without my family or friends. Slightly unnerving.

Before my parents left, we all went to a chapel service together, to kick off the school year. I remember feeling a heavy conviction from the Holy Spirit during the service, and a really strong sense that I needed to chart a new path for this new season. I had spent the last few years secretly doing my own thing, and perfecting the art of deception. As I sat there mentally arguing with the Holy Spirit, I knew I needed to surrender to God and start living truthfully.

The altar call was excruciating. My heart was pounding, and my mind was racing. To go forward and pray meant my parents would realize I had been wearing a mask. My biggest fear in life was disappointing them. I just couldn't bring myself to do it. In my mind, I was thinking I'd do it later after they were gone. But that didn't happen. At least not right away.

After a tearful goodbye the following day, my parents headed back to Anderson, and I was on my own. Classes started, and unfortunately, my rebellious heart was immediately drawn toward other kids who also rolled their eyes at all the rules. We started hanging out and going off campus, and before long, I was right smack in the middle of a group of kids who had the reputation of being "the rebels."

Everywhere I Look

Kappa Psi

A couple weeks into school, I started dating a guy who was also in that group, but he didn't seem as rebellious as the others. He was a senior, so he took it all a little more seriously. In November, I brought him home to meet my family, and my siblings all came over for us to have a meal together. He knew my dad and brothers were all preachers, but he was completely unprepared for what happened next.

As we all gathered in the kitchen to say the blessing together, my dad asked us to bow our heads in prayer, and suddenly all three of them, my dad and both brothers, hit the floor and started yelling out loud prayers and waving their arms around. Then they stopped and looked over at my boyfriend, who looked like he'd seen a ghost! Bursting into laughter, they told him to relax, that they were only joking. He breathed a huge sigh of relief, and we all had a good laugh together, but I think he was still a little intimidated by all those preachers.

After Christmas, as the second semester was just getting started, I went off campus with a group of girlfriends. We were only two weeks into the semester, but we were already getting antsy, so we decided to go visit a girl who lived off campus. And that's when our college friend got drunk. Drinking alcohol will get you kicked out of that school, and even being with someone who's drinking can land you in a whole lot

Off to College

of trouble, as I would soon find out.

When she came staggering across the parking lot, barely able to walk, we all knew this was not good. But I don't think I had any idea just how bad it would be. During supper, we were each called away from our tables and were brought to the administration building to be questioned. Those interrogations actually lasted the entire evening, and it was very late when I finally got out of there. I don't use the word "interrogations" lightly. It was one of the most terrifying experiences of my life. I strongly disagree with the way it was handled, but I can confidently say God used it all for good. You'll never convince me it's okay to lie to kids to get them to confess. That may be a tactic police investigators use, but I just don't think deans of a Christian college should use it. Regardless, I stuck to the truth, which was bad enough, and I came away with 141 demerits, and a few other punishments. Hitting 150 demerits will get you sent home, so I had to go the entire semester, basically, without getting 10 demerits.

Now, you have to understand that you can easily get demerits for not making your bed correctly or forgetting to wipe the bathroom counter down before you head to class. Imagining myself going the whole semester without getting 10 demerits was like imagining myself walking on water. It seemed completely impossible. And honestly, apart from the grace of God, it was.

Fresh Start

The day after the interrogations, I sat at my desk in my dorm room, and had a heart to heart with Jesus. Ever since my first day there, I had been feeling clear and strong conviction from the Holy Spirit, and I knew this situation I found myself in was actually a wake-up call. I didn't have any question it was God's mercy that kept me from being expelled, and I also knew it was time for me to stop running from Him. I was also pretty sure it would take a miracle for me to make it through the semester without getting 10 demerits. So I prayed at my desk that day and fully surrendered my life to the Lord. I asked God for forgiveness and for a fresh start. And also for a miracle. I really, really didn't want to get kicked out, mainly because of how badly it would hurt my parents.

As a child, I had enjoyed a sweet relationship with God. I had prayed, read my Bible, and had dreamed of being a missionary someday. But those high school years were crazy, and my heart was far from God during that season. I can say that all along, I felt bad about how I was living. The lies I told my parents were enough to make me feel a perpetual sense of guilt and shame. So even though my moment of repentance at college wasn't as dramatic as either of my brothers, it was a huge breakthrough in my own mind and heart. I knew something radical was happening inside of me. And it was so refreshing and beautiful.

Part of my punishment was getting moved to a different dorm. I'm still not sure why they did that, but I fully believe it was by the providential Hand of God. In the new dorm, my roommate was a girl named Andrea Rencher. This girl was definitely not in the group of rebels. She was actually the opposite. Andrea talked about God all the time, asked me about having devotions, and lived out her faith in front of me. Since I was trying to have a fresh start with God, having her in my life was incredibly encouraging and helpful. I really wanted to become the kind of person she was. I also met other great people in the new dorm. One girl in particular, Richelle Lawrence, lived across the hall. She was really sweet and kind of quiet. We never really became close friends at that point in our journey. But the connection was made, and God knew how badly we would need each other later on in our lives.

During this time, I started talking to my boyfriend about God and about wanting to live my life differently. His parents were on staff at the college, so he was also from a Christian family. But he didn't necessarily want to talk about spiritual things. I remember at one point he told me he was too private to share personal information like that. So I just respected his position and let it go. But we were actually on two different wavelengths spiritually, and it would be years before we both realized the extent of it.

Back and Forth . . . and Back Again!

We dated the whole school year, and somehow, by the grace of God, I made it through the last semester without getting too many demerits. I think I ended up with a grand total of 147. On the last day of classes, my boyfriend and I said goodbye for the summer, and in the conversation he told me for the first time that he loved me. We were apart during the summer, except for a couple short visits, but wrote letters and talked frequently, and in the fall, we were back at school.

Andrea and I requested to be roommates again, but our third roommate had graduated back in the spring, so we got a new roommate that fall. Valerie Bianco was the perfect fit for us. The three of us became best of friends, and we actually still are. We were literally only roommates for one semester, but we remained close from that point on. There's just something special about the bonds created in a college dorm room over late night laughter and heart to heart conversations.

Andrea, Val, and me, in our dorm room

It was the fall of 1986, and my boyfriend was graduating in December. He was trying to decide what he would do after graduation, and he had applied for jobs in several cities. I knew he was under a lot of pressure to make some big life decisions, but I didn't realize he was also questioning our relationship. Sometime during the semester, I started feeling him pull away emotionally, and when I asked him about it, he said he wasn't sure if he loved me and didn't know if we should stay together.

I was completely devastated. By this point I was crazy about him, and we had talked about marriage. My sweet roommates consoled me, and told me what a big mistake he was making. It was the first time I'd gotten my heart broken, and I was thrown off balance. This was the first sign of something being not quite right, but since we didn't actually break up, I chalked it up to him being unsure of his future in general, and I tried not to think about it. But his uncertainty and anxiety kept getting worse, and the whole semester was tainted by a dark cloud of heaviness. After he graduated, he went to stay with his parents, who now lived in Pennsylvania.

For several reasons, I decided to transfer to Bob Jones University after the Christmas break. I had had about enough of this college, and at Bob Jones I could live at home and be a town student. But more importantly, I could study Special Education. The other school didn't offer that, but at Bob Jones I could double major in Elementary Education and Special Education, so this is the route I decided to take.

In February, my boyfriend came down to visit and to decide if he wanted to stay in the relationship. After a few days together, he told me he felt like we needed to break up, and then he left for Pennsylvania. It was Valentine's Day and my birthday was two days later. Whew, not gonna lie, it was devastating. I cried for a few days, but then I washed my face, and decided to get on with my life. A week later, he called saying he felt like he'd made a terrible mistake and he wanted me back.

Too little, too late, buddy. I was done with the back and forth, and I told him it was over. Maybe it was just a crazy game, or he wanted what he couldn't have, but he was convinced he wanted me back and called continuously trying to change my mind. This went on all se-

Off to College

mester, and in May he offered to fly me up to Pennsylvania because he wanted to see me. He actually said he was hoping I'd fall in love with that place and decide to move up there.

But this idea was completely out of the question and I told him so. I had two more years of school, and I wasn't about to move all the way to Pennsylvania for a guy who couldn't make up his mind about me. But I did decide to take him up on the offer to fly me up there for a visit, because that did sound like fun.

I stayed at his family's house with his parents and brothers, and we had a wonderful week together. I had always loved his family, and it was sweet to see them again. At the end of the week, he told me he loved me and he was willing to move to Anderson to be with me. I didn't fully believe him, and I told him I would believe it when I saw it.

Surprisingly, he actually did it! Two months later, in the middle of the sweltering August heat, he moved to Anderson, got a job and an apartment, and started talking about marriage again. And then on Valentine's Day, one year to the day after he had broken up with me, he took me out to dinner and proposed. Trying to redeem the holiday, I guess. I think I was still expecting him to change his mind again, but he didn't. We spent that semester planning a summer wedding, and on July 16,1988, we were married.

This was one of those times when it was a huge advantage to be the pastor's daughter. The whole entire church pitched in to make my wedding amazing. They threw showers, made the food for the reception, decorated everything beautifully, and gave us a ton of gifts. Oakwood is full of kind-hearted people and they loved my dad. Helping me have a big, beautiful wedding was their way of loving my family well.

Having three pastors in the family made for an interesting wedding ceremony. My dad walked me down the aisle, where both of my brothers stood ready to greet us. One of them asked "Who gives this woman?" and the other led us in prayer. Then my dad stepped in front of us, between my brothers, to perform the actual vows. I loved having all

Everywhere I Look

three of them play a role in giving me away. My big brothers had always been so protective of me. And this felt like they were walking me into this new season of my life. Getting married can be a scary thing, but having all three of them there for me felt comforting.

It was a beautiful beginning to what I hoped would be a beautiful life together.

Rice Family photo at Oakwood

Glory Days

For my parents, this was a season of pure joy. All of their kids were doing well, and in-laws and babies were being added to our family. The year I got married, Rusty and Sharon moved to the Greenville area, so we all lived within 45 minutes of each other. Rusty started pastoring a church in Travelers Rest, SC. A few years later they had their first baby, Hannah Joy, and two years later, Angela Marie made her entrance.

Off to College

Sharon, Hannah, Angela, and Rusty

When I got married, I still had one year left in school—a semester of classes and a semester of student teaching. In the spring of 1989, my parents' second kid graduated from the school Russ initially couldn't stand. I graduated from Bob Jones University with a double major in Elementary Education and Special Education. We lived in an apartment in Greenville, where he worked and I taught students with learning disabilities. We saved up my salary for a down payment on a house, and after two years, we were ready to buy our first home and start thinking about having a baby. Things were moving along according to plan, and from the outside I'm sure we looked like we were doing fine. But trouble had begun to simmer, just below the surface.

Something strange was going on that I couldn't put my finger on. The "back and forth" which had defined our dating relationship, was now showing up in our marriage. But it didn't look the same. When we were dating, the ups and downs were about whether or not we should stay together. After we got married, that question was off the table, since we were both committed to the marriage. What went back and forth was the atmosphere in our home, and my husband's disposition in general. Some days he came home happy and in a great mood. Other days he came home sullen and agitated. When he was angry, he would have outbursts where he would throw things or kick things, and he didn't want to talk about whatever it was that was upsetting him. Sometimes he would give me the silent treatment and go to bed in a bad mood. It was incredibly confusing. We only lived in that apartment for the first two years of our marriage, but I have many disturbing memories of this behavior. I can vividly remember going out to our living room, late at night, and sitting there in tears, wondering if we would actually be okay.

I had no idea what this could possibly be, but I wasn't about to tell anyone about it. As you already know, I can wear a mask when I need to. So I didn't talk about this with a single person. I wanted us to be okay, and I hoped whatever this was would eventually pass.

Building Bridges

Can you see a pattern forming in my life? A pattern of hiding the truth, pretending to be someone I wasn't, wearing that fake mask? A lot of it had to do with pleasing people, and it's taken me years to learn how to live in the light of God's grace, and to be okay with my authentic self and my true reality.

I hope you aren't living behind a mask, but if you are, I want to encourage you to dig deep into the areas of your heart that need healing. Jesus said it best in John 8, "The truth will set you free." It really, really does! He longs to break the chains that hold us down. And He stands ready and willing to do this as soon as we're ready to let Him.

Father, would You bring healing now to anyone hiding in shame or living under the weight of pretense and fear? I speak peace and freedom over them now in the Strong Name of Jesus.

Chapter Ten
Wife and Mommy

It's what I always wanted to be. As a little girl, I loved playing with baby dolls more than anything else. I think I asked for a new doll every year for Christmas until I was a teenager. I didn't really care about having a career, although I loved teaching. But what I really wanted, more than anything, was to be a mommy.

And God graciously gave me this sweet privilege in August of 1991. Our first baby, Hope Ashlyn, was born, and I absolutely adored that child! We called her Ashlyn—she was the sweetest little baby, and such a joy to have around. She looked just like her daddy, with brown hair and brown eyes, and we both fell madly in love with her.

Ashlyn as a baby

I didn't go back to work after Ashlyn was born. We had never depended on my salary, but had chosen instead to save it. I decided to tutor in my home, to stay current in the field, so I established a little

Everywhere I Look

business and spread the word about it to friends and family.

Two and a half years after Ashlyn was born, we were blessed with our second baby, Kristen Elizabeth. With beautiful red hair, and a smile that would light up the room, Kristen added even more joy to our little family. She also had her daddy's eyes—even darker brown than her sister's. Two precious little girls. Our home was now filled with toys and baby stuff and lots of noise. So much fun!

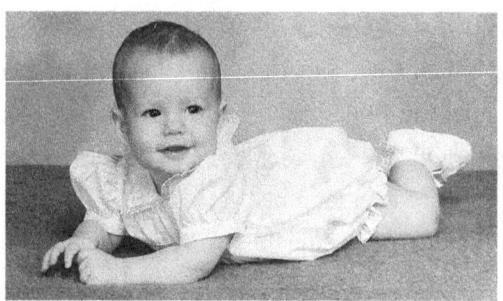

Kristen as a baby

When Ashlyn turned four, I started looking into schools in the area to try to decide where she should go. At a birthday party one day, I met another mom who was homeschooling her kids. I had never been willing to consider that option. In my mind, homeschoolers were all weird. The moms wore long denim skirts, and they had ten kids, and they probably lived on a farm and raised chickens and pigs. Not for me!

But this mom was different. She was actually normal. And she went on and on about the advantages of homeschooling. I still wasn't very interested, but I also had to admit it felt like God might be leading me toward this. She invited me to come to her home, where she could show me their "school room" and let me see how she did it. So I went to see it, and this little visit literally changed my life.

She had the cutest school room set up, with bright, colorful posters on the wall, and educational games everywhere. It all looked so fun! I checked out her curriculum choices, and again, I was impressed. Seeing her in action made me reconsider this option. I had recently gotten a few tuition quotes for Ashlyn to go to preschool, and I couldn't believe how expensive the schools were. I knew I could at least teach Ashlyn to read—that was my specialty. And I figured I could probably handle kindergarten math. I mean, how hard could it be? So I decided to just start with K-4 and see how it went.

We both absolutely loved it. I loved teaching her, and she loved learning. We only had "school" for a couple hours a day, and yet she was making great progress. I had been used to working with students who struggled to learn, so teaching a neurotypical child felt like a breeze in comparison.

I decided to continue homeschooling, taking it one year at a time, and reevaluating as I went along. On the side, I maintained my private tutoring business, but the longer I homeschooled, the more I loved it. And I didn't really plan to go back to teaching full time.

My parents still lived in Anderson, so they did a lot of babysitting and were very involved with all of their grandkids. They had a whole bunch by this time, and they were such amazing grandparents. Mom loved to have us all over for meals, so we did that as often as we could. For every birthday we got together at their house to celebrate. My dad loved taking the kids on "dates" and making them feel special. All of the Rice cousins loved staying at Grandma and Grandpa's house, and they grew up seeing each other all the time.

Change is in the Air

It was time to move. In 1996, some big changes started taking place in my little family. That February we sold our home and moved into a new house. We were hoping for more children someday, and our little three bedroom/two bath home had started feeling cramped. So we felt like it was time to move into a bigger one. That summer my in-laws moved to Greenville, and since we now had extra space, they moved in with us temporarily. They lived with us for ten months while my father-in-law was looking for work.

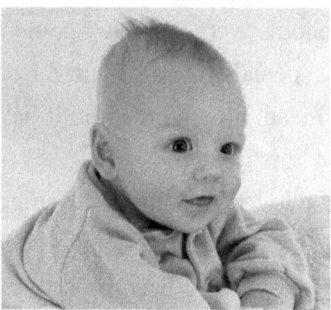

Josh as a baby

In 1997, we had the joy of welcoming a baby boy into our family. Joshua Donovan was such a sweet and happy little guy, and his big sisters adored him. Josh had blonde hair and blue eyes, so I finally had one who looked like me! Two years later, we were blessed with our fourth baby, Savannah Marie. She was a beautiful little baby, with brown hair and blue eyes, and was so incredibly precious. Her big sisters loved playing with their very own real-life doll. They pushed her around in their baby doll stroller, wrapped her in their baby doll blankets, and laid her in their baby doll cradle. Josh was just a two-year old, so it felt like we had two babies there for a while. Thankfully they were both easy babies, and the big sisters were a huge help. I say "big" like the girls were all grown up, but they were actually only five and eight. Still so little. But they were old enough to help me, and they both were great at it.

 I continued to teach the kids at home, even through all the baby craziness and newborn sleep deprivation. It was one of the sweetest joys of my life to be home with my kids, and to teach them and watch them grow. Having a good work ethic was truly one of my husband's greatest qualities. He was content to be the sole provider for our family, and he did a great job with that responsibility. I'm still very grateful for that.

Wife and Mommy

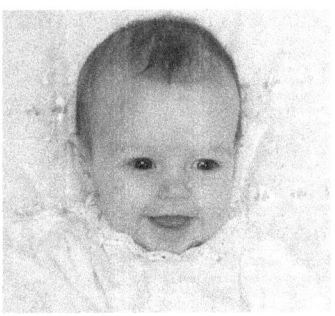

Savannah as a baby

By this time, we had settled into a church and had made many friends there. I continued to grow spiritually, but I still reverted to mask-wearing sometimes. When it came to our marriage, I was a pro at keeping our issues hidden. Things were often difficult, but I never talked to anyone about it. I also didn't share the story of how God had transformed me from the rebel and liar I had been, and part of that was because my own husband wasn't even aware of it all.

High school had been my season of utter stupidity and foolishness in my relationships with guys, but it was all covert and I had never told anyone the extent of it, especially not my husband. I was afraid that if he knew everything I had done, he wouldn't want to be with me. He'd already had so many fears and doubts through our dating years that I figured I better not share all of it. And at this point in my life, I was already a professional mask-wearer, so I didn't think a thing of it. He never needed to know. No one did.

But after we were married, I gradually began to feel the weight of those secrets. And during this time, God was also teaching me about how to walk in the light of the truth. I became so tired of having things in my past that he wasn't aware of, and I knew I needed to come clean. But I was terrified of talking to him about it all, because I had no idea how he would respond. As God worked on my heart, I became completely convinced it was the right thing to do. Looking back on it now,

Everywhere I Look

I can clearly see how God was rescuing me from a duplicitous lifestyle and from the bondage of secrecy and the prison of shame.

I never could have imagined the response I got from my husband. Not in my wildest dreams. What followed that conversation is actually difficult to describe, but it threw our marriage into a complete tailspin. When I made the confession to him, he felt the freedom to share a few confessions of his own, so we spent the next few weeks in an emotionally broken state. We were both in what felt like a fetal position emotionally, and we had to figure out how to regain our balance. It took a while, but we eventually decided to forgive each other and try to move forward.

But the process was terribly complicated, and we actually took different paths. I was constantly running to God with my broken heart, and He was teaching me how to forgive. My husband, however, wasn't sure what to do with his pain, and he became very fearful and filled with insecurity. This resulted in erratic and unpredictable behavior. Because I could see he was struggling to feel safe again, I promised to do whatever it took to earn his trust. I had been freed by God from that lifestyle years ago, and by God's grace, I had never betrayed my husband in any way. But he just couldn't believe me, and life became unbearably difficult. He decided to put restrictions on me to try to control the situation. The biggest restriction was that he wanted me to always have the kids with me, presumably to keep me from having an affair. Since I was willing to do whatever it took to help him trust me, and I knew I had nothing to hide, I agreed to that. But I had no idea how long it would go on, and how messed up we'd become in the process.

The really ironic part is that in my attempt to come out of hiding, I ended up in another world of secrecy. Now we were experiencing very serious issues in our marriage, but my husband didn't want anyone to know. He was ashamed of my past and of me personally, which led to disrespectful and degrading words and actions. He didn't want anyone to know about any of what was going on. His own parents were living

Wife and Mommy

right there in our house, and they had no idea. No one did.

And I just traded one set of secrets for a different one. Rather than being freed from my prison of shame, my husband and I entered a new one together that would take us down a dark, painful path. The enemy is sneaky like that.

Building Bridges

If you've ever had to live with secrets and shame, you know the weight of that burden. It's incredibly heavy. I hope and pray that if you're living a secret lifestyle, you will allow God to show you a path to freedom, and you'll have the courage to take the path out of hiding and into His marvelous light. Living in the light isn't always easy, but it is a place of peace and freedom. I know that now.

I've had well-meaning people tell me I should've left those skeletons in the closet, but I fully disagree. The Spirit of God was driving the train, not me. In Luke 8, Jesus tells us all that is secret will eventually be brought into the open, and everything concealed will be brought to the light and made known to all. God could have uncovered those secrets any time He wanted, but He told me to do it. He showed me the path, and I stepped out in faith, trusting Him to take care of me in the process. And even though the path became clouded with deep pain and discouragement, I know it was the path I was supposed to take, and God did take care of me. Every step of the way. It's actually when I started seeing His grace most clearly.

God's grace shines brightest in our darkest places.

Part Four

Looking Through

Seeing God's Grace in the Heartaches

"I have come into deep waters, and a flood overflows me.
I am WEARY with crying; my throat is parched,
my eyes fail while I wait for my God" (Psalm 69:2-3, NASB)

"Come to Me, all who are WEARY . . ."
(Matthew 11:28, NASB)

The courtroom was filled with a heavy, suffocating atmosphere. A dark cloud was hovering over us and my sister and I held each other's hands, trying hard just to breathe. How did we end up here? How did our family end up here? None of us ever really expected things to get this bad. My brother, Charley, sat stoically in front of us, his sweet, supportive wife beside him. And I remember thinking he looked kind of like a statue. Staring straight ahead, he was frozen and stiff, his face expressionless. I wondered what in the world was going through his mind.

My parents were also very still, but their faces betrayed their calm exterior. There was a look of deep sorrow in their eyes that I will never forget. Overwhelming sadness and paralyzing fear, all mixed up together.

And then there were the two very young girls sitting here with us. They had no idea how important this decision was. Their lives were about to be changed forever. As I sat there, trying to make myself breathe, they were the ones I was most concerned about. I figured the rest of us would be okay, eventually. We were all adults . . . but they were so young. Would they ever recover from this?

What I didn't realize is none of us would ever fully recover. What we were about to hear would change the dynamics, and even the trajectory, of our whole family. You can move on, adapt, adjust. But you can't recover what's been lost forever.

"O God, please cover my family with Your peace. Help Rusty trust You, remind Charley to keep his focus on You, and please guard my mom's heart from worry and sorrow. Please hold my dad's hand and give him peace. Help mom and dad to remember constantly that You are good and You will not forsake them now, but will run to them and help them. Help Sara see Your goodness through all of this. Help all of us to be drawn to You. Let our pain drive us deeper into You and teach us how to love and trust You more. I know You can use this for good in our lives, and You want us to grow and learn through this. Please accomplish that in each of us. Soften our hearts, remind us to look to You for strength and guidance, and give us more faith so we might learn to trust You more. Father, I thank You, in advance, for what You are about to do. May Your Will be done." (My journal entry- Thursday, April 8, 2004)

Chapter Eleven
The Unraveling

Have you ever pulled a string on your clothes, and watched in horror as the fabric started unraveling? There's no going back, is there? Sometimes in life we pull a string, or we watch someone else pull a string . . . and situations start to unravel. Lives can unravel. Marriages can unravel. Entire ministries can unravel. And sometimes, there's just no going back.

Our family was flying high for a few years there. My brothers were in the ministry, my sister and I were both married, and we all lived within an hour of each other. My parents were still serving the Lord at Oakwood, and grandkids were everywhere.

But life is never perfect, is it? My siblings and I were all doing well, for the most part, but we each had struggles simmering. I don't think any of us felt like they were serious enough to become the volcanoes which eventually exploded all over the place, so we mostly stayed in denial about them. Denial is a really happy place, but I don't recommend living there.

When Rusty and Sharon moved to Travelers Rest in 1988, he started pastoring a small, country church with a parsonage just across the road where they lived. At this point, after being a youth pastor for four years in North Carolina, Rusty was excited to get this position and opportunity. It seemed like a great move in the right direction.

Hindsight is 20/20, and looking back, one of the glaring dangers none of us saw at the time was Rusty still maintained close friendships with the guys he had known in his previous life. I remember hearing him talk about this, saying he knew them best and they trusted him, so he was in the perfect position to influence them for the Kingdom. He invited them to church, and had deep, long conversations with them about the things of God. But sometimes when life was hard or things were challenging, he would take off and go back to Winston Salem to take a break from everything. And this wasn't the best idea. We all remember what happened there.

When we're feeling weary, or frustrated with life, I've learned it's vitally important to be picky about who (or what) we turn to for encouragement or comfort, or even just for a distraction. For Rusty to go hang out with those old buddies was probably very relaxing and fun, but the danger turned out to be too great. Eventually he started sliding back into some of his old ways. Bad company truly does corrupt good character (1 Corinthians 15:33), and we saw this firsthand.

There was also another danger lurking. Some of the people in the little church had slipped into a very legalistic version of Christianity. I'm referring to a works-based way of relating to God, rather than relying on the finished work of Jesus. This can actually happen anywhere if we aren't careful. There's such a fine line here . . . We can be well-meaning and truly concerned one minute, and the next minute we're falling into a trap of judgmental self-righteousness without even realizing it. The religious spirit is such a subtle tool of the enemy, and it's as old as the Pharisees. It's focusing on the external instead of experiencing an internal change of heart, like when Jesus called the Pharisees "whitewashed tombs." He hated it then, and He still hates it now. We need to be on guard.

Once when Rusty invited his good friend to church, the people complained to him about the friend's long hair. This is the kind of legalistic nonsense I'm talking about, and it made Rusty furious. One year he canceled a Sunday evening service on Christmas, and the people almost lost their minds. It didn't matter that he felt like it was important for everyone to enjoy time with their family. They were rule-following

The Unraveling

Pharisees who HAD to be in church on Sunday nights. Rusty hated their legalistic attitudes, but he couldn't seem to get through to them. They were convinced they were right.

When you are surrounded by Christians who are not walking in God's love, and you also have friends who are unbelievers but are actually kinder than the Christians, you have a recipe for disaster. I'm not excusing anything that happened, but I do want to warn us all of the potential fallout when we get sidetracked by rules and fail to walk in love.

As the years went by, Rusty became more and more weak and spiritually vulnerable. Sadly, he began to spiral into very destructive behavior. The disconnect with the church grew, and then the disconnect spread to his marriage. He became attracted to other women and was inappropriately involved with some. Eventually, he started having an affair and had to resign from pastoring.

At first, Sharon didn't leave him because she was hoping and praying for their marriage to be restored. But after they left the church in Travelers Rest and moved to Anderson, Rusty continued having the affair. They spent the next three years in limbo, up and down, back and forth. During this time, Rusty continued down a very destructive path but tried to cover his tracks and pretend like everything was okay. Nothing was, though. It was a huge, painful mess. In October of 1997, their marriage officially ended.

Marriages unravel. Ministries unravel. In one horrible chain of events, Rusty lost his wife, his ministry, his home, and his way of making a living. The affair didn't last either, so he lost that too. He had already turned his back on God but after he lost everything, he did a complete 180 and plunged headfirst back into the drug world. After all, it was a way to make good money and he had all of his old buddies back there who still loved him and were happy to welcome him with open arms.

Everywhere I Look

Full of Holes

He lived on the streets again. This was before cell phones, so we had no way of knowing if Rusty was dead or alive. My parents had already lived through this nightmare once before, but for me, this was very different. I had been a kid before, with limited awareness of the severity of the situation. This time I was an adult, with my own kids, who were wondering what was going on with Uncle Rusty.

For the next seven years, his heart grew colder and harder toward Christianity. Occasionally he would pop back into our lives and act like nothing was wrong. Rusty has always had an incredible way of maintaining a happy exterior, and acting like everything's perfectly alright, even when it's obvious to everyone that everything is actually awful. When he came around, he would be the fun uncle who would bring gifts for the kids, and throw twenty dollar bills around like Monopoly money.

When he was AWOL, we all continued to get together at my parents' house for birthdays and dinners. The conversation would always include the situation with Rusty. *Has anyone heard from him lately? Is he okay? When will he be back in town? Does anyone know?*

I always wanted to discuss his spiritual state. It was truly baffling to me that in a few short years someone could go from being a pastor to completely walking away from the faith. I was in good company to discuss these theological positions and possibilities. Dad and Charley were both happy to let me process it with them, but it was still so hard to reconcile in my mind. Rusty was claiming now to be an atheist. He didn't believe any of it anymore. So how could he be a "believer" if he didn't actually believe? Yes, we had seen his previous transformation. None of us could deny that. My dad and Charley always pointed out the fact that he HAD truly been saved. We were sure of it. And they would remind me of all the verses in Scripture which teach eternal security. They stood by their position that he would be back. They were convinced he was a child of God, and nothing could ever change that, so eventually God would bring him back. But it was messing with my theology. If we're saved by faith, and well, now he has none, then how could I believe he would be okay?

Last family photo

During this time, I remember meeting him at a McDonald's, and while we were sitting outside eating ice cream, I mustered up the courage to ask him about his relationship with God. I could tell he wanted to shrug it off and change the subject, but I pushed for more. Finally, he said, "Look, Charity. I tried it. I tried the whole 'living for God' thing, and it didn't work. I believed the Bible, I prayed for stuff, but it just didn't work. So I'm sorry, but I just don't believe the Bible anymore. It's too full of holes. If you poured water on the Bible, it would gush out because that thing is full of holes."

This from a man who had preached from that Bible for ten years. I was so dumbfounded. And utterly heartbroken. I wanted to believe as strongly as Dad and Charley did that he truly was a believer . . . even though he no longer believed. It was all such a terrifying prospect.

Back on the Home Front

Meanwhile, I was continuing to have conflict in my marriage, which added to the weight I felt from my brother's situation. During this time, my husband lived in a constant state of hypervigilance and was always afraid I was going to cheat on him. The fear grew into intense jealousy. I assumed if I did everything he asked me to do his fears would decrease and eventually go away. But they didn't, and in fact they actually grew worse.

A strange thing happens when control enters a relationship. The more power and control one gets, the more power and control one wants. It's a dynamic that I've since learned a lot about, but at the time, I had no idea what was going on or what to do about it. I felt like I was on a leash with a noose around my neck. I had restrictions on where I could go, how I could dress, who my friends were, even what kind of music I could listen to. And the more time went on, the tighter the noose became. More rules were added. Less freedom was given.

My mom, who knew nothing about any of this, offered to start coming over every Friday night to babysit so we could go on a date. We managed to maintain this consistently for several years, even when things were incredibly tense and full of hidden conflict. I still wasn't allowed to be away from the kids, so this was my one time to get a break. But it was frequently a stressful time of fighting and arguing. We would sit down in a restaurant, and before we even ordered, he would accuse me of "looking at" a waiter, or "having a thing" for a man nearby. I'm confident now that there was a spiritual dimension to this, and I believe the enemy was playing mind games with him. But at the time, I was just so perplexed and frustrated. I tried to not even look around when I was with him. I would do my best to just stare straight ahead or look down. But whatever I did, I did NOT want to actually make eye contact with another man. That would be a big mistake, and the night would be ruined by all the conflict that would follow.

It was a very difficult way to live, but I honestly didn't think I had any other option. There were four beautiful children now to consider, and they were worth every bit of effort I could put into this marriage, no matter how challenging it sometimes was. I also knew I wasn't doing anything wrong, and this fear existed only in my husband's imagination, so I hoped he would somehow overcome these tormenting thoughts. I desperately wanted us to move past this and have a healthy marriage, especially for the sake of our kids, but I just wasn't sure how to get there.

My Spiritual Mentor

God gave me a new friend who would completely change my life in December of 1996, just two months after this behavior started. God's timing is amazing. Carol Williams and her family had just moved to Greenville, and I met her through mutual friends who introduced us because Carol was also homeschooling. She and I began to do Bible studies together weekly, and I loved digging into Scripture to find the answers I had been searching for. We added several other ladies to our Bible study—Karen O'Neal, Lisa Clark, and Lisa Allen, to name a few. That little group was such a huge source of joy and encouragement to me. Our kids all played together and became friends in the process, and we continued to meet for several years.

Carol was the only one who knew the severity of the situation in my marriage. I was still trying hard to keep our issues secret, mainly because I was afraid of how he would respond if I didn't, but also because I had a lot of shame around it, since I blamed my dishonesty for causing this mess. I shouldn't have carried that weight, because we had both been dishonest, and we had both shared secrets. But I was having mine constantly brought up again, and I was continually punished for mine. So it messed with my mind, and I felt responsible for the situation we were in.

My husband threatened to divorce me if I disclosed to anyone what was happening, but I made the decision to trust Carol with it because I desperately needed help. And she really did give me the help I needed. Just being able to verbally process it all was a tremendous help. She listened and gave wise feedback, and she taught me how to find my strength in God and in His Word. During those years, I learned to ask God for ways to show love and grace in spite of the tension in our marriage. I also learned to pray. Carol and I wrote out prayers for our husbands and kids, and I learned to pray Scripture back to God. It was the School of Intercession 101, and God has continued to teach me through the years in this school. At the time, I didn't know if my marriage would ever get better, but I knew I was growing in the process. God was showing me how to selflessly love others like He loves us. Carol was a beautiful example of this to me.

Carol and me

Building Bridges

Who are the people in your life God has strategically placed there for this season to help you? Stop and think about this for a minute. People come in and out of our lives. Some are there for the long haul. But some are there "for such a time as this," to guide you and encourage you in a dark season. Take a little while to thank God for giving you those people.

When I look back over my life, this is another area where I can see God's grace so clearly now, and I'm so humbled and grateful. He has

The Unraveling

been so faithful to surround me with people who helped me carry the difficulties and who loved me well through it all. I saw the love of Jesus on display, in so many tangible ways. And it not only strengthened me, but it set an example for me to follow. I have a responsibility now to pay it forward, and by God's grace I'm constantly looking for ways to do that.

If you are one of my friends who has done this—and you know who you are—I am eternally grateful. I thank God for you, and I pray for His favor and blessings to return to you a thousand fold.

Chapter Twelve
From Bad to Worse

He woke up in a hotel room and thought he was dying. His chest hurt, his arms were numb, and he didn't have the strength to move. It shouldn't have come as a surprise, considering the lifestyle he was living. For the past four years, Rusty had built a drug trafficking organization which kept him moving at an unearthly pace. He would deal drugs from Thursday night through Monday morning, day and night, with no sleep. Coke made this possible. On Monday morning, he would crash and sleep for three days straight. Then on Thursday he would be ready to go again. All day Thursday he would "bust up coke and bag it," then by Thursday night he would start hitting up his connections again.

By this point, Rusty had several connections in North Carolina, South Carolina, and Tennessee. He traveled this circuit continually, and made frequent trips out West when he needed more coke.

So when he woke up in a hotel room, thinking he was dying, it was not surprising. But what was surprising was he really, really did not want to die. He immediately thought about his girls. He hated the idea of them hearing that their dad had been found dead in a hotel room. And here he was again, wondering if God could hear his prayers. He decided it was worth a shot. He'd actually been feeling the same familiar conviction he felt back in his twenties. So his thoughts quickly turned to God, and he started begging for another chance. He tried to make a deal with God . . . He promised God if He would let him live, he would quit using.

And miraculously, he started gaining his strength back, and the pain immediately eased up. It was all too coincidental to brush off. He knew God had heard him and had answered his prayer. But there was one little problem. He only agreed to quit using. He didn't promise to quit dealing. So his lifestyle changed a little, and he gave up his ridiculous schedule. But he figured out other ways to maintain the business.

A year went by, and he was having problems left and right with his people. Rusty wasn't actually selling drugs most of the time himself. He was trafficking them, so he had people in each location he would distribute them to, and then those people would handle the sales. Even as I describe this, I want to scream in frustration at the waste of potential. Rusty had a brilliant business mind, but it was wasted on illegal drugs, and I can't help but wonder what could've become of his life if he had channeled that brilliance in the right direction.

But at this point, his energy was still being spent on making lots of money with drugs, and he did make plenty. He would tell you now the greatest sin driving him during this time was greed. He was obsessed with making money, and it consumed him completely and blinded him to the destruction all around him.

Some of this destruction involved the guys who were working for him. In the fall of 2002, a series of horrible events were unfolding. Several people ended up dead, either to suicide or murder, and on New Year's Eve, Rusty was arrested for the murder of one of them.

You Need to Sit Down

It was just a normal day for me. I was upstairs in our bedroom, picking up the kids' toys, and I got a call from my sister-in-law, Phyllis. The first thing she asked me was if I had seen the news on TV. I had not and didn't know what she was talking about. The next thing she said was, "Charity, you need to sit down."

That's never a good sign. It was the first time someone had ever said those scary words to me, but I did sit down, and she proceeded to tell me Rusty had been arrested, that the charges were very serious, and

From Bad to Worse

that he was being accused of murder.

Oh. My. Word.

What did she just say?? Did she say "MURDER?!"

I knew he had to be selling drugs. He always lied and told us he wasn't, but we all knew better. I had been afraid for years I would open up the newspaper and see his face on the front page. It actually kind of haunted me, and as time went on, I started to dread opening the paper for fear of seeing he'd been arrested. But I always thought it would be for drug charges. Never in my wildest imagination did I think it would be for murder.

I honestly couldn't imagine Rusty doing that. I know drug dealers are known for all kinds of criminal activity, and you hear all the time about drug deals gone wrong. But this was Rusty. He had such a big heart. He was so loving and fun and had always been so protective of me. He couldn't really do that, could he? Sell drugs, yes. Kill somebody? How could this be?

And then my mind went to my parents. Oh Jesus, please help my sweet parents! What was this going to do to them? Could they even take this kind of pain and survive it?

A few weeks later, I went with my mom to visit Rusty for the first time at the detention center. I'd never been in one before, and we had to go through all the screenings and metal detectors, and eventually we found ourselves sitting in a cold, sterile room with a few other people who looked as lost as we felt. I sat there, on the hard, uncomfortable metal chair, trying to imagine what my mom was thinking. This was Beverly Jo. The sweet baby girl born to Charlie and Eva Clingerman, who had lived her whole life for the Lord. My sister and I used to joke that Momma never sinned. We really couldn't think of any sin we'd ever seen her commit. She was as close to perfect as they come. And here she was, sitting in the waiting room of a detention center, coming to see her boy who was being charged with murder.

We didn't belong here. We were the preacher's family, for crying

Everywhere I Look

out loud! We were decent people. We were law-abiding citizens. And now here we were, lumped in with all these other people, and being examined and treated like we might be criminals ourselves. It's so humiliating, and I remember feeling so defensive of my mom. I wanted to scream out to everyone that of all people on this whole earth, Beverly did not deserve to be here going through this.

It was just the start though. It was only the beginning of a long, long road of sadness and frustration and humiliation. And that was only what we were feeling. Rusty had it so much worse.

Come to Jesus

We started hearing Rusty had gotten right with God. Charley and my dad had been visiting him, and they were saying Rusty was reading his Bible again and saying things they hadn't heard him say in years.

I'll be the first to admit my cynicism. Jailhouse conversions happen all the time, and why wouldn't they? Of course everyone is going to get right with God. They want out of there, and they know it'll probably take a miracle for that to happen.

But when I saw Rusty myself, I had to admit he did look and sound so different. He started telling me about what had been going on the past few years—the truth of what he'd been doing. He told me about the hotel experience and how he asked God to save his life, and He did. But Rusty didn't give up his business, so God had stayed on him about it for the whole next year.

And he told me that a year to the day after the hotel scare, he had pulled out of a parking lot and was driving down Haywood Road in Greenville when he saw blue lights in his rearview mirror. He said it was like God Himself was pulling him over. He had been arguing with God again for months by that point, and he recognized those blue lights as the end of his running. It was over. The whole mad pursuit of millions of dollars, running like a maniac, trying to outrun God's Spirit. It was all over. And he surrendered to God and felt immediate peace,

From Bad to Worse

even while they were placing him in handcuffs.

There are only two ways to get out of the drug world—prison or the grave. You can't just decide to stop trafficking drugs. You know too much, you know too many names, and you are a huge liability to all of those people. As Rusty explained all of this to me, over the course of several visits, I started to see a joy and peace in him I couldn't deny. He told me he was more free there in that jail cell than he had ever been on the outside in the drug world. He maintained he didn't commit the murder, and he said he'd been set up. But he didn't deny the trafficking, and he was prepared to serve time for that. He was just glad to be alive and have another chance at life.

When he first got to the detention center, he asked for a Bible, and he read it and studied it all day every day. Other inmates noticed and some started asking him questions. Some came to him for counseling or help with suicidal thoughts. Sometimes impromptu Bible studies would break out and inmates would start gathering around to listen. He had plenty to share because of his ministerial training and knowledge of the Bible, so he became their resident jailhouse pastor.

I asked him all my questions about eternal security. And I'll never forget his answer. He said he held that theological position now more than ever because he had tried his best to stop believing in God. For years, he pushed God away as hard as he possibly could. He even said for a few of those years God was actually silent, and for a little while he thought he had been right, that there really was no God.

But then God started speaking again. God's Spirit came chasing him down and would not let up. Rusty said he would get in a car and the radio would be playing a Christian station when he knew good and well he never would've put it on that station. Or he'd see a billboard with Scripture on it, or someone would randomly speak the truth to him. The Voice started coming back here and there, and then the pressure started to build, and it kept getting stronger and stronger until it was constant, and he knew he was eventually going to have to surrender. There was no denying God had not given up on him. It was literally like the Good Shepherd had left the ninety-nine and was coming after this one very lost sheep.

And because of this, Rusty explained he had no doubt about his eternal security now. He told me once you've been truly born again into the family of God, He will never leave you and He will never forsake you. Even if you try your best to push Him away. If you are His, He will find you. He will relentlessly pursue you. And He will bring you back.

Turns out, my dad and Charley had been right all along.

Building Bridges

Have you been through a season of theological shifting? Most of us have experienced this at some point (or maybe several points) in our walk with Jesus. When circumstances don't seem to jive with what we have believed, our faith can come into question, and sometimes it feels like the rug is being pulled out from under us.

Did you know God can handle your doubts? He isn't intimidated by your questions, and in fact, I believe He welcomes them. Wrestling with the Biblical text and even with God Himself is sometimes a necessary part of our growth. The journey of faith is often filled with confusing twists and turns, and we see examples all through the Scriptures of people who questioned God and cried out to Him in frustration and anguish when they weren't sure what to believe anymore.

It's okay to wonder and question and wrestle. What isn't okay is walking away from the faith and turning our backs on the one true source of wisdom who can actually guide us through the land mines of our own doubts and confusion. So run TO Him with those questions,

From Bad to Worse

not AWAY from Him. If we are truly His, He will come after us if we run away, like He came after my brother. But we sure can make a mess of things when we try to do life apart from God.

Chapter Thirteen
Layer Upon Layer

Ever have one of those years where so much change takes place it makes your head spin? 2003 was that year for my family. In a lot of ways it felt like the bottom was falling out.

Rusty was in the detention center the whole year. Charley was working feverishly to figure out every detail of Rusty's case and get the legal counsel he needed. My mom needed to have hip replacement surgery that fall, and when she was in the hospital, we started seeing signs of something wrong with my dad.

We couldn't put our finger on it, but he was definitely forgetting things and was just not himself. In 1999, he had retired from pastoring but was still preaching revival meetings and teaching at the Bible college. My mom also retired so she could travel with him. But none of us realized she was becoming more and more responsible for my dad. She was now in charge of their calendar, their finances, and even grading papers and calculating grades for his classes. My dad was doing less and less, but we didn't realize the extent of this until my mom was in the hospital for her surgery.

Afterwards when she was in recovery, we were all in the hospital room visiting her, and my dad asked her about some upcoming revival meetings. She explained what trips were next, and a few minutes later, he asked again. It was like it hadn't registered with him, and he seemed confused. But even as she tried to go over it all again, I could see he was not really tracking, and I remember feeling kind of sick watching this. It felt like someone was turning the lights of my awareness on,

Everywhere I Look

and after that, I started noticing more red flags. He got turned around in the hospital when he was going back to the car after one of his visits with her, and that was really strange, considering he had been visiting people in this hospital several days a week for years as a pastor. And in general his navigational skills had always been amazing, so this was pretty alarming. Without mom at home that week, he just seemed agitated and confused. We all started realizing how much he had been relying on her.

Sara, Charley, Phyllis, and I all started comparing notes after this, and the more dots we connected, the more concerned we became. Sara is a nurse, and my mom and dad trusted her judgment, so she started pressing on them to have Dad evaluated by a neurologist.

At first, they both resisted. Dad had been discussing his memory issues for a couple years with his primary care physician, and he had told my dad the stress of pastoring was probably the cause. So Dad had decided to retire, and was expecting this to do the trick. But here we were, several years past his retirement, and things weren't getting better. They were actually getting worse. Eventually, Sara was able to convince them to see a neurologist. Not long after that, he was diagnosed with Alzheimer's Disease. He was only in his sixties. He had retired at the age of 63, and although he didn't have a diagnosis until he was 67, we had seen signs back before retirement but didn't recognize them.

Since my maternal grandmother had had Alzheimer's, we would not have been surprised if my mom inherited it. But my dad didn't have any family history of this disease so his diagnosis came as a complete surprise to all of us. We knew something was wrong, but honestly, I think we were more prepared for a brain tumor or, really, any other disease. The Alzheimer's diagnosis left us in complete shock. And since we were already in the middle of the heartbreaking mess with Rusty, this just added another layer of pain and stress.

I think it's pretty safe to say Charley felt the weight of all this the most. By now, he was the dean of the Bible college, so he was con-

Layer Upon Layer

stantly having to pick up the slack for my dad. He had to step in and teach classes for him, and also try to figure out what to do about easing Dad out of this teaching position after thirty years in it. Charley also felt responsible to help Rusty get out of jail. And I'm sure there was part of him that just felt alone in all of this because he was the last man standing. Dad's health was failing and Rusty was incarcerated. So, like it or not, Charley was becoming the patriarch of our family. And that's a pretty heavy load to carry. Not to mention a sad one. Especially considering how close the three of them had always been. He was losing two very important people simultaneously. Actually, we all were. It felt like both Daddy and Rusty were both getting a terminal diagnosis at the same exact time.

The Trial

It lasted a week, and we all sat there every day in the courtroom, listening carefully to the testimonies and the lawyers, and trying hard to reach our own conclusions. When court was in recess, we would sit in the same waiting area as the family of the victim. That was awkward. But my dad, being the guy who could make friends with anyone, actually struck up a friendship with the father of the victim. The two of them sat and chatted like old army buddies.

After a week of testimonies, the jury left to deliberate, and they were out for what seemed like an eternity. When they came back into the courtroom, they told the judge they were not able to reach a decision. The judge immediately issued an Allen Charge. He berated them for not having an answer and sent them back to deliberate again with a very stern warning. He said the families want a verdict, and we are NOT going to have a hung jury here. Make your decision and come back with a verdict.

And so they did. They went out and deliberated again. When they filed in the second time, I analyzed their faces carefully and tried to read their minds. Two of the jurors looked like they had been crying.

Everywhere I Look

Most of them wouldn't even look at us. Not a good sign. We all sat there, holding our breath, and I remember thinking about how hard my heart was pounding.

The judge looked over at us, and it was our turn to get a stern warning. We were not to make a peep when the verdict was read. No crying, no talking, no noises whatsoever. If we made even a sound, we would be immediately escorted from the courtroom.

And then it was time for the foreman to read the verdict. He stood, opened the paper, and read the words to us: guilty of murder in the first degree. I could never have predicted how hard it would be to not make a single sound. My instinctive gasp was like a reflex I couldn't control, and I had to physically force myself to hold back noise trying to escape from my mouth. My sister and I both struggled to keep ourselves from crying. It's so hard to describe that feeling, but it almost seemed like we were watching someone's death. Symbolically, of course. Rusty was still sitting there, alive and well, wearing his suit, and looking normal. But his life was taken from him at that moment. And it was an excruciating thing to witness.

After a few minutes, the judge handed down the sentence. Besides murder, Rusty was also guilty of trafficking cocaine and possession of illegal firearms, so he received a life sentence for the murder, 25 years for trafficking, and 6 years for the firearms. Life plus 31 years: two sentences to run concurrently, with a mandatory 85% of it to be served.

Basically, he would spend the rest of his life in prison.

The Aftermath

When someone dies, it's customary to have a big meal after the funeral. I'm not sure how this practice got started, and it seems a little strange, but it's what we do. And in a weird way, it's comforting to gather around a table, and process the events together over a meal.

When we left the courthouse, we all went back to my mom and dad's house. No one felt like eating. No one really felt like talking. We

Layer Upon Layer

just all sat quietly, lost in thought, trying to process what had just happened, and trying to imagine what this would look like going forward. I remember sitting outside by myself on the swing which was on Mom and Dad's front porch, rhythmically swaying back and forth, staring into space. Like I said, it felt so much like a death. He was gone, and he wasn't coming back, and our lives would never be the same. But there was no meal, no comforting conversation, and certainly no sympathy cards or beautiful plants. When a drug dealer is put in prison, our society generally cheers. The criminal got what they deserved. Good riddance. Get them off the streets, and let's get on with our lives. Knowing most people would feel this way just added several layers to our pain.

This was my brother. For my parents, this was their beloved firstborn son. For his daughters, this was their daddy. And for all of us, this was family. He wasn't just some horrible criminal to us. We loved him so much, and it was excruciating to watch him walk out to a van in shackles and ride away. For all of us, it was a very isolated grieving process we had to experience. No one else would grieve with us. No one else would feel this deep pain, and no one else would even understand, really. We had to walk the lonely path all by ourselves, and process these conflicting emotions on our own.

I personally was dealing with a lot of anger. I was mad at the investigators who left so many questions unanswered. There were so many holes in their case. I was mad at the lawyers who were joking around right after the sentencing and talking about going to the lake together later. I was mad at the star witness who kept contradicting himself and making things up as he went. I was mad at the judge for coercing the jury to make a decision when, clearly, they weren't in agreement. I was mad at the crying jurors for betraying their own consciences. I was mad at Rusty for putting us all through this. And I was mad at myself for being mad.

But give me five minutes, and the anger would turn to sorrow and then to fear and then to a million questions. What was this going to do

Everywhere I Look

to Rusty's girls? Would they ever recover? And what about my poor parents? Daddy was already struggling. What would this do to his mental state? And Sara, who had to go back to Florida and back to work where no one knew what she was going through? And Charley? . . . oh man. Charley. I could see this was going to send him over the edge. He had worked so hard to try to figure out a way to get Rusty out of this mess, and it all came to a screeching halt when the verdict was read. Would he be able to let this go? Would he live now for the appeal process and drive himself crazy still trying to get Rusty out?

So many unknowns. So many emotions to process. We didn't know it at the time, but it would take years to untangle them all and learn how to walk in peace again.

Somewhere along the way God gave me a poem by Amy Carmichael which Elisabeth Elliot liked to quote. And I finally began to understand that in order to have peace, I had to accept the situation. I couldn't forget it, or push it away by staying busy, or ignore it, or lie down in pseudo-submission. I had to come to the place of true acceptance.

As it turns out, Rusty would actually be the one to teach us this himself by the way he accepted the situation. And over the years, one by one, we all followed his example.

Here is the poem which so beautifully describes this powerful process:

In Acceptance Lieth Peace
by Amy Carmichael (1867-1951)

He said, 'I will forget the dying faces;
the empty places. They shall be filled again.
O voices moaning deep within me, cease.'
But vain the word; vain, vain: Not in forgetting lieth peace.

He said, 'I will crowd action upon action,

Layer Upon Layer

    the strife of faction shall stir me and sustain;
    O tears that drown the fire of manhood, cease.'
But vain the word; vain, vain: Not in endeavor lieth peace.

    He said, 'I will withdraw me and be quiet,
        why meddle in life's riot?
    Shut be my door to pain. Desire,
    thou dost befool me, thou shalt cease.'
But vain the word; vain, vain: Not in aloofness lieth peace.

    He said, 'I will submit; I am defeated.
    God hath depleted my life of its rich gain.
    O futile murmurings, why will ye not cease?'
But vain the word; vain, vain: Not in submission lieth peace.

He said, 'I will accept the breaking sorrow which God tomorrow
Will to His son explain.' Then did the turmoil deep within me cease.
Not vain the word, not vain; For in acceptance lieth peace.[3]

Building Bridges

    Is there a situation in your life you need to accept? Are you struggling to see God's goodness or to find peace in the middle of your pain or difficulties? I can tell you right now you will need God's grace to do that. Lean hard into His grace.

    It was only by God's grace any of us were able to accept our painful situation and find a path forward. And it definitely didn't happen overnight. There was a process involved, and we each moved at our own pace. But as you will see, God healed our broken hearts, and He helped

Everywhere I Look

us find peace through accepting our new normal and through trusting Him with it all. He will do the same for you.

Chapter Fourteen
Though I Walk Through the Valley

Anybody remember what happened in 2008 to the housing market? Well, I can tell you more about it than I wish I could because it deeply affected us. We had purchased land several years before and had worked for months with a builder to finalize the plans to build a house on it. We learned about the property from our good friends, Dan and Regina Cranston. It was down the street from their home, so this meant we'd be neighbors. They also had four kids, and they homeschooled too, so we were all excited about living so close to each other. In 2006, we finally started the process of building our dream home, and 13 months later, in 2007, we moved into it. But because of the volatile market, we very soon found ourselves in an "upside down" mortgage when the housing market crashed.

It was a beautiful home on four acres, with a peaceful little creek running through the back of the property. We wanted space for the kids to run around, and we also wanted to give my parents a place to live, so we built a basement apartment for them. By this point, my mom was needing more and more help with my dad. He still knew who we all were, and he could carry on conversations with us, but he couldn't be left alone, and he needed a lot of help with daily tasks. So my parents sold their home and moved in with us.

All of this would have been a wonderful idea for a strong and healthy couple. And we certainly appeared this way to a lot of people.

But our marriage was already in deep distress, so I'm not sure why we kept pretending like we were okay. That definitely came back to bite us.

The turmoil which had consumed us for the last ten years continued to escalate, and the added financial pressure sent us over the edge. We were struggling constantly, and we desperately needed help.

A couple years before this, we had actually experienced a little reprieve for a short time. In 2006, things had come to a head, and I had finally gotten a counselor. My husband had fought that for years, but the situation had become very serious. By this point, several of my friends were aware of our problems. They had seen things up close, and eventually had an intervention with me, insisting I get help. They were actually very concerned for us. That conversation was unbelievably intense and painful. I sat there, paralyzed by fear, wondering how I would survive on my own and how I would take care of the kids. I hadn't worked full time for fifteen years! But I knew my friends were right. The situation was terribly unhealthy, and it just kept getting worse and worse. So I told my husband I wasn't coming home, but I would meet him in a counselor's office. I fully expected him to file for divorce right then and there, because he had threatened to if I ever went to a counselor. But to my great surprise, he immediately softened, and started calling around to find a counselor to meet with us.

He was able to get one, and we started meeting with him. I wish I could say it helped. We actually met with several different counselors, but our situation was very complicated, and most people didn't know what to do with us. Eventually we did have a breakthrough, and things looked good for a little while. I wanted so badly to be the poster couple for a reconciled marriage, and for about six months I thought we would be. We started attending a new church, and started sharing with everyone how God had rescued our marriage. We were even asked to give our testimony in church, and it truly seemed like we were going to be okay.

But the changes that had occurred did not last. And when the fi-

Though I Walk Through the Valley

nancial burdens of 2008 added to the stress levels, the tension in our marriage came back with a vengeance. It didn't happen all at once. Things like this rarely do. It was a slow escalation, but eventually our notoriously up and down relationship was back in a very serious mess.

The Long, Slow Good-bye

Even though our marriage was struggling, it was such a joy to have my parents living with us. I'm so thankful they were able to, and again, I'm grateful my husband was a hard worker and was willing to help them. They pretty much stayed in their apartment and were so easy to have around. My kids loved going into their area and watching TV with them or getting help with their schoolwork. I was still homeschooling, and our schoolroom was also in the basement, so the kids went back and forth between the schoolroom and their grandparents' apartment. My mom had always been such a wonderful teacher, and she was happy to help my kids. She was also happy to keep her refrigerator stocked with cans of soda, which I rarely bought, so the kids loved going in there to have a treat.

All of 2007 was like this. For several years my dad stayed in the same stage (which would now be considered "stage five" of the seven stages of Alzheimer's). We didn't realize 2007 would be his last year in that stage. We enjoyed a whole year of having him there, being his pleasant, goofy self, and watching a lot of Andy Griffith. But when the decline started, things went downhill fast.

In the spring of 2008 we realized the disease was starting to progress quickly. Although he still knew who we all were, he was making less and less sense when we tried to talk to him. Often it seemed like he was talking in his sleep. Sometimes if I touched his arm, and said something like, "How's my daddy?" he would snap out of it, and smile at me sweetly and say, "How's Charity?" and we'd be back to normal. But sometimes when I tried that, he would look at me and continue in his hallucination, talking complete nonsense.

Everywhere I Look

I absolutely despised that wicked disease. It was stealing my daddy from me, bit by bit. And I desperately wanted him back. In June, after a series of horrible events, we had to make the gut-wrenching decision for him to be home-bound.

Rusty had been assigned to a prison which was four hours from our house. So going to visit him was an all-day ordeal. By now, we had all gotten used to this new life. It had taken us a few years, but we had accepted things, and we were now accustomed to making the trip down there to visit him. Mom and Dad went once a month, and even though Daddy was getting more difficult to handle, we all were glad he was still able to go see him.

In June, Mom and Dad came home from a visit with Rusty, and as soon as they walked in the door I knew something was wrong. First, let me say that my mom never cries. I could probably count on one hand the times I've seen her cry. But this day, I could tell she had been crying. They came in and she dropped her bags on the floor, and said, "Never again!" Then she broke down in tears and told me how Daddy had gone absolutely crazy on the drive home. He had gotten confused and had become convinced they were going in the wrong direction (this had started happening frequently). He had started yelling and screaming, even threatening to pull the keys out of the ignition. She had stopped at a gas station to try to get him to calm down, but he had jumped out of the car and was trying to get in other people's cars! It was a total disaster, and she decided it was the last time they were doing that.

These are the kind of events which were heartbreaking on so many levels. I hated to see my mom cry, and I hated to see my dad lose his mind, and I hated the idea of Rusty never seeing my dad again. I spent several months in a state of perpetual sadness. It felt like every day we were losing Dad a little more, and there wasn't a single thing we could do about it.

One day right after this, I was driving along, thinking, grieving,

Though I Walk Through the Valley

praying . . . and suddenly the song on the radio burst through my sad thoughts. God did this often. He would break into my darkness and shine His grace. When I heard the words of the song, it felt like the voice of God was literally singing over me. I can't even describe the kind of peace and comfort that washed over me. Even though I was driving, I felt like God was picking me up and telling me to look at Him and listen carefully to His voice. It was sobering and comforting all at the same time. The next morning, my devotional by Oswald Chambers said this:

"What makes God so dear to us is not so much His big blessings to us, but the tiny things, because they show His amazing intimacy with us—He knows every detail of each of our individual lives." [4]

So very true. I could never count all of those "tiny things" God did through those dark days. They were happening constantly. His grace, even in the darkness, was everywhere I looked.

Reaching the Finish Line

In July, just a month after we decided Dad needed to be home-bound, things took another turn for the worse. It was becoming impossible for us to take care of him, and we had to make the difficult decision to place him in a nursing facility. I was actually kind of in denial, and not quite ready for this step. But when I went with them to his neurologist appointment, and the doctor saw the condition my mother was in, he convinced me we had to do this or I would lose both of my parents. He looked at me very seriously and said, "You need to do this for your mom as much as for your dad."

So I had to take a deep breath and quickly process it all. We had reached our limit, and I had to face that harsh reality. Dad was admitted that day to the hospital for a three-day evaluation, and then he was transferred to a nursing home.

But he never really settled down. The unmanageable behavior which had caused us to take this step only increased in the facility, and they ended up sedating him to keep him from hurting himself or others. It was horrible to watch, and when visitors came to see him, it was so heartbreaking to see the confusion on their faces when they saw him so completely uncontrollable.

After only three weeks in the facility, his condition had deteriorated so much that the doctors had to have a very sobering conversation with us. They told us he was not taking in enough nutrition to sustain life, and we were nearing the end. We could either leave him there, or take him home for his final days under hospice care.

We chose to bring him home. When the ambulance transported him to my house, they opened the door and lowered him out into the sunshine, and he spoke what would be his last words to me. I was so happy to see him, and I ran over and said, "Hey Daddy! How are you doing?" He smiled and responded cheerfully, "Wonderful!! Won, Der, Ful!!" And it really was wonderful to have him home, even under such heartbreaking circumstances.

Sara had been up from Florida for several weeks, and we all took turns sitting with him around the clock. He came home on Tuesday, July 29, and he only lived for five more days. I had no idea five days could seem like such an eternity. They were the hardest five days of my life. Sometimes he was actually coherent and would even recognize people who came to see him. Other times he slept for hours, and we monitored his breathing, wondering if he would take another breath.

I will never forget his last words to my mom. She was sitting on the edge of his bed, and he reached up, gently patted her cheek and said, "Love of my life." Yep, that's what she was. The love of his life. Russ and Bev. Those two kids who fell in love at the tender age of 14 and were faithfully married to each other for 53 years. I think I can honestly say I've never seen a sweeter love.

Daddy died on a Sunday, which was his favorite day of the week. And his funeral was on 08/08/08, which I think would've made him smile. We had all gathered around his bed that Sunday morning, know-

Though I Walk Through the Valley

ing the end was near. In the background, a CD was playing his favorite music. He always loved the music of Lance Carpenter, a personal friend of his, who was well-known in our circles for his simple Southern Gospel melodies accompanied by masterful guitar.

As Daddy was taking his last breaths, Lance was singing words taken from the book of Job: "The Lord giveth and the Lord taketh away. Blessed be the Name of the Lord." Mom was holding Daddy's hand with her right hand, and holding her left hand up to Heaven, and tears were streaming down her face. Her lips were whispering the words that Lance was singing, and I will never forget that sacred scene.

She was walking him home.

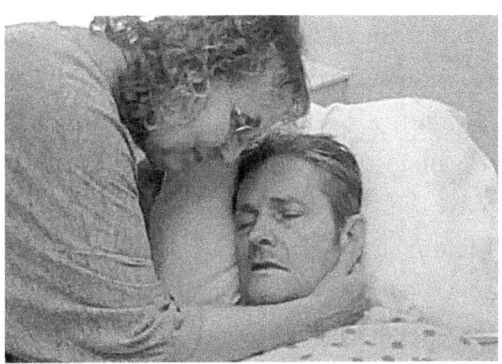

Russ & Bev

Legacy

The night before my dad's funeral, we gathered at the mortuary for the viewing and visitation. I don't know what I was expecting, but it wasn't this. Hundreds of people were lined up, and we stood there for hours as person after person came to pay their respects.

I did not realize until that night the extent of his influence. Maybe I had a little idea of it, but to hear story after story literally for hours?! I was completely blown away. So many people shared personal, intimate information. Couples he had met with, people he had counseled, pastors he had mentored. Several married couples told me they didn't know if they would even still be together if he hadn't helped them. I couldn't count the people who told me he led them to the Lord. My dad also had the rule Billy Graham had—he was never alone with a woman. So my mom went with him whenever he needed her. And many people told me my parents had met them, often in an emergency situation, sometimes in the middle of the night, or at the last minute. When someone needed them, they dropped everything and went to help.

As a kid, this was sometimes annoying to me personally, but I don't remember holding any bitterness about it. It was just momentarily frustrating, but it was also expected. That was just our life. It's part of being a preacher's kid.

But now I was hearing the other side of those situations, and it gave me a completely different perspective. As his child, I just saw him get up and go, but I didn't see what he actually went and did. Hearing these stories gave me a glimpse into the other side of all of those experiences. It made it all make sense, and it made it worth every ounce of frustration I had ever felt.

He was letting God use him to literally save marriages and sometimes to save lives or to save ministries. He lived his life influencing people for the Kingdom and bringing them closer to the Lord.

What a legacy!

Dr. Russell W. Rice

Building Bridges

Have you lost someone you love? Relationships are all so different, and each person touches our lives in different ways and to varying degrees. I had lost my grandparents by this point, and both of those losses were profound and painful. But losing my dad was a whole new level of sadness. I've had many people tell me the pain of losing a parent does not even compare to the pain of losing a spouse or losing a child. Some deaths are subconsciously expected, and some are tragically unexpected. I know this brings a different context altogether to the experience.

But death is awful, no matter how you view it. It's just so gut-wrenchingly horrible to say goodbye to someone you love. And the grieving process is a very confusing and unpredictable mind game.

My friend, Valerie Bianco (college roommate, remember?) had been trained in grief counseling, and during this time when I lost my dad, she gave me some great advice that I followed carefully. She described grief as something like emotional nausea. It builds up and builds up, and you have to get it out. So she actually recommended scheduling time for it. She told me to put it on my calendar, get away from everyone, and process the grief. She said to go and spend some time thinking about my dad, looking at pictures or cards or things I loved which reminded me of him. During this "appointment with grief" I could cry and pray and even yell if I needed to, but I would have an opportunity to get it all out, to cleanse away some of those hard emotions, and to experience some relief. Then later, whenever the emotional nausea would well up again, I would need to schedule another appointment with grief. Val predicted that at first I would need to do this pretty frequently, and then as time went on, the space between those appointments would grow farther and farther apart. And she was exactly right. I did that, and they did grow farther apart. But even now, years later, I still find a need to do this sometimes. Now it's usually on his birthday, or some other date that hits me like a ton of bricks. Or when I'm writing a book about him! (Reliving this has been harder than I would've imagined, but also strangely therapeutic).

So I'm passing on this really good advice. It's okay to sit in your grief. The Jewish people call it "sitting shiva," and if you aren't familiar with that, do a little research. It's an interesting process, and I feel like most of us don't give ourselves the space we need to grieve well. The people we love and have lost are worth it, and it's okay to create plenty of space to grieve their loss.

And what about your legacy? Do you think about this?

Seeing all those people waiting in line to talk to us and tell us what my dad had done for them—that changed my life! It completely shifted my perspective of his ministry, and it challenged me to consider my own life and legacy.

I want to challenge you with this thought too. How wide is your Kingdom influence? How deep is that Kingdom influence? God loves people. Don't ask me why! But He does. And He calls us to be His hands and feet, to love them as He does. And to bring them with us into His kingdom.

If my dad did anything, he loved people. And he loved them well. He used to have a little engraved keepsake sitting on his office desk which kept his favorite quotation in front of him. The words are a sobering reminder for all of us:

"Only one life, 'twill soon be past.
Only what's done for Christ will last." [5]

Chapter Fifteen
A Different Kind of Death

Have you ever heard someone refer to divorce as a kind of death? If you've never been divorced or affected by divorce, you might think that's an exaggeration. But if your life has ever been ripped apart by this awful experience, then you probably understand the comparison. In so many ways, it definitely is a death. Just a different kind of death. It's the end of a life that was built together, and the death of a million dreams. And afterwards neither of the people are ever the same. Layers of identity are stripped away, and a new identity must gradually develop. And during the transition, there is a season of emptiness and void which is excruciating and confusing.

During the ups and downs of my marriage, I read books, watched videos, did research—anything and everything I could think of to try to figure out what was happening. I learned a lot about relationships and what it takes to make them healthy. There are actually many kinds of marriage relationships. Some are incredibly fulfilling and peaceful with just occasional setbacks. My parents had this kind of marriage, and what a gift it was for me to witness that growing up. Many marriages have more consistent conflict. And among the ones which have consistent conflict there are three categories: disappointing marriages, difficult marriages, and destructive marriages. I'll try to explain the differences between these.

At one point or another, all marriages fit into the "disappointing" category, even the most peaceful ones. When we experience unmet expectations, we feel disappointed. Since we're all human, we all mess up, and when we sin against each other, it's disappointing and hurtful. But some relationships experience more disappointments than others. Difficult marriages, on the other hand, are relationships that have an added layer of chronic intensity. Maybe they have a handicapped child. Maybe they've had one financial setback after another. Maybe one partner has a debilitating illness or disease or they've experienced multiple job losses. There are many scenarios which can cause serious difficulties in the relationship. But in a destructive marriage, one or both people are actually being destroyed, bit by bit. It's why we use the term "toxic" to describe this condition. There's a poisonous element bringing actual destruction to the personhood of someone and to the relationship. It may be infidelity, addiction, abuse, or chronic dishonesty and deception. There are actually a whole host of behaviors that can erode trust and literally kill the marriage relationship. In our case, both of us were being damaged. You can see how all of this was hurting me, but I want to clarify here that it was hurting my husband too. His insecurities had hijacked his thinking, and eventually the destruction affected every area of both of our lives.

Calling it What it is

In Leslie Vernick's book, *The Emotionally Destructive Marriage*, I learned valuable information about emotional abuse. I had never called what I experienced "abuse" because I didn't have any black eyes or broken arms. But when I read the following description I could not deny the way I related to every word of it.

"Emotional abuse systematically degrades, diminishes, and can eventually destroy the personhood of the abused. Most people describe emotional abuse as being far more painful and traumatic than physical abuse. One only has to read reports of prisoners of war to begin to understand the traumatic effects of psychological warfare using emotionally abusive tactics—and this is when the behavior is perpetrated by one's enemy. When the abusive behavior is perpetrated by someone

A Different Kind of Death

who promises to love and cherish you, it is even more devastating and destructive." [6]

At the beginning of Leslie's book, she has a quiz for the reader to take to see if their relationship is truly destructive. When I took the quiz, I remember feeling so defeated. We were off-the-charts messed up. No question we were in the "destructive" category. And because I had spent most of our marriage pretending like everything was okay, most people had no idea how destructive it actually was. Even my kids, who did know some of it, did not see all of it. I kept so much from them to try to protect them. Only my closest friends knew, and that was only because they were very perceptive and by this point, they had begun to witness it themselves. I never wanted to talk about it so I wore the familiar mask again. Denial was so much easier. And the prospect of divorce continued to paralyze me with fear.

As I learned more and began to identify and analyze our relationship, I realized we had been bouncing back and forth between difficult and destructive for the entire marriage. But in 2011, the escalation toward destruction took off like a freight train without brakes.

By this point it had been fifteen years since I had confessed to him the inappropriate activities that happened before I met him. His insecurities had only grown more intense over the years, and this new financial pressure was causing my husband to experience extreme anxiety and depression. Eventually the need for control returned to our marriage, and this time it was even worse than it had been before. The big difference was that I was not the same person I had been before. I had spent the last several years learning and growing, and I now recognized how unhealthy and codependent I had been earlier to go along with the unreasonable and destructive behavior. So when this returned, I did not respond as I had before. I had learned how to stand up and how to speak up.

Another difference was that we were now in a church with a counseling ministry, and I had actually become a part of this ministry. Like

Everywhere I Look

I said earlier, I wanted so badly for us to be the poster kids for a beautiful, reconciled marriage, so when we went through a brief season of improvement, I was quick to talk about it. Back then I had been singing the praises of the temporary changes we experienced in our marriage, and some of the pastors asked me to join the lay counseling team and start learning how to help women who were in difficult marriages. I was thrilled to see God use what I'd been through to help others.

But the more involved I became with the counseling ministry, the more jealous my husband became. He resented any time I was away from home, especially if it had to do with the church. His jealousy became more and more intense, but this time I didn't try to hide it. I went to the counseling team for help.

At first they did not really understand the gravity of the situation. After all, we were new to the church, and from their perspective, things had just recently gone south. But I recognized the old patterns returning, and I refused to go back to that way of living. So I tried desperately to help them understand our history and what was currently going on in our home. It took quite a bit of untangling for them to get a clear picture of the situation, but eventually they did.

Disintegration

As our church elders became more involved, they met with us frequently to try to mediate. Their intervention was not welcomed by my husband, and his behavior at home became worse. The outbursts of anger escalated and created an atmosphere of fear and instability in our home. He wasn't abusing us physically, but his rages involved smashing and breaking things, or throwing things across the room or against a wall. I was afraid the aggression would eventually become directed at us, and I was very concerned about how all of this was affecting the kids.

It's understood in the field of domestic violence that emotional and psychological abuse often escalate to physical abuse, especially

A Different Kind of Death

if boundary lines are being drawn. When power and control issues are present in a relationship, the one in control will experience volcanic emotional explosions if their position of power is threatened, and this will often escalate to physical explosions if they can't figure out how to regain control. Physical abuse includes the obvious forms like hitting, slapping, and kicking. Thankfully I did not experience any of those. But it also includes physically restraining someone against their will, and my husband had actually done this a few times through the years. Each time was an isolated event that I minimized in my mind.

However, in December of 2011, he again used physical force to restrain me during a particularly aggressive fit of rage. And this time was different. He also destroyed nostalgic items and a picture of us during this episode, so when he used physical restraint in that context, it was a lot scarier. All of this crossed a line, and if I'm honest, nothing was ever the same. After this, our family started down the long road which eventually ended in divorce.

Help is on the Way!

During all of this, I have to point out, I was consistently seeing the grace of God break through the heavy, dark clouds. One of the ways it happened was in the way God provided a counselor for us who brilliantly understood what was happening. And he helped our church understand.

The way David Pennington came into our story is a beautiful demonstration of how the Spirit of God guided me. The first way I heard his name was actually through my mother-in-law. She and I have always had a very sweet relationship, and when I talked to her about what was happening, she recommended a book, *Trial By Fear*, which she had read. She gave me her copy, and it was a very helpful book. I felt like the author understood exactly what I was dealing with, and turns out, he lived in the same town we lived in. After I read the book, I wondered if I should try to contact him, but I never followed through.

Everywhere I Look

One day as I was driving near Bob Jones University, I remembered my mother-in-law had said she thought the author of that book, David Pennington, was a counselor on staff at Bob Jones. I immediately felt a strong sense that I needed to pull in there and see if it was true. I went into the administration building and asked, and was told he was not on staff but he had a counseling ministry in town. They gave me his email address, and when I got home I again did not immediately follow up. But God kept reminding me, and I decided to try to look up his phone number. I thought an email might get lost in cyberspace, and a phone call might be better. But I couldn't find a phone number for him, so again, I dropped the ball.

A couple weeks went by, and during a meeting someone brought up David's name out of the blue. I got his number and decided to give him a call. When I was with my friends, Cathy Johnson and Laurie Fillmore, I told them about all of this. I asked them to hold me accountable to call him, because I was struggling to follow through. By this point, I was so burnt out on counseling and was afraid to start over with yet another one. I was afraid I'd end up disappointed again. I was also a little hesitant to go outside the realm of my church's "authority." My view was a little distorted because I was so used to someone else telling me what to do. During this process, I had been slowly moving out from under my husband's authority, but rather than standing securely and solely under God's authority and learning to hear His voice, I had placed myself under a different human authority, my church. I do need to say it felt very reassuring to have them helping me, and I'm grateful for their support and guidance. But I wasn't emotionally healthy enough to stand on my own two feet yet, despite the progress I had made. I wanted to run everything by them and let them call the shots. It just felt safer, and I was desperate for security.

Right after that, my friend, Cathy, told me she had heard David's name again when someone recommended him to her. That was it. God was clearly leading me to this man through multiple sources, and I

A Different Kind of Death

knew I needed to actually get his help.

In the first meeting I had with him, David listened carefully to me as I explained our complicated history. For years, I had hesitated to call our relationship "abusive," but David immediately called it that. He introduced me to the "Power and Control Wheel,"[7] a graphic organizer which displays the different ways abuse occurs in relationships. The wheel is divided into eight sections, each listing the various tactics used to exert power and control. I had been experiencing emotional and psychological abuse in all eight categories. Typically, power and control are gained through fear and intimidation by using isolation, emotional and verbal abuse, minimizing, blame-shifting, gaslighting, and threats. When fear and intimidation no longer work, the situation almost always leads to physical abuse. In our case, as I had taken a stand against the emotional and psychological abuse in my marriage, the rages escalated and eventually did lead to that physically aggressive incident. God used that conversation to open my eyes to what was actually going on and how serious the situation was. I could no longer live in denial.

I was grateful beyond words for David's explanations and the clarity they brought to my mind. It was all starting to make sense, and I felt like I was coming out from a fog of confusion. When you are in a crisis, anxiety literally hijacks your ability to think rationally. So it was a gift from God to have him recognize what I was going through and help me find a path toward freedom and healing. From that point on, our church included David in our care plan, and he came to the meetings I had with our elders. He had a very clear grasp of our situation, and did an amazing job of communicating that with the elders and counselors of my church. David also helped me untangle my own confused thinking, and he encouraged me to lean on God's Spirit for wisdom and guidance. For months he met with us, individually and then later as a couple, and he did his best to help us find healing.

I wish I could say we did. But as time went on, it became very clear that healing wasn't happening. The control issues kept coming back, and my husband's emotional outbursts returned every time we tried to live together again. And every time he went into a rage, I braced myself for the possibility of him crossing lines again and becoming physically aggressive. Our neighbors, the Cranstons, were deeply involved with trying to help us. Dan is a physician, and he was a faithful and helpful friend to my husband. Regina spent hours with me, letting me process and helping me think clearly. They stood with us and wisely navigated those tricky waters. I know this isn't easy to do, and I'm still so grateful.

Dan & Regina Cranston

We also had a lot of help from our friends, Paul and Lisa Clark. We'd been friends with them since our kids were little, and Lisa had been in my ladies' Bible study which had been such a huge help to me for years. Paul and Lisa were available constantly during this season of instability. The Clarks and the Cranstons both opened their homes to us during the necessary separations. Russ and Carol Williams also gave the kids and myself a place to stay when we needed it. These couples and many others were 2D images of grace which helped me see 3D images of God even in this awful darkness. God literally surrounded us with some of the best people on this planet, and I'm still so overwhelmed by the way they all loved us so well and so sacrificially.

A Different Kind of Death

Paul & Lisa Clark

But despite all their best efforts, we kept having the same recurring issues, and I eventually reached a point of no return. David had actually predicted that it could happen, but I didn't really believe him. I had always been able to push through and keep trying. But David had seen people "hit a wall" emotionally, and he warned us both it could happen if my husband's mindset didn't change. He had probably seen it happen enough to recognize that we were getting close to that point. And he was right.

The very last time my husband lost control and destroyed something, the destruction wasn't even as extensive as it had been in the past, but it was the last straw for me. It literally felt like a death blow to the relationship. After that, I felt dead inside, and I refused to risk putting myself or the kids through another event. I had nothing left to give. My husband continued to ask for another chance, but eventually he got sick of trying to get me to change my mind, and he lost all hope of seeing the marriage restored. When that happened, he decided to file for divorce.

So in 2014, after two years of intense counseling and multiple separation and reconciliation attempts, and then another year of legal separation, the divorce was final.

It was time to pick up the pieces of my life, and find a path forward for myself and the kids.

Everywhere I Look

Grace in the Dark

If I could show you the journals I kept during this season you would read story after story of God's amazing grace. I didn't spend a lot of time describing the tornado swirling all around me. There are bits and pieces scattered throughout the pages, but the overwhelming majority of journal entries describe what God was doing in my own heart and the sweet ways He was carrying me. Scripture verses, poems, song lyrics, sermon excerpts, book notes, profound quotations . . . pages and pages of the beautiful grace of God in my life.

Let me just give you a few examples . . .

June 5, 2012

-Deut. 33:12 *The beloved of the LORD dwells in safety. The High God surrounds him all day long. (ESV)*

-Ps. 32:10 *Steadfast love surrounds the one who trusts in the LORD. (ESV)*

-Ps. 125:2 *As the mountains surround Jerusalem, so the LORD surrounds his people, from this time forth and forevermore. (ESV)*

I've had several moments lately where God's love just kinda washes over me and completely surrounds me. Sometimes it's unexpected and seems to come from out of nowhere. Sometimes I have to go looking for it . . . but each time I'm reminded that it's always there, whether I 'see' or 'feel' it - or not. Yesterday, I got this mental picture of a phone booth . . . as a picture of God's love that 'surrounds' me. I'm standing inside the phone booth of God's love and nothing can touch me—I'm safe from the enemy. I'm secure and protected. Because I'm in His love, I can rest and be totally at peace. It's always surrounding me whether I see it or not. If I close my eyes, I don't see the phone booth anymore. I can stand there with my eyes closed and imagine that maybe it's not there and I'm standing there in the open, vulnerable and unprotected. This will make me fearful, worried, anxious, maybe even terrified. But

A Different Kind of Death

it's all unfounded fear- fear that's not based in reality. The truth is, if I just open my eyes and see that the phone booth surrounds me, I'll be at peace again and the fears will flee. Perfect love drives away fear! (1 John 4:18) There is no room for fear! There's also no room for insecurity. I am "in His Love" which is really just another way to say "in Christ" because Jesus is the tangible expression of God's love. I am forever secure, because I am forever "in Christ." (Romans 8:1, 1 Corinthians 1:30)

June 7, 2012

Another beautiful picture of God surrounding me with His Love- even better picture than the phone booth . . .

In a cocoon, a caterpillar is transformed into a butterfly. Inside my cocoon of God's Love (expressed through Jesus, "in Him") God is transforming me into His image. When He looks at me, He sees the 'cocoon' of Jesus surrounding me (justification). What's happening on the inside of the cocoon is my sanctification.

August 2012 (a series of events)

1. I woke up one morning to a text from a friend. She had written out 1 Samuel 30:6 for me- "David strengthened himself in the LORD his God."
2. Mom came out on my back porch one afternoon and told me she wanted to encourage me and that the Lord had reminded her of Daddy's sermon on Ziklag (1 Samuel 30) where David "encouraged himself in the LORD his God."
3. I looked up that passage in my Daddy's Bible and read his sermon notes:
4. "When faced with devastating circumstances, David and his men had two different responses. His men were 'embittered' and spoke of stoning David. But David did two things–

- *Encouraged (strengthened) himself in the LORD his God*
- *Inquired of the LORD (What should I do?)"*

Daddy's illustration said "sun-butter/ sun-clay (The heat of the sun can soften our hearts like butter, or harden our hearts like clay. Same heat, different response)."

August 21, 2012

During this wait, God keeps communicating truths to me, and often it will be the same truth or verse coming to me from several different people or places. Back on June 20, God gave me the sweet reminder of Jeremiah 29: 11-14, "For I know the plans I have for you, says the LORD . . . " I wish I had written down all the times He gave it to me over the summer. Seems like every time I turned around there those verses were again.

The other day, my mom came up and handed me a piece of paper. She said Aunt Joy had called and said she was praying for me and felt like God wanted her to pass on some verses to me. Mom handed me a little pink slip of paper, and on it she had written: "Jeremiah 29:11-12."

Sweet words from God.

October 2012

"Have you come to the Red Sea place in your life, where in spite of all you can do,

There is no way out, there is no way back, there is no other way but through?

Then wait on the LORD with a trust serene, 'til the night of your fear is gone;

He will send the wind, He will heap the floods, when He says to your soul, 'Go on.'

And His hand will lead you through- clear through- Ere the watery

A Different Kind of Death

walls roll down,
No foe can reach you, no wave can touch, no mightiest sea can drown;
The tossing billows may near their crests, their foam at your feet may break,
But over their bed you shall walk dry shod in the path that your Lord will make.
In the morning watch, beneath the lifted cloud, you shall see but the Lord alone,
When He leads you on from the place of the sea to a land that you have not known;
And your fears will pass as your foes have passed, you shall no more be afraid;
You shall sing His praise in a better place, a place that His Hand has made."
-Annie Johnson Flint [8]

Feb. 26, 2013

From Jesus Calling:

"I am leading you, step by step, through your life. Hold my hand in trusting dependence, letting Me guide you through this day. Your future looks uncertain and feels flimsy- even precarious. That is how it should be. Secret things belong to the Lord (Deut. 29:29) and future things are secret things. When you try to figure out the future, you are grasping at things that are Mine. This, like all forms of worry, is an act of rebellion: doubting My promises to care for you. Whenever you find yourself worrying about the future, repent and return to Me. I will show you the next step forward, and the one after that, and the one after that. Relax and enjoy the journey in My presence, trusting Me to open up the way before you as you go." [9]

Everywhere I Look

March 18, 2013

Isaiah 43: 1-3
Thus says the LORD, your Creator, O Jacob,
And He who formed you, O Israel,
"Do not fear, for I have redeemed you; I have called you by name; you are Mine!
When you pass through the waters, I will be with you, and through the rivers, they will not overflow you. When you walk through the fire, you will not be scorched, nor will the flame burn you. For I am the LORD your God, the Holy One of Israel, your Savior." (NASB)

From George Müller:
"God delights to increase the faith of His children. We ought, instead of wanting no trials before victory, no exercise for patience, to be willing to take them from God's hands as a means. Trials, obstacles, difficulties and sometimes defeat, are the very food of faith."[10]

Generally attributed to Charles Spurgeon:
"I have learned to kiss the wave that throws me against the Rock of Ages."[11]

June 18, 2013

My brother Rusty's words, from a conversation I had with him during a visit to him in prison at Lieber Correctional Institution:
"If we could just really get a glimpse of what God is doing when things are hard, if we could focus in on how He's changing us, how it takes extreme heat and pressure to form a diamond, then maybe we could do what Paul says and rejoice because God really is making me more like His Son."

THIS is God's plan to prosper me! My circumstances may not look very "prosperous" but the key here is how I define prosperous. If I define it by my circumstances, then I reveal that my heart is set on "things below." But if I define "prosperous" as my sanctification and becoming like Jesus, which is TRUE PROSPERITY, then that reveals that my heart is set on "things above"- what truly matters!

Building Bridges

If you or someone you love is in an abusive relationship, I want to urge you from the depths of my heart to get help now. Don't wait. Don't assume it will always stay at the level it is now. Don't believe the lie that this is okay or it will magically get better. Without serious intervention, it will likely continue to escalate. And it's not okay to accept that behavior. I believed I was "showing grace," but through therapy and counseling, I began to understand that it was enabling. It isn't loving to allow someone to continue in destructive patterns of behavior, and it isn't what grace looks like. Grace leads us AWAY from destruction rather than binding us to it.

If you aren't personally affected by abuse, consider with me any areas you need to surrender to God. Where is He stretching you, teaching you, molding and shaping you? That often involves pain and heartache. We live in a fallen world, and He uses those painful situations to transform us into the image-bearers we were created to be. The sooner we yield to the transformation process, the better. It can be a very difficult process though, and sometimes it takes a long time for us to get to the point of surrender.

Through these difficult years, God kept giving me a vision of the correlation between my circumstances and the children of Israel when they came out of Egypt. I often wanted to "look back" at the security I had in being a married woman, even if that marriage was a mess. I was scared of the path forward, and my past life was at least familiar,

Everywhere I Look

although painful. Over and over, God's Spirit kept telling me to trust Him completely. I didn't know how I was going to provide for myself or the kids, find a job, find a place to live, move forward into the scary unknown. But He kept telling me He was going before me, and preparing my path . . . I just needed to keep my eyes on Him. I couldn't see the whole path, but I did have enough light for each step of the way. And that was all I needed.

It's all you need too . . . just take one step at a time.

Eyes focused on Jesus.

Ears listening for His voice.

Heart aligned with His heart.

Soul resting in His love.

With His help and by His grace, you too can find a path forward.

Chapter Sixteen
Let's Do This!

During the years after my divorce, I watched God take care of us in a million big and small ways. One of the sweetest provisions came in His way of guiding me to a place of employment. I hadn't worked outside the home for years, so this process was very intimidating to me. But my daddy had always encouraged me to get my college degree, so I would have "something to fall back on," and I'm so glad he did! It was now time to fall back on it. I started chasing down leads for teaching positions, and eventually struck gold.

My friend, Karen O'Neal, from my ladies' Bible study days, was now working at The Pearl Center for Learning. I think I saw this on her Facebook page and asked her about the place. She encouraged me to reach out to the owner, Suzanne Ringger. So I did, and Suzanne asked me to come in for an interview.

It was the summer of 2013, during a crazy time when we were living in our friends' backyard. Brian and Andrea Hardyman had offered to let us stay in the RV behind their house until we could get on our feet again. So I literally got ready for my interview in an RV and went over there and tried to impress her. By the grace of God, it somehow worked, and she hired me. I needed a college course for my training, so I signed up for it, and found out I would need to go to a small town in Florida for this class. I also applied for the scholarship the program offered, and was thrilled when I received it. So I just needed to figure out my housing arrangements while I would be in Florida. My mom told me my Aunt Charity's daughter, Penny, had a second home in Florida, so I decided to reach out to her and see where it was. Turns out, it was five minutes from where the class was being held, and it was actually empty for the summer. Penny told me she'd be happy for me to stay there while I was taking the class. So now I had the class paid for and an entire house to myself at no cost!

This was the first in a series of events where God cleared the path for me, and made a way where there seemed to be no way. I was charting a new path for myself and for the kids, but God was going before us. And He allowed me to see this over and over. I had never experienced a season like this before in my life. Every time I turned around, God was demonstrating the reality of His name, Jehovah Jireh—the God Who Provides. My faith grew exponentially through these years, and I started understanding what the book of James is talking about when it says we can actually consider it "joy" when we go through trials:

"Consider it pure joy, my brothers and sisters, whenever you face trials of many kinds, because you know that the testing of your faith produces perseverance. Let perseverance finish its work so that you may be mature and complete, not lacking anything." (James 1:2-4, NIV)

I was beginning to see grace like I had never seen it before.

Charley's Diagnosis

After working at the Pearl Center for a few years, I had almost completed my certification for educational therapy. Upon completion of the first class back in 2013, I had been able to practice as an educational therapist, but I had continued to work toward professional certification. I had one last class to take, and then I would officially be a Professionally Certified Educational Therapist. So during the summer of 2016, I went back to Florida for the final class.

Everything went well, and I completed all the requirements successfully. On the last day of class I drove to Orlando to see my sister and my mom. After my divorce, Mom had moved to Florida to live

Let's Do This!

with Sara, and I was excited to visit with them for the weekend before heading back to South Carolina.

But when I walked in the door of Sara's house, I knew something was wrong. She told me to come in and sit down. This was the second time in my life where I heard those horrible words, and I immediately tried not to panic. She told me Charley had just gotten a scary diagnosis, and she had waited to tell me until I finished my class. He had been having some weird symptoms for a while, but that guy would never go to the doctor, so he put it off until it was very obvious something was wrong, and his wife, Phyllis, had insisted on getting a medical opinion.

They had been living in West Virginia for a while now. In 2006, Charley became the pastor of Mount Jackson Baptist, a quaint little church in the beautiful mountains of Athens, West Virginia. After pastoring Bethel Baptist Church for twenty years, God had led him to make some changes, and he and his family made the move to West Virginia. Nestled in a peaceful college town, Mount Jackson was a wonderful place for a fresh start.

Rusty's incarceration and my dad's illness and death had taken a toll on Charley, and navigating all that pain had been a challenge. The enemy of his soul had never really let up on him. When he had decided years ago to join the winning team, the spiritual forces of Hell were unleashed, and throughout his life the spiritual attacks never went away. He didn't talk about it much, but occasionally he expressed to those closest to him that demonic spirits would occasionally still torment him. When he was discouraged, he was more vulnerable, and he could actually still see and hear them. The pain and discouragement following Rusty's incarceration and Daddy's death made him more susceptible to the spiritual attacks. So thankfully, God provided a change of scenery, a new ministry, and a reset which helped him regain his equilibrium.

Everywhere I Look

Charley's family

By 2016, he had been at Mount Jackson for ten years, and the people loved him dearly. In addition to pastoring, Charley enjoyed playing his guitar and leading the congregation in praise and worship. Phyllis was also involved with the music ministry and various other ministries in the church. They had both settled in and were enjoying serving the Lord there.

But then these strange symptoms started emerging, and it was puzzling to both of them. Charley had had pretty severe heartburn and acid reflux for years. When it seemed to get worse, and he was struggling to swallow, he figured it was just more of the same. The initial diagnosis seemed to indicate he was right, because nothing seemed to be wrong with his gallbladder like they suspected.

But then things got worse, and he wasn't just having trouble swallowing. His overall pain levels were increasing and he had an alarming lack of energy. Phyllis was getting really concerned, and she convinced him to go back to the doctor for more tests, and this time they finally got answers. Charley had a large tumor in his esophagus, and they wanted to send him to Wake Forest's cancer center in, of all places, Winston-Salem, North Carolina.

When I arrived at Sara's, she gave me this news and told me we were getting ready to call Charley. He had just emailed her a copy of the medical report, and when she called, she put him on speaker so the

Let's Do This!

three of us could go over the report together. Because she's a nurse, she was able to interpret it pretty quickly. Not only was there an esophageal tumor, but the report also indicated spots on his liver and his spine. It appeared to have already metastasized. I've already mentioned Charley was a genius, so there was no confusion on his part. He knew immediately how serious this was, but honestly, I couldn't believe how calm he sounded. His voice didn't even sound concerned, much less fearful. He was just discussing it all, as if we were discussing the weather. This was just the beginning of the fearless way he faced this.

The Ultimate Healing

Charley's doctors had instructed him to go to the cancer center the following Monday, so he planned to preach on Sunday as usual. In fact, just a couple days earlier, on that previous Wednesday, he had taught a weekly Bible study at church. He didn't feel well, but he still did it. And he figured that would be the case again on Sunday. But before church, he was trying to get ready, and didn't have the strength to. He had to admit he wasn't going to be able to preach, or even get to church. This is when his family decided they were heading to the cancer center immediately instead of waiting until the next day.

Sara and I had already made adjustments to our schedule and were heading to the cancer center on Monday. I left Florida and drove back to South Carolina, where I unpacked and repacked, then left Monday morning for North Carolina. My kids all came too, some driving their own cars by now. By the beginning of that week, our entire family was making their way to the hospital. We pretty much invaded the place.

I will never forget the look on Charley's face when I walked in his hospital room Monday evening. He was sitting in the hospital bed with a cheesy grin on his face and when I hugged him, he said, "Guess where I'm going, Charity!"

Everywhere I Look

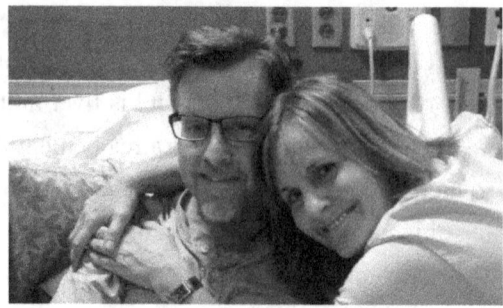

Charley and me, in the hospital

Now, you have to understand that in a family filled with pastors, we all had plenty of experience with death. Funerals are an integral part of a pastor's job, and we had all grown up going to them and being familiar with death and grief and funeral homes. We had also had a million conversations about death and dying, and probably an unnatural curiosity about the whole experience. It wasn't uncommon for us to sit around my mom and dad's table and ponder what happens when you die. Do the angels carry you to Jesus? Do you see your body as your spirit soars to God? Is there music? A celebration in Heaven? What's it like to actually see Jesus face to face?

Well, Charley was pretty sure he was soon going to find out, and he was actually excited about the prospect. Let me clarify though. I don't mean to give the impression that he wasn't torn about leaving us, especially about leaving Phyllis and his kids and grandkids. His love for his wife was one of the sweetest I've ever seen. He was absolutely crazy about her. So all of the emotions were experienced that week. But overwhelmingly present was the joy he clearly had about what was in store. And I know that made our experience completely different than if he hadn't been so peaceful and joyful.

We had no idea on Monday that the whole hospital experience would last less than a week. For the first couple days, the oncologists were running tests, getting scans, and trying to determine a treatment plan. Charley and his family discussed where they would live while

Let's Do This!

he went through treatment, and we all discussed the options. But on Wednesday, things shifted, and we were told the cancer had completely destroyed his liver and it was starting to shut down. His lungs were also starting to fill with fluid, and this meant he wouldn't be strong enough to even leave the hospital. He would likely only have days to live.

At one point, by God's grace, Rusty was able to call and talk to him. Everything had happened so suddenly that we had not even been able to make him aware of Charley's diagnosis. We aren't able to call Rusty, but he is allowed to call us, so we hoped he would call at some point for us to let him know what was happening. When my phone rang and I saw the number, I stepped out into the hallway and broke the awful news to him. His tone shifted dramatically and I heard him sighing and taking deep breaths. After processing this heartbreaking information, he immediately asked to speak with Charley. I went back into the hospital room and handed the phone to Charley. Then I stepped back to watch them talk and to take in the reality of what was happening. Those two brothers, "Rusty and Randy," best friends through all the ups and downs of life, were saying goodbye over a phone call. Another sad result of that devastating incarceration. But I'm thankful they were able to take what they could get. It was a sweet gift from God that they were able to have that conversation.

By the middle of the week, Charley was showing signs of being very uncomfortable. They were giving him oxygen and pain medication to ease this, but it was clear he was struggling. Even then, he maintained a positive attitude despite the pain and weakness. At one point Phyllis showed him a video of his granddaughter, Abigail, reciting Psalm 23. She was only three years old, but she recited the entire thing. At the end, her sweet voice rose in excitement as she exclaimed, "and I will dwell in the house of the Lord . . . FOREVER!!" It brought a smile to everyone's face, and Charley was staring at the video with joy and excitement in his own eyes. He nodded and quietly said, "Let's do this!"

On Thursday, he deteriorated quickly and the doctors did not think he would live through the night. That evening, we wanted to give him some time with Phyllis and his kids, so the rest of us filed out of the hospital room. A few hours later, everyone said their goodbyes and left the hospital except Phyllis, Sara, Mom, and myself. We had decided to stay the night, so the four of us settled in and tried to rest, but none of us could actually get to sleep. Charley did though. He actually slept soundly, and we took turns keeping an eye on him as he rested.

Sometime in the middle of the night, Charley roused from sleep and blurted out in frustration, "Good night! Am I still here?!" We all laughed and cried and tried to tell him yes, he was still with us. And then, to our complete surprise, he sat up and started telling jokes!

The next morning when he woke up, he was joking around again, and seemed to have no pain. This was weird, because they had stopped giving him pain meds the night before. When they came in to check on him, he told them he wasn't feeling any pain, so they decided not to give him any medication. And they actually didn't give him any for the entire day on Friday.

We called it our "miracle day" with him. He sat up in bed, talked and told stories, and looked like he was completely healthy. Several friends came by that day to see him, including Gary Williams, his life-long friend from our days in Edenton. The whole entire day Charley was telling jokes, watching Andy Griffith, and being his normal, crazy self. At one point, one of the nurses came in and said she heard us down the hall laughing and carrying on, and she wondered if we were having a party in there. We all looked at her and nodded. Yep, that's right. We're enjoying every minute we have with him, and we're confident about where he's going. Why not celebrate? That's exactly the way he wanted it.

Let's Do This!

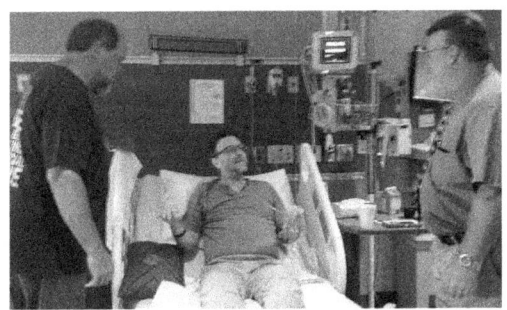

Charley & friends, in the hospital on our "miracle day."

That evening he was visibly tired after such a fun but exhausting day. So we all said goodnight and tried to get some rest. The next morning he did not wake up. He slept peacefully all morning, and at some point, Summer's dad, Sam, brought in a CD player so we could fill the room with music. Sam is an incredible pianist, and he had a recording of himself playing some hymns. While those were playing peacefully in the background, Charley took his last breath. I like to think those hymns created an atmosphere of worship that gave him the peace he needed to bid us all goodbye.

While we were processing what just happened, and the medical team entered the room to take over, I couldn't help but imagine what Charley was experiencing. All those questions we had discussed, all the curiosity we had about this transformation, all the unknowns suddenly became known to him. His life didn't end in that hospital bed. It just transitioned from here to there, from black and white to color, from shadows to reality. What a beautiful thought.

Charley was an amazing big brother, and he taught me so much. He was such a knowledgeable theologian and true lover of God. His words, his sermons, and his life made a huge impact on mine and taught me how to live. But during that week, the lessons he taught me exponentially surpassed all the theological knowledge he had ever passed on to me. His peace and confidence during his final week on earth taught me how to face death with joy and anticipation rather than fear or dread.

Everywhere I Look

After years of teaching us how to live, he spent his final days teaching us how to die.

As Voddie Baucham put it: "Sometimes God is glorified when sick saints get well. But more often than not, God is glorified when sick saints die well."[12]

Charley showed us how to die well. And God was indeed glorified.

Being crazy with my big brother!

Let's Do This!

Building Bridges

Are you afraid of dying? Did you know the fear of death is actually described as a bondage in Scripture? Hebrews tells us that through His death Jesus destroyed the power of death and delivered us from this slavery.

"He too shared in their humanity so that by His death He might break the power of him who holds the power of death—that is, the devil—and free those who all their lives were held in slavery by their fear of death." (Hebrews 2:14-15, NIV)

We can see this fear all around us. Most people live their entire lives dreading and being terrified of death. Even Christians, who have the hope of eternity with Jesus, often cling to this life as if this is all we get.

I love how Francis Chan describes this. In a famous sermon illustration, he brings a long rope onto the stage. He says to imagine the rope going on and on forever, and then he says to imagine the rope is a timeline of your existence. At one end of the rope, he has about two inches of red duct tape, and he says the red portion represents your time on earth. "You've got a few short years here on earth," he says, "and then you've got all of eternity somewhere else." He goes on to challenge us to consider that most of us only live for the red part. It's all we think about. We're consumed with protecting it and clinging to it. We often don't even consider the rest of the rope which represents all of eternity. [13]

Charley had a window into the spirit realm most of us don't have. He often wished he didn't have it, but God used his enhanced perception of that realm to give him an anticipation for Heaven. The enemy had used it for evil, but God used it for good. Charley knew death would eliminate all of his struggles against the forces of Hell, and he would at last be free from all spiritual warfare. He also knew that because of his faith in the finished work of Jesus, the end of this life on earth would only be the beginning of eternal life in the presence of God. And with all of this in mind, he was able to face death fearlessly, and even with excitement. He had fought the good fight, he had finished the race, and he had kept the faith (2 Timothy 4:7). And he knew, without a doubt, what was in store for him.

I want to live with a faith like Charley's which paints a vision of eternity so clear and so strong it displaces all fear. Especially the fear of death.

Rice Family

Part Five

Looking Ahead
Seeing God's Grace in Our Healing

"And He will be the stability of your times,
a wealth of salvation, wisdom, and knowledge;
The fear of the LORD is his treasure."
Isaiah 33:6 (NASB)

"The LORD is my shepherd. I shall not want."
Psalm 23:1 (ESV)

We decided to drive by our old cabin. It had been a fun but exhausting weekend, and Dollywood always made us feel better. It was our place. So nostalgic and sweet to be there again. After our sad and disappointing year, a group of kind and supportive friends collected money and surprised us with a vacation to Pigeon Forge, TN. The four kids and I enjoyed every minute of it, even though thoughts of our new reality occasionally popped into my mind. I worked hard at pushing those thoughts away this weekend.

On our way home, we passed the road which led to Oak Haven, the resort where we used to own a vacation cabin. Seemed like another lifetime. But the kids immediately started asking to go see it. So we did. Driving through the gate, we were all transported back in time. Back to a few years before, when we came up here every May for our family vacation. We would spend an entire week hitting all the tourist traps: go-karts, mini golf, gem mining. And we always made sure to visit our special place, the Apple Barn, with its restaurant, gift shop, and the kids' favorite—the candy shop. The highlight of the trip was always Dollywood. Every year we looked forward to coming up to these beautiful Smoky Mountains.

And this trip was good for us. As we drove through the resort, the steep, winding road led us up to cabin #37. I drove slowly around the little cul-de-sac, and we all stared at the place where we used to feel at home. It wasn't ours anymore though. We had to give it up just like we had to give up so many things in the last few years. After their dad and I divorced, the kids and I said goodbye to more than just a cabin. We had to leave the dream home we had spent over a year designing and building, our four and a half acres with a little creek, our zipline, our neighbors—the Cranstons, who were like an extended family. And we had to give up our financial security. We had to kiss our old life goodbye, and start a new one. Now we were staying in our friends' backyard, living in an RV.

Driving out of Oak Haven, I tried to help us all look on the bright side.

"You guys really have a unique perspective now," I said. "We've had two opposite experiences. We've been rich and we've been poor, and that'll help us all understand so many more things in life. You'll be able to relate to people on both ends of the spectrum."

My oldest daughter didn't miss a beat. She summed up her opinion quickly, and it probably reflected everyone else's too.

"I liked being rich better," she said, and we all laughed in agreement.

Yeah . . . me too, babe. In many ways, money did make things easier. And now that I had to figure out how to financially survive, I had a deeper appreciation for the money my husband had provided for us.

But money doesn't buy everything. It doesn't buy emotional security, which I had found is sometimes more important than financial security. Money also doesn't buy a good marriage, unfortunately, and it certainly doesn't buy peace . . . the one thing I had desperately longed for all those years.

One thing was certain though. Rich or poor, we were learning a very important lesson—the secret the Apostle Paul was talking about in Philippians.

"I have learned to be content whatever the circumstances. I know what it is to be in need and I know what it is to have plenty. I have learned the secret of being content in any and every situation, whether well fed or hungry, whether living in plenty or in want. I can do all this through

Everywhere I Look

Him who gives me strength." ~Philippians 4:11-13 (NIV)

Finding contentment.

Maybe, just maybe, this is where healing begins.

Chapter Seventeen
Let the Healing Begin

Joy and Sorrow

Wouldn't it be nice if emotional healing could be a process that's tied up neatly with a bow? We have pain, and then we heal. The end. Put a bow on top. Unfortunately, as long as we live on this planet, that's not actually how it goes. The healing journey is so multi-layered, and is often a big tangled mess rather than a nice linear progression. It can also be a long and confusing process. Just when you feel like your heart has healed, along comes more pain. And then some more. Sometimes you think your heart has healed, and then something happens that takes you back a couple notches or opens those wounds again.

My experience of healing has been a long process where I've learned to simultaneously hold joy and sorrow, one in each hand, and I've learned to trust God a little more with each painful experience I've been through. That trust is actually what has facilitated my healing. Looking back now, I'm amazed at how God gently and faithfully guided my healing journey. I had no idea what I needed. I just knew I wanted to follow Him, and I trusted Him to heal my broken heart.

It came in so many ways, and it happened so incrementally it was almost imperceptible at the time. In the jumbled up mixture of good and also more pain, I was learning more and more about how to rely solely on God and to get my strength from Him. I'm still learning, and I'm sure I always will. My circumstances certainly didn't precipitate the healing. They were still unpredictable and often disappointing. Sometimes very painful. But through it all, healing was happening in my heart despite my circumstances. My heart was fully set on God now. I had lost so much, but I had also gained what my heart truly needed . . . security and stability in God alone.

The Kids

In the aftermath of the divorce, my biggest concern was my kids. For the last twenty years of my life, it had been my joy to pour into them, and they were the number one reason I was willing to remain in a destructive marriage. I mistakenly thought it was always in the best interest of the children to stay in a marriage. But when the escalation of the destruction was affecting them, I started questioning the value of what I was clinging to. It wasn't a healthy mindset, but I had been willing to put up with anything personally to hold our family together. When I expressed this once to a counselor, I remember saying, "I'll put up with anything to avoid a divorce. I can't stand the thought of my kids coming from a broken family." It felt like she smacked me in the face when she said, "They already do, Charity. You can't avoid that, because your family is already broken." Those words were a wake-up call for me. When I became aware of the damage it was doing to the kids to remain in that environment, I couldn't keep telling myself it was in their best interest for me to stay. As the destruction escalated, it was obvious it was hurting them too.

Once it was final and official, the kids were the ones I worried about the most. I had homeschooled them all, and had already taught Ashlyn and Kristen all the way through to graduation. While they were in high school, I continued to homeschool, but they also went to a co-op two days a week. After they turned 16, they started taking dual-enrollment courses at a local university, and both of them went on to graduate from that college. Josh and Savannah were still in school when we went through the divorce, so even after I started working I continued to homeschool them, and they also took classes at the co-op. Amazingly, by the grace of God, all four of them were doing well, and it was clear the difficult season we had gone through had served to make them more resilient. The five of us were closer than ever, and very protective of each other.

We still had a lot of storms ahead of us, but we had each other, and we were seeing the faithfulness of God everywhere we looked. And that was a huge comfort to all of us.

Savannah, Josh, Charity, Ashlyn, & Kristen, 2014

Serving in Slovenia

Hindsight truly is 20/20. I had no idea why God was leading me down certain paths along this healing journey, but as I look back over the process, several milestones stand out clearly. One of them was how He led me to become involved with mission work.

Being a missionary had been on my heart since I was a little girl. Remember how I had dreamed of going to Africa and teaching children there about Jesus? My daddy loved missions and when I was a little girl, missionaries were my heroes. During mission conferences at my dad's church, I would literally run around getting their autographs in my Bible. For my entire adult life up to this point, going on a mission trip was out of the question. I wasn't even able to go on a beach trip with my friends. So I certainly wasn't able to go to the other side of the world. But now . . . well, now I could.

Everywhere I Look

In early 2014, I was sitting in a church service one Sunday night, and a missionary from Ethiopia was speaking. Something he said instantly made me listen up. He was explaining how education is an open door into many countries, and teachers can go into places other people can't. I had recently gotten back into education so this caught my attention, and I started praying about this opportunity. I felt the Spirit of God strongly pressing me to go to the front afterwards to speak to the pastor about this. So I did.

Our missions pastor listened to me explain my thoughts and he was excited to hear God was leading me toward this. He asked me to email him about it, and he also gave me the name of someone in our church, a girl named Kathy Sibley, and he told me to call her.

I left feeling a little apprehensive about that idea. I didn't know who she was and I didn't have the courage to call her out of the blue. I figured I'd try to work up the courage, but then days turned into weeks and I never did. The following fall when I was serving in the children's ministry one Sunday morning, I noticed the name tag of another helper. It was Kathy Sibley! So I went over and told her the mission pastor had told me to talk to her. She asked me if I was a teacher, and I said "Yes!" And then she said, "You're supposed to go to Slovenia with us!"

Kathy & me

Let the Healing Begin

I'm gonna be honest . . . I didn't even know where Slovenia was. And I didn't know who this person was, but she went on to tell me she and some others had gone there on several mission trips to teach English and to share the Gospel. They had specifically been praying for God to call more people to come with them, and she immediately recognized I was responding to that call.

I was so excited when I heard this because the Spirit of God was confirming everything so clearly as she spoke. We stayed in touch and began to make plans for a mission trip the following summer. I told all of my kids about this, and asked them to pray about whether they should go too. Everyone did, but only Savannah felt like God was calling her to go. She was only 15 at the time, so she was the youngest person on the team.

The two of us started going to the planning meetings once a month, and as the trip was approaching, our excitement grew. This was a lifelong dream for me, and I can't even express how thrilled I was to have this opportunity. I soaked in the information, and spent time studying and preparing for our trip.

One of the ways God started immediately stretching my faith was in regards to the financial provision for the trip. Kathy and the others who had gone before shared with us about fundraising and trusting God to bring in the money. Savannah and I had to each raise over $2000, so we were looking at a total of almost $5000. Especially scary since I had absolutely no way to do that without God's help. I followed all the steps, sent out letters, and set up an online fundraiser. At first only a few donations came in, and I started to panic. I kept praying for God to provide, but I literally felt like He was telling me to relax and wait, that He was giving me an opportunity to learn how to trust Him in this unknown territory. I knew He was stretching my faith, but it was still scary. After a few months, the money came pouring in all at once. Within a couple week's time, all of it was in, with enough to even cover our passports and phone bill. The last time I needed to transfer money from the online fundraiser to my account in order to pay the church, the amount was $940. I transferred it to my account and the next morning, I got an email from the church with the financial statement attached. It listed all the donations which had come to the church for us, and the balance we owed. I wrote down Savannah's balance, and my own balance, then added them together. The total was $940! It brought me to tears. God really is in the details!

On Friday, June 26, 2015 we left the church, drove to Charlotte, and boarded a flight to Munich, Germany. We had a 10 hour layover there, so we got to explore a little and enjoy a day in Munich. So much fun! Then we flew to Slovenia that night, landed in Ljubljana, and spent the night at the missionary's home. I was absolutely blown away by the beauty of this country. How had I never even heard of it? It's incredibly green, with rolling hills and the majestic Alps in the distance. The capital city of Ljubljana has a gorgeous river flowing through the center, beautiful old buildings, cobblestone streets, and a castle looming on a nearby hill. It has a distinctively European feel to it, very cozy and quaint. I was instantly in love!

The next day we drove to Croatia for a week of kids' camp. There were ten of us on the team—two guys and eight girls. The guys had a big age discrepancy—one was a teenager, and one was in his sixties. The girls had a big range too. I was the oldest and Savannah was the youngest, with everything in between!

We learned Slovenia had formerly been a part of Yugoslavia, and had only become an independent state in 1991. Until then, it had been under communist rule, and the predominant religious influence had and continued to be atheism. Many of the kids who came to camp had parents who were atheists, and they had grown up under that influence. So the Gospel was very new to many of them. The Slovene pastor told us God had specifically given him a vision of reaching the next generation and building the church from the ground up. They had then set their minds to train people through Child Evangelism Fellowship, an

Let the Healing Begin

organization which focuses on reaching children with the Gospel, and they started having camps to reach as many kids as possible. We had the privilege of coming to help with one of those camps.

Each morning the adults had coffee and devotions together (some of the best coffee I've ever had in my entire life, by the way). Then we had breakfast with the kids, a morning service and activities, and an English lesson. Kathy and I taught English, the other girls helped out with activities and games, and the guys jumped in and did whatever was needed. Zach Martin, our teenage guy, was especially loved by the kids. He just had a way of connecting with them, and the kids all flocked around him. He also volunteered to emcee the evening programs and some of the group games, and he was constantly joking around and keeping everyone laughing. I never would've imagined that in a few short years Zach would be my son-in-law!

Zach & Savannah in Slovenia

The Love of God

On Thursday of that week, the Slovenian National Television crew came to camp and wanted to interview several Slovene workers and two people from our American team. Kathy wanted one guy and one girl from our team to be interviewed, and she asked Zach and me to be the ones to do it. We both agreed and went off to individually pray and process before the interview. This would be televised over the entire country, and I specifically asked God to give me whatever message these people needed to hear. I don't remember all of the questions but I do remember them asking why we came all the way from America. My answer was not planned but the Spirit gave me the words. I said God wanted to give them the message that He loves them. In a couple other answers, I found myself again emphasizing the love of God. After they finished my interview, Zach came over and prepared for his. He had not heard mine, but when they asked him, I was surprised to hear him also emphasizing the love of God! In the translation of the word "Gospel" they called it "the happy news," which I still think is such a great way of saying it. They asked Zach, "What is this Happy News you've come to tell us?" And his answer was God loves them and sent His Son to be their Savior. I loved how God had given us both the same basic message, completely unrehearsed or planned.

But what was really amazing was something we learned the following week. After camp, we drove back to Slovenia, and then to a town called Velenje. An American missionary needed our help there, so our team went and taught English in an elementary school and helped with their Good News Club. That's a backyard program for kids to attend daily for a week, where they learn songs and Bible stories, and enjoy games and other activities. One day the missionary took us to visit an old castle, and we climbed a hill overlooking the city. We were there to do a prayer walk around the perimeter of the castle and before we prayed, he spoke to us for a few minutes about this beautiful country. He explained the history of atheism and how so few of them believed in God. This has driven many of these beautiful people to despair, and even to take their own lives. He told us Slovenia has one of the highest suicide rates in the world, and he was convinced it was because they had never known the love of God. He encouraged us to show these people God's love, to lavish that love on them, and to speak of it any chance we got. He said traditional methods of evangelism of jumping straight to "You're a sinner and you need a Savior" weren't successful

Let the Healing Begin

there. He said it takes a long time to build their trust and they need to see and hear about the love of God before they are taken down the "Romans Road." Did you catch what I just said? The message needed to be that God loves them. Period. My mind quickly went back to those interviews. The message of God's love was what came out of my mouth and also out of Zach's mouth. We didn't know how badly they needed to hear that. But God knew!

We were there for two weeks, and it was a life-changing experience. In a foreign country you get to witness the "bigness of God," which is amazing in and of itself. But to see God at work, and to see His love for people, to sing and worship while others are singing and worshiping in another language—it's all such a unique, spiritual experience. God used it to expand my vision beyond my own little life and my own pain. He carried me up and gave me the 30,000-foot view of what He's doing in this world.

Getting my eyes completely off of my circumstances and onto His greatness was exactly what I needed.

Teaching adults in Slovenia

Building Bridges

This life is filled with pain and disappointments, and we're all on healing journeys. What's yours been like? Can you identify points along the way where God has been gently healing your brokenness and transforming you into wholeness?

As long as we stay focused on our circumstances or on our pain, it only hurts more. I don't mean we should minimize it or stay in denial. Facing it honestly is necessary. But our focus can still remain on the Lord, even while we work through our pain. In his book, *Healing What You Can't Erase*, Christopher Cook explains there is strength in having a "fixed focus."[14] He accurately notes, "Times of shaking come to all of us. But there's great strength to be had when our focus is fixed, especially *in* the shaking." He then quotes his life verse:

"I have set the Lord always before me; because He is at my right hand, I shall not be shaken." (Psalm 16:8, ESV)

Chapter Eighteen
Unexpected Gifts

Have you ever gotten a gift from God which only He could give you? Stop and ponder this thought. It happens to all of us, but we don't always recognize it. He doesn't just love the people of Slovenia. He loves each of us deeply and He knows the desires of our hearts. And He loves to give us good, good gifts.

One year after our first mission trip, Savannah and I got to go back to Slovenia with the team from our church again, and it was just as amazing as the first trip. This time I got to teach adults, and that was a really fun experience. Those sweet people completely expanded my view of their country and helped me understand even more their culture and lifestyle. It was fascinating.

After our mission work was completed, Savannah and I stayed in Europe for a few extra days. On our first trip the year before, we had discovered how close we actually were to Italy. Savannah had begged me to find a way to go there, but it wasn't in the plan that year, so I told her if God ever let us come back, we'd find a way to see Italy.

When He actually did lead us to go again the following year, she reminded me of my promise. We discussed it with Kathy and the church, and started making a plan to stay a couple extra days after everyone else left. So at the end of our time there, our team all headed to the airport, and everyone flew back to America except us. She and I rented a car and took a road trip through Italy!

What a crazy, exciting trip it was. Hands down the scariest thing I've ever done, but so very worth it. Just the two of us, making our way to Venice, and then continuing on down to Rome, seeing the sights and stopping for lots of pictures along the way. We didn't have enough time to actually tour anything, but we didn't care. We were in Italy, and we were enjoying every single minute of it!

We rode in a gondola in Venice, and toured the beautiful city. Then the next day we drove down to Rome, and took a subway to the Colosseum. We tried to see Trevi Fountain, but it was closed for maintenance and was dry as a bone. Bad timing. We ate pizza and spaghetti and gelato, and held our purses closely, since everyone had warned us about pickpockets. But no one had warned me about driving in Italy. Bad enough I couldn't read the road signs which were all in Italian, but half of the roads didn't have signs anyway or even lines on them. Cars just criss-crossed all over those cobblestone streets, with mopeds and motorcycles dodging in and out of traffic. It's a miracle I didn't run over someone!

Savannah and me in Rome, Italy

The whole time I was relying completely on my GPS to tell me where to go, but sometimes the internet blanked out on me, and I couldn't get it to tell me anything. Sometimes it did give me directions, but how was I supposed to know which "right at the roundabout" when there were three or four right turns at the crazy roundabout? By the time we made it to our hotel, I threw myself on the bed and told Savan-

Unexpected Gifts

nah we'd just have to live in Italy forever because there was no way I was getting behind the wheel again!

I eventually got up my nerve, though, and we headed out of Italy and back to Slovenia to catch our flight home. It had been unnerving to drive a rental car in a foreign country, but suddenly I felt like I could conquer the world. If I could do THAT, I figured now I could do anything.

On our return flight, we had a three hour layover in Paris. Before the trip, I asked around to get opinions about whether we should try to go see the Eiffel Tower. Everyone I asked said I didn't have enough time. Until I asked one of our team members, Damaris Daugherty, who had traveled quite a bit. She didn't even hesitate to tell us to go for it. And she gave me clear instructions. When we landed, she said, be the first ones off the plane. Hop out of your seat, grab your things and move to the front. When you get off the plane, look for the baggage claim sign which will take you to the exit. As you walk out of the exit, you'll see taxis lined up. Jump in the closest one and tell them you need to get to the Eiffel Tower and back to the airport in three hours. Shouldn't be a problem.

I decided it was worth the risk. What's the worst thing that could happen? We miss the flight and have to stay in Paris? Well, okay! So we went for it, and it happened exactly like she described. We asked the taxi driver if he could wait for us to take some pictures, and he was happy to accommodate. We jumped back in the taxi, he raced (literally) back to the airport, and we even had time to spare. We have some hilarious photos of two crazy, excited people in front of the Eiffel Tower to prove it!

I had no idea the courage that extra little trip would require, but stepping out and doing a really scary thing changed something inside of me. We knew God was with us, every step of the way. It all went too smoothly and angels had to be guarding us. A million things could have gone wrong, but I had a strange, unexplainable peace and confidence.

Everywhere I Look

I knew in my heart this trip was a gift from God, and I had no doubt it would go well. Even when what we were doing did actually feel scary, it was a strange emotional mixture of fear and confidence. And it shifted something in me. It was a milestone in my healing journey.

Zach and Savannah

The following year I wasn't able to go, but Savannah did, making it her third trip. And it was on that particular trip when something sparked between her and Zach. About halfway through their trip, I was talking to her on the phone and she said, "I've been hanging out with Zach a lot on this trip!" And I could hear it in her voice. At the end of the trip, I went to the airport to pick her up, and the two of them walked out together. Yep, there was no mistaking it. Those two were falling for each other!

This was in 2017, and they dated for the next year and a half. In December of 2018, in downtown Greenville surrounded by sparkling romantic Christmas lights, Zach proposed and she said yes! They decided to have a short engagement, so they planned a March wedding. We jumped into action and put together a surprisingly gorgeous wedding in only three months.

Falls Park is a magnificent place in downtown Greenville with tall trees, paved paths, beautiful flower gardens, and a huge suspension bridge crossing a stunning waterfall in the center of the park. It's just down the street from where they got engaged, and beside the park is a charming wedding venue. We gathered there on March 16, 2019 for this wonderful event. They had their wedding photos taken in the park with all that beauty surrounding them, then we went over to the venue where Zach and Savannah's youth pastor performed the ceremony. It was a picture-perfect day, and after a night of food and dancing, they rode away in a white horse-drawn carriage to begin their new life together.

Unexpected Gifts

And Baby Makes Three!

For Christmas 2022, Savannah told me she wanted to get a picture of the two of us in front of my Christmas tree. So she and Zach came over, and he got his phone ready to take the photo. She and I fixed our hair, put our arms around each other, and looked at Zach. He held up the phone and told us to smile at the camera, then he said all the normal things, "Ok, look right here, smile, say cheese . . . " And then he said, "Savannah's pregnant!" It took a split second for those words to sink in, and my face went from a frozen photo smile to a big-eyed look of total shock! I didn't realize it, but he was actually making a video, not taking a picture. It's a pretty funny video to watch now. I literally lost my mind for a few seconds and screamed my head off. What a fun way to find out my baby girl was going to have her own baby.

On August 17, 2023, Savannah gave birth to a handsome baby boy. Greyson Michael Martin made his grand appearance, and instantly stole our hearts. He is the sweetest little good-natured baby. All smiles and cuteness. What a gift from God!

And I still love how it all started on a mission trip.

Savannah, Zach, and Greyson

Building Bridges

For most of my adult life I dreamed of going to Europe. I joked around about it, and secretly hoped somehow someday I'd get to go, even though it never looked like a realistic possibility.

But on these two trips, I was finally getting to see the beautiful continent. God actually gave me so many desires of my heart with those trips. I got to serve Him in Slovenia and be a part of a mission team—a childhood dream come true. And I got to see Italy and France—another dream come true. I remember the moment when this all dawned on me. I was actually praying, thanking God for everything He had allowed me to experience, and His Spirit brought this to my mind. It felt like He was saying, "You wanted to be part of mission work because of your love for me. And I wanted it to be in Europe because of my love for you. I just gave you the trip to Europe you've always wanted."

And even beyond that, unexpected gifts came from those trips too. The first trip paved the way for the next and the next, and through the last one, our family was blessed with a wonderful son-in-law and a beautiful baby.

Sometimes when we pause and make space for gratitude, we can see even more clearly His incredible love and His sweet gifts of grace. Some of them are gifts we could very literally never get anywhere else. Take some time to ponder this and ask Him to reveal the gifts He's given you which you may never have taken time to fully appreciate.

Gratitude definitely brings healing!

Chapter Nineteen
Beauty from Ashes

When we walk through fires, it sometimes feels like all we come out with are painful burns. But we serve a God who brings beauty from ashes. Throughout this journey, each of my kids have experienced their own personal pain and healing, and I've watched their faith grow and deepen in the process. Some of them went through deeper valleys than the others, but all of them have had to personalize their faith and make it their own.

My oldest daughter, Ashlyn, walked through an intense personal fire for several years. In her second year of college, she met a guy who was a ministry major and a youth pastor at a local church. That all seemed so wonderful . . . on the outside. But there were bright red flags everywhere. He swept her off her feet, but he wanted to keep her a secret—always a bad sign! She later found out this was because he already had a girlfriend. Well, they had technically broken up, but it wasn't completely over, and he was playing games with both girls. Right out of the gate, their relationship was filled with ups and downs and very serious problems. There were several break-ups because of his chronic cheating. But after each break-up he would "get right with God" and convince her he was a changed man.

At one point in December of 2012, she tried to break it off for good, but he started coming to our church after that. He went through counseling, and even started serving in the counseling ministry and in the youth group. Everyone in leadership adored him, and Ashlyn was hopeful he had truly changed. They got back together and in March of

2014, as he was teaching in the youth group, he called her up to the stage and proposed. Everyone was so excited for them, but I have to admit, those of us who had witnessed the entire relationship felt very apprehensive. They went through premarital counseling, and had to postpone the wedding twice because of his anger issues and continued infidelity (this time with his best friend's wife). But despite all of this, they kept getting back together and were married in April of 2015. For the next several years, she found herself navigating a terrible relationship filled with deception and habitual infidelity. As if that wasn't bad enough, he often abused alcohol, and was verbally, emotionally, and physically abusive. It was my worst nightmare to see her going through this—even worse than my own abusive marriage. I desperately wanted to help her.

But parenting an adult, I have found, is tricky business. There's an interesting progression that happens as our kids grow up. During their teen years, we have to begin giving them independence, incrementally, but we still frequently step in with clear direction and guidance. As soon as they are adults, the dynamic abruptly shifts, and we have to step back and wait to be invited into that space. My parents did this beautifully. I don't know if they even had conscious awareness of it, and I don't remember them telling me about these steps, but I remember when it happened. As soon as I got married, as a young and naive 21 year old, my parents stopped handing out advice, and I had to ask for it. I remember wondering why they went a little quiet with their thoughts, but anytime I opened the door and asked them about anything, they were still filled with wisdom and great advice. But the big difference is I had to ask for it. As my kids have become adults, it's been natural for me to follow that pattern. I know I haven't done it perfectly, and there's a learning curve, for sure, but I've seen a lot of people fail to step back at all. They just continue to offer non-stop advice to their adult kids, and I think the kids probably resent it.

So here I was, learning to be a single mom and learning how to

Beauty from Ashes

parent adults at the same time. I was trying not to insert too much unsolicited advice, but Ashlyn was clearly in a terrible situation. We went back to our church for help, as I had done in my own nightmare, but we didn't get the same response. For one, Ashlyn's husband did an amazing job of fooling everyone, and each time he seemed genuinely repentant. So she kept going back. After multiple affairs, the trust was completely destroyed. She couldn't bring herself to give him another chance, but the church insisted she should. In their minds, as long as he was repentant, her response should be to forgive and reconcile.

Forgiveness vs. Reconciliation

Let me pause here to say, there's a world of difference between those two words. Forgiveness is what we offer someone in order to set both of us free. We set them free from our judgment and condemnation, and we set ourselves free from grudge-holding bitterness. It's a wiping of the proverbial slate. But it is not always followed by reconciliation. That's a whole other animal requiring much more from both parties. For the offended party, it requires a vulnerability and willingness to possibly be hurt again. For the offender, it requires a process of rebuilding the trust which takes time and a whole lot of work and patience.

Relationships cannot be maintained without trust. And trust is a very difficult thing to rebuild. There is no clear cut timeline, for one thing. It may take one person a lot longer to trust than another depending on about a million variables in that person's own life and history. In addition to the timeline, the actual offense plays a big role in whether trust can be re-established, and how far the offender is willing to go to rebuild trust. For instance, in the case of habitual infidelity, including digital infidelity (pornography) words hold very little weight. You can tell me all day long you'll never look at porn again, but the minute I start seeing all the signs—unreasonable anger, emotional distance, disappearing for long periods of time, off-the-charts selfishness—the trust begins to erode.

Everywhere I Look

Let me just add here that pornography addiction and emotional affairs are just as horrible as physical affairs. They crush a person's spirit and are extremely destructive patterns of sin. Don't believe me? Read what God Himself, in the flesh, had to say about it in Matthew 5:28—"Anyone who looks at a woman with lust for her has already committed adultery with her in his heart" (NASB). That's not just my opinion—it's God's. Don't let the enemy deceive you into minimizing that sin. It's very sad to me when so many pastors and churches insist a woman stay in a marriage where the husband is constantly cheating on her with porn or emotional affairs, but legalistically conclude she doesn't have "real" Biblical justification for divorce. I wonder what Jesus would say about such Pharisaical thinking.

So trust is a very tricky thing, and for someone whose betrayal includes a physical affair, or in my daughter's case, multiple affairs, they literally may not be able to rebuild the trust. Especially if the person only appears repentant temporarily, but keeps returning to that sin.

Ashlyn kept trying to trust again, but he kept destroying her trust. She also had a heartbreaking series of events during this season which added more layers of pain. In November of 2017, she found out she was pregnant, and even though their relationship was terribly unstable, we all celebrated this new life, and hoped somehow their marriage could be healed, especially for the sake of this new baby. But a couple months into the pregnancy, she miscarried, and the loss was devastating. They were actually separated at the time, so she came back to my house from the hospital, and I helped her recover. We spent those days grieving the loss together, and crying out to God for healing.

A few months later, her doctor discovered a large cyst on one of her ovaries. It was causing her pain, and was so large it needed to be removed. During the surgery, the doctor had to actually remove the entire ovary, and Ashlyn woke up to face that news. Now her chances at pregnancy were jeopardized, and she had to grieve another loss and potentially more pain.

Beauty from Ashes

Not long after her recovery, she discovered he had had another affair. She had to play detective, yet again, to get to the bottom of it, and she ended up finding out about several other girls he had been with or was texting/sexting. He eventually confessed, again. But this time, there was no capacity left for her to trust. Even though our church wanted her to go back to him, she decided not to. It turned out to be the right decision.

After this, she was finally able to start her own healing process, and I was so proud of her resilience and courage. She took some time to heal, and eventually bought herself a house, and found another church to settle into. She had already been a caseworker for our county's department of social services, and she was spending her days taking care of children in abusive situations and bringing them into foster care. She went on to become a supervisor at DSS, and she continues to excel at her job to this day.

New Beginnings

A couple years later, when she least expected it, God brought someone into her life. Right before this, she and I were in a church service at a place I was visiting, and the pastor asked us to lay hands on the person beside us and pray for them. Ashlyn was sitting beside me, so I put my hands on her shoulders, and prayed for God to continue to bring healing to her heart and for Him to bring a good man into her life. I'll never forget what she said to me afterwards. She thanked me for praying for her, but wanted to be clear—finding a man was the last thing she wanted to do. She was doing just fine on her own, thank you very much, and she had no desire to find a guy. We both laughed together at her raw honesty, but I still hoped and prayed God would bring a good man into her life. As painful as marriage has been in our family, I still believe in it. And I hoped someday she would find love again.

After Ashlyn had settled into her new church home, she decided to sing on the worship team. Robert Queen had been playing drums on the church's worship team for several years, and she immediately caught his eye. Before long, he asked her out, and a few months later he came over to meet with me. He wanted me to know he was in love with my daughter and wanted to marry her, but even more importantly he wanted to share with me his own story of grace and redemption. With all the messy pain in our rear view mirror, I was surprised at my own ability to offer him my blessing and my trust. I think it was God's grace, because I was still pretty wounded from my own divorce, and I was definitely still jaded from hers. But I really liked this guy, and I hoped and prayed he would treat her with the love and respect she deserved.

Ashlyn & Robby's engagement

Did you hear about weddings that took place during the Covid-19 pandemic? Ashlyn and Robby's wedding was one of them. They got married on April 18, 2020, while the whole world was in lock down. This didn't stop them, though. We just all had to practice social distancing. We gathered outside and watched from a distance. And we all stayed six feet apart! We even have a funny picture of the beautiful couple with Ashlyn's siblings, all standing six feet apart with their hands playfully covering their mouths.

Robby has been such a wonderful addition to our family. He has a huge servant's heart, and his love and care for Ashlyn has been a sweet thing to watch. Even though she wasn't trying to find someone, someone found her! And their story is yet another picture of grace. After all the pain she went through, she is finally enjoying a healthy relationship. And two years after their wedding, on March 5, 2022, God blessed them with a beautiful baby girl. Mila Ellis has brought so much joy and laughter into all of our lives. It's been so fun to watch them parent her and pour into her. In a lot of ways, their story reminds me of my grandparents' story. Remember Charlie and Eva and all the pain they had experienced? And the way God brought them together and gave them that sweet baby girl, Beverly Jo? I watch Ashlyn and Robby now, and can't help but think of the circle of life, and the incredible way God picks up the pieces of our broken lives and creates something beautiful.

Beauty from ashes. Grace upon grace. Everywhere I look.

Ashlyn, Mila, and Robby

Building Bridges

Maybe you're reading this and you've been through a painful experience, and you're still only seeing ashes. Maybe you're wondering where the beauty is. It's a valid point, and it's true we don't always get a "happily ever after" like Ashlyn did. Sometimes we have to wait until "someday" to understand it all and get a glimpse of beauty. It's okay to grieve that and make space for lament. There's a whole book of the Bible which is literally named Lamentations so I think God's okay with it. 'Lamentation' simply means an expression of deep sorrow. To lament is to acknowledge grief and pain, in God's presence. And that last part is what makes it a healthy practice. If we grieve apart from God we risk sinking into depression and despair. Apart from God we can easily become hopeless and sabotage our own healing.

But to grieve in God's presence is to take all of our pain and very intentionally process it with Him. It's important to realize He also grieves over the painful circumstances of our lives. This world is a broken place, and things are not as they should be. God knows our pain whether we take it to Him or not. I've been in the ashes with no beauty in sight, and I understand that pain. It's not a fun place to be. But I'm so glad I wasn't alone in those ashes. God was "sitting shiva" with me, and thankfully, one of His beautiful names is "Comforter."

So it's okay to process our pain with God. Lamenting brings healing.

Chapter Twenty
The Birth of a Ministry

"Hey Preacher Rice! Let me introduce you to my parents! Mom, Dad, this is Pastor Rice!"

Wearing a bright orange jumpsuit, the inmate standing by our table was beaming from ear to ear. His voice was filled with joy and excitement as he told his parents how Preacher Rice's church had helped him come to know God.

Mom and I were at Lieber Correctional Institution visiting Rusty, watching this surreal scene unfold. The visitation room was filled with square tables and uncomfortable chairs where families and loved ones were visiting, laughing, and trying to talk over each other. One wall was lined with vending machines, so almost everyone was snacking on chips and candy. Some were playing board games or cards, just enjoying a little piece of normalcy. When you're with the ones you love, you can sometimes momentarily forget you are inside a maze of concrete walls, surrounded by fences topped with layers and layers of coiled razor wire.

I sat there watching in complete amazement as Rusty stood up and shook hands with his friend's parents. Just hearing this guy refer to Rusty as his pastor was incredibly surreal to me. After a few short months of being at this place, Rusty had started holding Bible studies and teaching classes. What he would later call "the most fruitful ministry of his life" had been born. Men all over this maximum-security prison were hearing stories about what was going on, and were asking for transfers into the dorm where this church was meeting.

Everywhere I Look

The ministry grew and grew, and for years, every time we came to visit, Rusty would tell us incredible stories of salvation and deliverance. People were giving their hearts to the Lord left and right. He was offering the gift of eternal life to people who had given up on life. If you think about it, the "soil" here was about as fertile as you could get. Men in this prison were here for life. They generally did not have much hope of ever getting out, so that fact alone drove many of them into deep depression and suicidal ideation. Presenting a different narrative to them of joy beyond this life, and also joy in this present life, was like giving water to people in a desert who were dying of thirst. They soaked it all in and sprang back to life!

During these years, friends and family members contributed Bibles and songbooks to Rusty's ministry, and many donated money. With the money which came in he would buy food from the canteen and serve meals to the other inmates. The food in there is terrible, so inmates jumped at the opportunity to eat delicious food, and Rusty built friendships and relationships with them through this outreach. He would then invite them to church, and many of them gave their lives to the Lord.

The church in the prison was similar in many ways to churches we've all attended on the outside. Once a person was saved and started studying the Bible, they wanted to be baptized. So Rusty asked the correctional officers for a trash can large enough to be used as a make-shift baptismal. He filled it with water and held baptisms for his new converts. The newly saved men also wanted to give generously to others, so they regularly "tithed" their food and possessions (no one has actual money in there), and Rusty filled a pantry with food and basic necessities to donate to inmates who didn't have family to provide for them.

As the ministry grew, Rusty needed helpers, so he prayed and asked the Lord to help him choose men to serve as "deacons" in his church. Some led the singing, some managed the pantry, some served food, and some helped in the church services. Eventually, some of them felt led by the Spirit to request a transfer to a different dorm so they could start

The Birth of a Ministry

new churches and Bible studies. Rusty's church called these guys their "missionaries." One inmate felt called to the mission field of Death Row. This prison housed the only death row in South Carolina, and this man asked for his work assignment to be serving food to those on death row. He got the job, and spent years giving them food and telling them about Jesus!

At some point, my mom asked Rusty to write a letter to the friends and family who were contributing to his ministry, and he did it. She took his letter, typed it up, and mailed it out to everyone. They started doing this every few months and continued for several years. When she couldn't keep up with it anymore, my sister and I took it over for her. The mailing list grew, and we sent out letters a few times a year. Christmas was always a big occasion for donations, and Rusty was able to stock his food pantry and hold Christmas parties for the inmates.

For a while, Rusty was also sending us written testimonies from some of his church members. These stories were absolutely mind-blowing. Many of these guys were just normal, everyday people whose lives took a crazy turn somewhere along the way and spun completely out of control. One of them described having a wonderful little family, with a wife and two little kids. Then one day their house burned down, and they were left with nothing but the clothes on their backs. Shortly after that, on the way home from a beach trip, they were in a terrible car accident and his little boy was killed. The layers of grief and stress from all of this drove him to abuse pain medication, and he became so lost in his addiction he ended up taking another man's life. Now here he was, spending the rest of his life in prison. That's how easily a life can turn upside down.

But some of the inmates had extensive criminal backgrounds that were equally mind-blowing. One guy had actually been a murderer who cannibalized his victims! He was so dangerous the prison kept him in solitary confinement for years. Occasionally they tried to assimilate him into the mainstream prison population, but each time he posed a threat and had to be returned to solitary confinement. Apparently you are only offered that opportunity a limited number of times, and on his last possible attempt at re-entry, he was placed in Rusty's dorm. Rumors had spread about him, and most of the guys were fearful of being anywhere near him. But Rusty invited him to church, and the man gave his life to Jesus! His miraculous transformation was instantaneous, and he became a faithful member of Rusty's church, singing in the choir and serving others with joy. Rusty said he reminded him of the man in Luke chapter 8, who had been demon-possessed and mentally disturbed. After Jesus healed him, he was "sitting at the feet of Jesus, clothed and in his right mind." (Luke 8:35, ESV)

Prison ministry is an interesting thing. Rusty himself had ministered in prisons when he had been a pastor, going in for a couple hours and holding a service or teaching a devotional. But all of those experiences didn't compare to his prison ministry at Lieber. I remember him telling me about some guys who had come in to preach at his prison like he had done so many times back when he was a pastor. They came in there with an air of superiority, and seemed to pity these men rather than view them as equals in God's eyes. After they left and went back to their comfortable lives, the inmates were still sitting in prison. Those men weren't able to truly relate to what these guys were going through, and they weren't able to actually minister to them. But Rusty could. He was one of them and he truly understood them. He knew their struggles, their desperation, their fears, and their deep levels of regret. He didn't get to leave and go home like those other men. He was in the trenches with these guys 24/7. And this gave him credibility which went a long way in earning their trust. He was able to minister to them like no outsiders ever could. It was a unique position, and an incredible opportunity. Seeing all of these people healed and set free was actually part of Rusty's own healing.

The Birth of a Ministry

Rusty with his girls and grandkids

After feeling so defeated and thinking God could never use him again, he was able to look back over all of his failures and see the hand of God in his life. He had turned his back on God (so many times) and had made such a mess of things, but here he was . . . forgiven and restored! In so many ways and on so many levels, healed.

Building Bridges

Have you ever felt like you've disappointed God or gone beyond the hope of return? I assure you, it's not too late. God loves to redeem and restore. He is a faithful Father who longs to see us turn to Him, our only Source of true joy. Even when we make a mess of things, He can turn those circumstances and use them for our good and for His glory.

Some of our most fruitful ministries are birthed through our own personal struggles and mistakes. One of the greatest benefits of going through difficult seasons is the compassion created in our hearts which wouldn't have existed otherwise. Because Rusty had experienced the same pain as his fellow inmates, he was able to relate to them and minister to them in ways you and I never could, no matter how hard we try.

Everywhere I Look

And in the same way, after we have gone through difficult seasons, we can relate to hurting people in new ways. We move beyond "sympathy" into the realm of "empathy." When you sympathize with someone, you acknowledge their pain. But when you empathize, you feel their pain. There is a world of difference.

God never wastes our pain! If we surrender our disappointments and failures to Him, He will teach us to use them to help others. And seeing them helped through our experiences will actually bring healing to our own broken hearts.

They say "hurt people, hurt people." That's often true. But you know what's also true?

Healed people, heal people. Restored people, restore people.

And people who have received grace, show grace!

Chapter Twenty-One
Tsunami of 2016

I've read that when a marriage ends, people typically need one year of healing for every five years they were married.[16] I don't know if there's actual scientific data to back it up, but it does seem reasonable to me, given all the complexities involved with the ending of long-term relationships. What I do know is even after two years of healing, my heart was nowhere near being ready for a new relationship, but a new relationship hit me like a tsunami, and I'm still trying to understand what happened.

Do you remember when I mentioned a middle school boyfriend who came back into my life after 35 years? This was the summer of 2016, during the same time I was losing my brother. I've had counselors since then point out that my level of vulnerability was heightened because of those circumstances, but at the time I didn't realize it. I did feel like I was sleep-walking through life. It's hard to describe now, but my mind was so distracted by the pain of losing Charley, I honestly felt like I was in a daze.

I had already lost my dad, and I had essentially lost Rusty too. I had lost my marriage and my husband as well, so losing Charley meant there were no men in my life. Remember my security in my childhood included two very good men—my dad and my grandpa. And in adulthood, I still had those two amazing men, plus my two big brothers and my husband. Lots of men I depended on for security and strength. One by one, I lost them all, and when Charley died, my support system was completely gone. I did not have any conscious awareness of how great the loss was, but in retrospect I can see I was grieving more than the loss of my brother. I was grieving the loss of this entire male support system, and the gaping hole in my life left me very vulnerable.

So when my middle school boyfriend showed up in my life, I know now I was subconsciously longing for someone to fill that void. It was also a pleasant distraction from the pain, and with this new relationship, all my reasoning skills literally went out the window. He sent me a friend request on Facebook, and we started messaging each other, just catching up on life. After a few weeks, we decided to meet up in person, and that's when I completely lost my mind. Being with him took me back to my childhood. We reminisced about the school we grew up in, our old friends and former teachers. We had so many shared experiences of a much happier time. He and I had first met when he was in second grade and I was in third, and our earliest memories of each other were of racing on the playground. He was one of the fastest boys and I was one of the fastest girls, so we both vividly remember those competitions. And as I mentioned earlier, my mom had been his fourth grade teacher, and he had memories of me coming into their classroom each day to get my lunch money. It was a small school, so we literally grew up together.

And when we were in middle school he had asked me to "go with him." Anybody remember calling it that? We were "a couple" for only a few months, but it was long enough to go on my first "date" at the Asheville Mall I mentioned earlier. It was a sweet, innocent relationship, back in carefree days, long before life hit either one of us. Now that we'd both been hit pretty hard by life, reminiscing about those simpler days stirred up a whirlwind of emotions.

After only three months, we decided to get married. Why wait when you're almost fifty and ready to get on with life? I've known plenty of healthy marriages that started with very short dating periods, so it didn't really scare me. Especially since I felt like I already knew him. I was also depending on one very strong aspect of our relationship—we both loved Jesus. He leaned a little more toward charismatic theology and worship than I was used to, but that didn't bother me. If anything, it intrigued me. I had never really been around anyone who spoke in tongues or believed in miraculous manifestations of the Spirit, but I was open to learning about it. So I felt like we had a good foundation and anything else could be dealt with through our solid connection in Christ. My kids were apprehensive, but supportive. My friends were even more apprehensive, but happy for me. I was happy for myself! It was about time I had a happily ever after. It wasn't until we were back from our honeymoon that things started hitting the fan. I've learned that things shift after the vows are made. Sometimes dramatically. It's happened twice in my life. Suddenly, there's a new level of comfort, and the real side of people emerges once they feel safe enough to expose it.

Sadly, a lot of very unhealthy issues were exposed—toxic behaviors and habits which can easily crush the life out of a marriage. Another thing I've learned through all of this is that when we normalize destructive behavior for years and years, our brains become so accustomed to it that we lose the ability to recognize red flags. We kind of go color blind, where we might see "flags," but they aren't bright red. Everything looks gray and the red doesn't stand out like it should. Looking back now, I'm amazed at how many warning signs I didn't recognize when I should have. I had already lived through similar circumstances and the red flags should have jumped out and scared me enough to make me run like my hair was on fire. But that didn't happen. If anything, my familiarity with some of what I saw lulled me into complacency, and I figured I was fully equipped to handle it.

This is another common mistake people make. I wish I had known all of this earlier, but my work with cognitive development in the last few years has given me insight into all of this. When our brains normalize unhealthy patterns of behavior, strong neural pathways are formed, and we can sometimes be drawn to the very same kinds of situations which have hurt us in the past. The familiarity is actually what's attractive. This is due to the fact that the brain also searches for the familiar because it lowers our anxiety and helps us feel more in control. The unfamiliar is scary, but the familiar helps our brains relax. Now that I have this understanding I can see why I wasn't afraid of what should have terrified me. It was all very familiar.

Very soon after the wedding, I woke up and realized how serious the situation was. The spell was broken, and the harsh reality jolted me out of my lovesick stupor. We were married in October, and by Christmas, I knew we were in deep trouble. Because of our earlier connection in life, I had felt safe and assumed I knew him and could trust him. But unfortunately, 35 years can do a number on a person. People can change a whole lot over that many years. And I realized pretty quickly he wasn't who I thought he was.

Getting another divorce, however, was out of the question in my mind. I had fought for 25 years to avoid the first divorce, and even though another difficult marriage was the last thing I wanted, here I was. And I was ready to fight for its survival. Again.

My "Wives" Group

In an attempt to get help, I looked up groups on Facebook to find other women who could relate to my situation. In one particular group, a girl named April responded to some of my questions, and I could tell she was a "Believer." After a little while, she contacted me personally and we talked on the phone for over an hour. We couldn't believe how similar our husbands were, and we were both trying to figure out how to heal the brokenness in our marriages.

April introduced me to Marco Polo, a video messaging app where you leave video voicemails with your friends to keep in touch. She and I started Marco Polo'ing almost every day, getting to know each other and giving each other feedback on the situations that arose in our marriages.

Tsunami of 2016

Before long, she wanted to introduce me to another girl she had met through the Facebook group. This girl was named Charity, too, which kind of blew my mind. I've only known a handful of Charity's in my life, so it was fun to have a friend with this name. To differentiate us, she referred to me as Charity Margaret and the other friend as Charity Rose. A little while later, April brought Jenny into our Marco Polo chat. She was also in a similar marriage, so the four of us instantly became friends. The crazy part was April was in Arkansas, Charity Rose was in Georgia, I was in South Carolina, and Jenny was in California. Our friendship started growing fast, and we video messaged all the time, but we had never actually met in person. Now there's an unusual friendship!

After video chatting for about a year, we decided we wanted to actually meet each other in person. So we made plans for a trip to Gatlinburg, Tennessee in the beautiful Smoky Mountains. I can't even accurately describe how fun it was to see each other in person for the first time, after we'd been communicating for a year on a video screen. It almost felt like meeting a celebrity. We screamed and hugged when we first saw each other, and instantly felt like old friends. In fact, when people saw us having so much fun together they would ask if we had been college roommates, and we loved telling people we had actually just met. The looks on their faces were hilarious!

The best story we have of this was when we were having lunch one day at the Apple Barn. We met a couple as we were all waiting to be seated and enjoyed telling them we had all just met. Later when we were inside, they were seated near us and saw how much fun we were having together. When they left, they came over and said goodbye to us, and we found out later that they had paid for our meal! Their kindness overwhelmed us, and we knew it was a sweet gift from God so we thanked Him for that. But we wished we could've thanked them too. That night we were back in Gatlinburg, walking through downtown, and were completely surprised to bump into the same couple. We got the chance to thank them, and we told them we had specifically talked about how we wished we could, and how kind it was of God to give us the opportunity. They love Jesus too, and said He had told them to buy our meal. We were all amazed at how He orchestrated our little encounters and how encouraging it had all been.

It was such a fun trip. The whole entire thing! A little oasis of joy in the middle of my very dark circumstances.

Charity Margaret, Charity Rose, Jenny, and April.

Our "wives" group continues to keep in touch, and April has made several trips to my neck of the woods for conferences and for a writing retreat we did together. She and I are both working on a book now, and actually Jenny is too! So we're having the privilege of seeing God use our painful circumstances for good. When you can pass on the comfort to others which God has given to you (See the first chapter of second Corinthians) it brings a whole new level of purpose to your pain.

An All-Time Low

Even though God was meeting me in my pain, and bringing encouragement from unexpected places, that second marriage continued to be a disaster. We saw counselors, therapists, and pastors. Nothing changed. I watched a million YouTube videos and listened to a million podcasts, trying to understand what I was dealing with. Even with all

Tsunami of 2016

my previous experience with mental health struggles, and my educational experience with processing disorders, nothing could've prepared me for this level of relational dysfunction. The last time I insisted on getting counseling, he thought it over for a couple days, then calmly told me he felt like it was time for us to go our separate ways.

We were married for six years. And I gave it my best shot. If I'm honest I have to admit that was mainly because of my pride. I literally could not stand the idea of being divorced twice. How could this possibly be happening to me? I had spent my entire adult life standing firmly against divorce, unwilling to let that be my story, and here I was facing another one!

The prospect of this sent me spiraling into depths I had never experienced, even during the first divorce. New levels of pain. Intense feelings of despair. And a strong determination to never trust again. That last one was probably the most damaging. All I wanted to do was crawl in a hole somewhere and shut out the whole world. I wanted to close off all my emotions and never, ever feel again so I could never, ever get hurt again. It was a defense mechanism I couldn't consciously control. I knew it couldn't possibly be healthy, but I had no idea what to do about it.

But thankfully, God did.

Building Bridges

Have you ever found yourself in a story you did not want? Have you ever felt like you hit rock bottom? Some people call it a broken spirit or the dark night of the soul. Whatever you want to call it, it's a miserable place to be. I knew God was there with me, but I had no idea how to get out of that pit.

Everywhere I Look

The next few chapters will tell you how God brought me out and what He accomplished in my heart during the process, but if you are there right now, I want you to know you aren't alone. We are never alone. There is Hope in the darkness and His Name is Jesus. Let Him pick you up and carry you out of that awful place. It may take a while and He may ask you to do a few things along the way you don't understand or don't want to do. Resolve to give Him your "yes" and then watch Him turn things around.

All of the pain and pressure, even what feels like a crushing, is producing something beautiful and valuable that can only come through an intentional process orchestrated by a sovereign God. He knows what He's doing, and He can be trusted.

> *"The roots can only grow in stony, difficult ground.*
> *The pruner's shears cut deep. The grapes are crushed*
> *and kept in the dark for decades. For the*
> *sake of the sweetness. For this very moment."*
> *-Theo of Golden* [16]

Chapter Twenty-Two
Sawubona

Are you familiar with "small groups?" In most of the churches I've been a part of, people are encouraged to join a small group for encouragement and accountability. They are usually made up of 10-15 people who meet in homes regularly to study the Bible and pray together. It's a great idea, and for most of my adult life I loved being in these.

But when I found myself trying to navigate a second dysfunctional marriage, hanging out with several married couples was incredibly painful. My friends, Regina and Dan Cranston, invited me to theirs and I went for about six months. The people were all so sweet, and I loved being in the Cranstons' home again, but inevitably I would crash emotionally on my drive home. What was meant to be an encouragement was making me spiral into discouragement, no matter how hard I tried to fight it.

One day, as I was having coffee with a friend, God gave me a wonderful, unexpected gift. Remember Kathy Sibley from my Slovenia trips? Her name is Kathy Young now, because God brought a wonderful husband to her, and we've maintained a sweet friendship ever since our Slovenia trips. As we were having coffee that day, I was verbally processing my experience with the small group. She listened attentively then told me she wanted to extend an invitation to me. In fact, that very morning Jesus had specifically instructed her to invite someone to the book club she'd been attending, but she wasn't sure who He meant for her to invite. And now, as I was sharing all of this with her, she knew He meant that invitation for me.

Everywhere I Look

I asked her to explain, and she said the book club was a group of women who loved God, and enjoyed reading and discussing books. They met once a month, and the conversations were always encouraging and spiritually motivating. She said the women in the group are married, but the conversations aren't about marriage. They are centered around God and spiritual growth, and she felt like it might be just what I needed.

So I decided to give it a try. This was in the fall of 2020, and the book club had already been meeting all year, reading books about trust (ironically). I got in on the tail end of the study, and each January they switched the topic, so after Christmas we started reading and discussing friendship. The leader of the book club, Traci Newkirk, had been an acquaintance of mine from our homeschooling days, and I already knew several of the women in the group from years ago when we went to church together. The next year, all of 2021, as we focused on friendship, Traci asked us to commit to one-on-one activities throughout the year to actually build friendships. Each month we drew someone's name and we had to meet outside of the book club to get to know each other. This went a long way in helping us all get to know each other, and I had no idea at the time how much I would need these connections.

That fall, my marriage was completely imploding. We had lived in separate parts of the house for two years, and by June of 2021, I had reached the end of my rope. This is when I had asked for another round of counseling, but he had told me he was unwilling and we needed to go our separate ways. Shortly after that he got a lawyer, drew up an Order of Separate Maintenance, and in November he moved out.

Emotional Healing

Two months later, our book club began a new study. In fact, the entire group was restructured into a process/growth group rather than a book club. Traci, our leader, was working on her Master's degree in counseling, so we all became part of her educational journey. She

Sawubona

shared with us what she was learning, and our meetings morphed into group counseling sessions. It couldn't have been better timing for my own healing journey. We named our group "Sawubona," which is a South African greeting that means "I see you." The word conveys the worth and dignity of each person by communicating the individual is seen in their entirety—their experiences, their passions, their pain, their strengths and their weaknesses.[17]

In January, we started our new focus for the year: processing emotions. We worked on identifying and naming our emotions, and processing them in healthy ways. We read books like *Emotionally Healthy Spirituality* by Peter Scazzero (highly recommend), and *People Fuel* by John Townsend (I also highly recommend). Using the book *People Fuel*, Traci taught us about the relational nutrients humans need to be emotionally healthy. The book categorizes these nutrients into four quadrants, referred to as Q1, Q2, Q3, and Q4.[18]

Quadrant 1 is called "Be Present." This means when someone is sharing information with you, especially personal experiences, being present involves attunement and containment. Basically just being there. Sitting with them in their situation. Quadrant 2 is called "Convey the Good" and it involves giving positive feedback and encouragement. Quadrant 3 is "Providing Reality." It takes the feedback a step further, bringing clarification and insight, and possibly a new perspective. Quadrant 4 is "Call to Action." This is where advice is given, and recommendations are put forth.

Most people seriously lack a lot of these relational skills. As you can see, the quadrants progress from simply a position of listening and attuning, to gradually engaging in gentle confrontation. How many of us are even aware of these steps? I feel like most of us hear someone explain their frustration or pain, and we jump too quickly to Quadrant 4 and start spouting off advice. In our process group, we all realized how easy it is to do this. Traci asked us to practice "staying in Q1 and Q2" with each other, meaning, don't rush to give advice. And whew!

Everywhere I Look

That was easier said than done. We all caught ourselves starting out in Q1 and inadvertently jumping to Q4. We might start off with, "Wow, I'm so sorry. That sounds so painful." And then stumble right into, "But don't worry . . . " or "Maybe you could . . . " We found out it takes intentional thought to simply listen and identify with someone's pain, and stop right there. We all want to fix it and make it go away. Their pain makes us uncomfortable, and we squirm under the pressure.

In order to learn these new skills, with each meeting that year, we spent time going around the room sharing our emotions and learning how to respond to each other. One of our activities involved taking turns naming one emotion we had felt recently, and giving a two to three sentence explanation of why we felt it. Then one person (usually the one who was struggling most intensely) would do a "deep dive" and we all practiced responding with Q1 and Q2 relational nutrients. We called it "going in the well" and then having the others sit with us in the well. Let me explain by telling you about my own deep dive into the well.

We started our meeting as usual, with each of us looking at the sheet of paper listing a million emotions, and trying to identify which one we were currently feeling. I was in the middle of the year-long separation, moving toward my second miserable divorce. I'm not one who usually deals with a lot of anger, but I had to admit anger was my dominant emotion that evening. As I gave my two sentence explanation, I felt tears starting to well up, and I hated how intensely emotional I became. When it was time for us to choose one person to "go into the well," it obviously needed to be me. So Traci set the timer for 15 minutes, and I started verbally processing my anger, trying to identify where it was coming from and why I was feeling it. I was surprised at how incredibly angry I was. I was mad at myself most of all, for getting myself into another bad marriage. I was mad about the whole stupid, annoying marriage itself, and what a huge disappointment it had been. I was mad at both of my former husbands who had hurt me so deeply, and I was

Sawubona

mad I no longer had any desire to ever be married again. And while I was at it, I was mad about a few other things too. I was mad about how my mom was struggling with dementia. I hated seeing her like this! I was mad that my brothers couldn't help me with her. And I was mad that my sister lived so far away, and the heaviest weight of this was falling on me, and I was mad that I didn't have a husband to help me carry it.

All of this anger came spewing out of me, and I was shocked at how much there was. After my 15 minute emotional puke session ended, Traci asked the other ladies to sit with me in the well, and she cautioned them to "stay in Q1 and Q2." They started speaking to me, responding carefully to my words. They gave one or two sentences which addressed my pain and anger by speaking life and truth into each of my complaints. For instance, I had said something like, "I'm so mad at myself for being so stupid and getting myself into this. I thought I was a decently intelligent person, but how could I be so dumb?" And one of the ladies responded to that statement by telling me she had always considered me one of the most intelligent people she knew. I never knew that, and her affirmation was powerful! For each statement I had made, these ladies put their words on top of my emotions like an overlay of grace which changed the entire appearance of each situation. Their words were very literally like a healing balm to my wounds, and it all clearly demonstrated Proverbs 18:21(ESV)—"Death and life are in the power of the tongue."

I sat there with tears streaming down my face, letting their words wash over me. That night when I got home, I wrote down everything they had said—I listed my points of pain and their beautiful words of love while I could still clearly remember them all. I still have that list.

Everywhere I Look

Sawubona Girls

Sitting with Jesus

The next morning, I got up and had my "coffee time with Jesus." I literally sat on my couch and took all of those same complaints to Him. I figured if what those ladies said had been such a great healing experience, then I should see what He had to say too. So I got out my list, and asked Him about each of those points. He knew my anger better than I did myself, and He understood the situations better than I ever could, so I asked for His take on them. As I prayed and poured out my heart, I listened for His Spirit's response to each of them and wrote it all down. I'll share a few things He clarified to me.

My second marriage, as crazy as it was, served several purposes in my life, and taught me a whole lot of things. It brought new insight and wisdom, and even new friendships and experiences. But it definitely was unhealthy and God was just as sad as I was that it didn't survive. It frustrates Him too when people refuse to grow and their hearts remain stubborn. But He loves that guy, and will continue to pursue him. It's out of my hands and is no longer my responsibility. There is freedom and release in that. And I can be grateful for the freedom without being angry about it.

And as for my mom, well, Jesus had such a beautiful perspective

Sawubona

He gave me that day. He reminded me that this is Beverly Jo, the sweet baby who was miraculously gifted to Charlie and Eva. Here she was now, years and years later, but still their baby girl. How would they view the opportunity to care for her in this fragile state? How would they want me to view it? Jesus also reminded me about how my mom was the love of my daddy's life. He would've been so honored and happy to care for her, but he didn't get the chance. I, however, do have the chance. No need to be mad because my brothers aren't here to help. They also aren't getting this opportunity. And I need to be grateful I have my sister, and that she is willing and able to step in at any time to help me. What I actually have here is a golden opportunity to love and serve my sweet mother, who has loved and served me and many others her whole entire life. What a gift! What in the world is there to be angry about?

Getting God's perspective on each of these situations completely changed mine.

Joy and sorrow, held simultaneously. What truly is painful and hard in the natural realm, can be seen through a different lens in the spirit, and joy can actually be experienced right smack in the middle of the pain. The healing is tangible and beautiful, like a kaleidoscope of emotions which all form an intricate design of grace.

I'm here to tell you it's true, and it is real. And I'm living proof.

Building Bridges

Do you have any situations you need to take to God right now and get His perspective? If we stay in our own heads we actually play right into the hands of the enemy. God has the best perspective of every situation we go through, and taking the time to get His input will radically

Everywhere I Look

alter how you see it.

    I'm going to remind you, at this point, of something I mentioned at the beginning of this book. When you look at a stereogram, those weird pictures with hidden 3D images, your vision shifts strangely and a new perspective comes into view. If you blink or look away, it disappears. You have to stare intently at the image for your brain to internalize it. This is what was happening on my couch that morning as I sipped my coffee and asked Jesus for His perspective. He shifted my view, and new images came into focus. The more I have stared intently at those new images, the clearer they've become, and I'm internalizing the truth of them a little more each day.

    Father, please help us come out of agreement with any lies of the enemy, which are strategically designed to cause us more pain. Help us come into alignment and agreement with the truth of what You reveal to us. Shift our views from our circumstances to the bigger picture You are creating and to the transforming power of Your Spirit at work in our lives.

Chapter Twenty-Three
When Cancer Brings Healing

It was such a beautiful day for a wedding. I received wise advice from my boss, Suzanne Ringger, about my role as mother of the groom. She told me I just needed to do three things: show up, shut up, and wear beige! I still laugh when I think of those words. I was actually wearing a pale pink dress, but overall, I was enjoying the day and relieved to not have as much responsibility as I'd had when I was the mother of the bride. I'd already had that honor with Ashlyn and Savannah, so this was the third wedding so far. As fun as that role had been, this one was a lot less stressful!

Josh and Hunter's wedding

Josh was twenty years old and in college when he met his future wife, Hunter Wengrow. Although she was a year younger, Hunter had already graduated from college and was working a full-time job and getting ready to buy her first house when they met.

When she came into the family, I was at an all time low. It was 2017, one year into my second marriage, and I was trying hard to navigate the mess of toxicity. Josh and Hunter wanted nothing to do with my current husband, and as much as I understood, it was still a painful situation. So this beautiful wedding day was a little bittersweet for me.

My husband had not been invited to the wedding, understandably, so I was there without him. Josh's father, my former husband, was also there, and we were sharing the typical parental wedding responsibilities. By now, we had both settled into this new normal and had a really pleasant, cordial relationship with each other. Forgiveness had happened a long time ago, and we were getting good at being around each other in social settings. But it was a weird feeling for me to be at our son's wedding, yet married to someone else and experiencing all kinds of dysfunction in a new marriage. Not at all the circumstances I had hoped for and dreamed of for Josh's wedding day.

Nevertheless, I was so happy for Josh, and so were his sisters. Hunter was a beautiful bride, and they made a stunning couple. The wedding was gorgeous, but I have to admit, as happy as his sisters and I were for him, we were also very aware of how everything was changing and, in a way, we were losing him. For several years, Josh had been the man of our family. It wasn't fair to him, and he was way too young for the heavy responsibility, but he was just that kind of guy. He rose to the occasion, and stepped into the role even though none of us would've chosen it for him.

In a strange way, he was walking a similar path to the one my dad had walked. Living with his mom and three sisters, Josh grew up quickly like my dad had, and he became protective of us all, just like my dad had been with his family. And now, things were shifting and we could all feel it.

The month before this wedding, Savannah had had her own beautiful wedding. We had two weddings six weeks apart, and just thinking back on that time makes me a little exhausted. It was so much fun, but boy, it was a busy time. Somewhere in the mix of engagements and

When Cancer Brings Healing

wedding plans, my kids all had a series of disagreements and misunderstandings which left everyone in a weird place emotionally. And since we were already in a heightened state of emotion due to the simple fact that our family dynamics were shifting, those misunderstandings were intensified. No one was upset enough to put up walls or shut each other out completely. We all loved each other too much to let that happen. But still, there was a little tension hanging in the air.

After the wedding, Hunter and I had dinner a couple times, and we both tried to dispel the cloud of confusion and misunderstanding. But neither of us knew how to make it all completely go away. I was still in a terrible marriage, and she and I couldn't see eye to eye on that situation. She knew how toxic it was and I'm sure it made no sense to her for me to remain in the relationship. It made no sense to me either, actually, but I felt paralyzed by the prospect of a second divorce, and I was still praying for a miracle. Josh and Hunter had drawn a line for their own protection and were not willing to have any kind of relationship with him, and they had also made it clear that if they had children, the kids would not be allowed to be around him.

So when they announced her pregnancy in the spring of 2020, my mind was immediately bouncing back and forth between elation and apprehension. I was going to be a grandma for the first time! We were going to have a BABY in the family. The thought of this made me want to scream and shout and dance. But then I would remember this baby wouldn't be allowed in my home, and if I stayed in this marriage we would have continual chaos surrounding that situation.

Joy and sorrow. One in each hand. And I was learning once again how to hold both simultaneously.

Another Terrifying Diagnosis

While Hunter was pregnant, her mother was fighting colon cancer. Her mom was only in her forties, and her mom's father had also had colon cancer, so Hunter and her sisters all had genetic testing which confirmed a hereditary condition known as Lynch Syndrome. This meant they were all at risk of developing colon cancer. At her doctor's suggestion, she decided to get a baseline colonoscopy after the baby arrived.

On November 14, 2020, Josh and Hunter welcomed Adelaide Raine into the world. She was born during the Covid-19 pandemic, so unfortunately, no one was allowed to be at the hospital with them. They sent out lots of pictures, though, of a beautiful, healthy baby girl with a head full of dark hair. Becoming a mom had been a dream come true for me, but becoming a grandma was absolutely next level. I fell madly, head over heels in love with that baby girl!

Six weeks after Addie's birth, Hunter went for her scheduled colonoscopy. Kristen and I stayed at their house to watch the baby while she was gone. Hunter's mom drove her to and from the appointment, and when the two of them got back and walked into the living room, we teased her at first about how hungry she must be from fasting. But she had a strange look on her face, and I thought she looked like she might cry. Hunter's mom looked at us and quietly said, "They found something."

My heart dropped. I handed the baby to Kristen and ran over to them. *What? What did she just say?!* Her mom repeated herself then added that it looked like a fist-sized tumor, and they wanted to operate immediately. Now the room started spinning, and I did the only thing I knew to do. I put my arms around Hunter and said, "We are not going to hesitate to take this straight to Jesus." And I started praying over her, begging God to take this away, to remove every bit of this, to calm our anxious hearts, and to bring complete and total healing in Jesus' Name.

We found out shortly after this that the tumor was in fact cancerous, and Hunter's doctors wanted to remove her entire colon. They saw potential for recurrence and felt like removing only a section of it would still leave her in danger. So at the young age of 22, she underwent a total colectomy. With a six week old baby, she had to face life and death decisions, and I'm still in awe of the way she handled it with such calm

When Cancer Brings Healing

and maturity. Hunter is a deeply spiritual girl, and her faith in God was in full view during this entire traumatic experience. She and Josh both amazed us all with the way they handled this terrifying situation.

During the weeks which followed, Josh and Hunter needed a lot of help. As strong and independent as they both are, this wasn't something they could navigate on their own. Josh had to go back to work, and he was also still completing coursework for his college degree. Hunter was recovering from major surgery, and learning how to live without a colon. And they had a newborn to take care of.

Since Ashlyn was working from home because of the pandemic, she offered to go over to their home during the day and work from there. Most days I drove over there after I got off work to relieve Ashlyn or Hunter's mom or sisters and help out in the evenings. Kristen and Savannah pitched in whenever they could and whenever they were needed. The awful situation this cancer caused was actually providing one good thing—time and space for us to love and serve them and build strong relationships.

Hunter and I spent hours and hours together during those weeks when she was recovering. We talked about our own childhoods, the experiences of our lives, and our likes and dislikes. We found out we had a lot in common, and we began to form a bond which was more like a friendship than a mother/daughter-in-law relationship.

During one of our conversations I mentioned my book club (Sawubona) and she seemed interested, so I invited her to come to it. I wasn't sure if she would actually enjoy it, considering we are a bunch of 40-50 year old women. But Hunter's an old soul and has wisdom beyond her years, so I figured she would probably fit right in. And she absolutely did. As soon as she was well enough to go, she started attending our meetings. She added a refreshing insight and perspective to the group, and sharing those times together added a new layer to our growing friendship.

When my second marriage fell apart beyond repair, any remnants of former disagreements between us completely vanished. The weekend after he moved out I hosted a baby shower for Ashlyn, who at that point was pregnant with Mila. Hunter was able to come to my home and feel comfortable in it. I was also able to babysit Addie now, so I transformed one of the bedrooms in my house into a nursery and filled it with toys for her.

As crazy as it sounds, Hunter's diagnosis changed the dynamics in our family in a positive way. When you are faced with the reality of how fragile life is, petty disagreements and misunderstandings fade completely into the background. Suddenly, what's really important takes front and center, and everything is put into perspective. In our case, cancer was actually the catalyst for healing.

I would never wish that nightmare on her, and I hated seeing both of them go through it. But I did see the hand of God in all of it. Hunter has completely recovered and is cancer-free, praise God! But her life was permanently altered because of it, and she has had to learn how to manage without a colon, which isn't easy, I'm sure. But that girl never complains. Ever. It rarely even comes up, and you'd never know she is having to deal with ongoing considerations because of it.

After her surgery, Hunter's doctors told her if she wanted to have more children, they should go ahead and do that, since this condition could eventually make it necessary to have a hysterectomy. So a couple months later they announced their second pregnancy. Hunter's body had already been through so much, and this pregnancy proved to be a little more complicated. She had to be on bed rest due to a rare form of anemia, and she was monitored continually by several specialists, including her oncologist and obstetrician.

But thankfully she made it to full term without going into labor early, and on May 16, 2022, Eloise Rose came into this world! Ellie has beautiful red hair and big blue eyes, and this little girl has added so much joy to our family.

When Cancer Brings Healing

Hunter, Adelaide, Eloise, & Josh

Josh and Hunter now have two precious girls, only 18 months apart. After going through a two-year nightmare, they came out stronger than ever. And our family is too. Life is precious, and we all have a deeper understanding of that now, and a deeper appreciation for each other.

All gifts of grace. Everywhere I look.

Building Bridges

Remember Tim McGraw's song, "Live Like You Were Dying"? When it first came out, everyone was talking about it. It was a huge success and had a profound impact on our whole society. When death comes into the conversation, everything changes. Suddenly things are put in perspective and we see more clearly how precious life really is.

Have you been through an experience like this? Maybe you've been on the receiving end of a diagnosis, or maybe it was someone you love. How did you respond? I fully believe we're given a special grace in certain situations, and this is one of them. Hunter and Josh had it all over them. They never seemed terrified, and were instead marked by a supernatural calm and steadiness which HAD to be grace. What they

Everywhere I Look

were going through, especially as brand new parents, should have easily sent them into full blown panic. But it didn't. They did have a ton of people covering them in prayer, which I'm convinced plays a part in this. But they also chose to keep their eyes on God. I believe God responded to their faith and to our prayers by giving them a special grace.

And the same grace is available to every single one of us when the storms of life hit. If we look to Him, cry out to Him, and keep on trusting Him, His grace will carry us through our darkest times.

Chapter Twenty-Four
Layers of Healing

Are we humans bipartite or tripartite? Now there's a fun rabbit hole to explore! In Christian circles, this is often debated. Bipartite refers to the position that man is made up of only two main parts: body and soul, but the tripartite view holds the position that we are made up of three: body, soul, and spirit. I personally see a clear distinction between soul and spirit, but I won't lay out all of my reasons for this here.

My body needed healing from the trauma I had experienced, but not in ways you might think. I'm not talking about bruises; I'm talking about physical symptoms which were caused by the emotional chaos. I used to get migraines all the time, and I was constantly catching colds and viruses because my immune system was shot. During the 25 years of my first marriage, every single winter I could count on getting a horrible cold which would make me lose my voice and I'd feel terrible for days. Even though I was home the majority of the time homeschooling my kids, this would happen several times a year. I just accepted this was normal, and assumed I must have a weak immune system.

After my divorce all of these issues seemed to disappear. When I started teaching, I was certain being surrounded by kids constantly coughing would make me sick. I even remember warning people at work that when winter hit I'd probably miss a few days because it happened to me every year. But in the twelve years I've been teaching there, I could count on one hand the times I've missed work because of being sick.

I know now my body was responding to what I was experiencing emotionally. I've also seen this phenomenon in many people I know who have experienced emotionally destructive relationships. A common physical response is gastrointestinal issues, but I've also heard of migraines and immune dysfunction like I experienced.

So even though I was unaware, God knew my body needed a reset. He also knew my soul did too, and He led me through an amazing process for that.

The way I see it, our souls are made up of our mind, will, and emotions. And our spirits are where we connect with God. I needed healing in both soul and spirit. My mind and emotions were all out of whack, and spiritually I still had a lot to learn which would hugely influence my healing. I'll cover that in the next chapter, but let me just tell you here about the process God took me through to heal my soul (mind and emotions) and my body.

Relational Healing

Emotional healing from a painful divorce is a tricky thing. It's multi-layered and involves personal healing and sometimes also relational healing. I already described how God brought a huge part of my emotional healing through Sawubona. That was a work He did in my own heart. But I'm thankful He also brought healing to my relationship with my first husband, especially for our kids' sake. After a long term marriage and a difficult divorce, the two people involved may or may not experience any amount of reconciliation. Every situation is different, and it isn't always possible. In my case, even though the marriage wasn't restored, reconciliation did happen, but it took willingness and cooperation on both our parts.

Thankfully, my former husband has experienced a lot of healing himself, so our tumultuous past now seems like eons ago, and actually feels like another lifetime altogether. Healing in our relationship wasn't immediate, but we gradually became more and more comfortable around each other. We both remarried, so the new relationship that

Layers of Healing

grew between us was based on our mutual love for our kids, and the desire to make things easier for them. When you have four kids together, there are endless opportunities to be in the same place at the same time. Graduations, weddings, monumental birthdays and events. And in our case, grandbabies arrived on the scene, and brought even more of these opportunities.

By the grace of God, we now have a good relationship. And I actually have a sweet friendship with his new wife. Most people are shocked when they learn she and I have gotten together a few times, just the two of us, to intentionally build a relationship. My kids are her step-kids, and my grandbabies are also her grandbabies. She's also been through a devastating divorce, so we both understand the depth of pain and destruction it brings, and the work it takes to heal from it. Having a good relationship was important to both of us, for our own healing, and for the healing it would bring to the entire group of people we both call family.

In the process of writing this book, the three of us had many discussions. I wanted their input, and I worked hard to honor their perspectives and wishes. It hasn't been easy to relive some of the most painful events of our lives, and it certainly hasn't been easy to navigate the vulnerability necessary to tell about them. But if our story helps anyone avoid what we went through, then the vulnerability it has required to share it will have been worth it.

Cognitive Healing

Did you know the brain can actually experience growth and change? My own brain needed a lot of healing and change, but I didn't even know it. One of the programs we use to help our students at the Pearl Center is called FIE, Feuerstein's Instrumental Enrichment. It was developed by Reuven Feuerstein, a Romanian-born Jewish man who survived the Holocaust. He was a clinical, developmental, and cognitive psychologist who was called upon to help survivors of the Holocaust recover from their trauma. He believed in the neuroplasticity of the brain, before that was even recognized as a thing, and he developed a program to help these survivors recover their cognitive functions. It was hugely successful and continues to be today. He established the Feuerstein Institute in Jerusalem, Israel, which is still training practitioners in his theory, assessments, and interventions. Our therapists at Pearl are trained in FIE, and we see incredible results from this program.

Several years ago, our director, Suzanne Ringger, decided to reach out to a local ministry which has an addiction recovery center for women. She wanted to use FIE with these ladies, so she and my friend and fellow therapist, Karen O'Neal, started holding ten-week classes to help these women understand they could literally change their brains and establish new neural pathways which would help them in their recovery. After a couple years, I joined them and started teaching classes. It's been an incredibly successful experience, and one of the most rewarding things I've ever done. These ladies are so precious, so hungry for help, and they are like sponges, soaking up every bit of information we teach them. Many of them have expressed that this information is life-changing, and it truly is. I always fully agree with them when they say this because it has changed my own life dramatically.

God knew I needed this—my mind needed this, and my emotions needed this. When you change your mind, you actually change your emotions too, and I've seen this happen to me. As I've understood the power of a growth mindset and the ability of the brain to rewire itself, I've seen my own thinking improve and in response, my emotions line up with my new thinking. And then what follows is my behavior, which is how it literally changed my life. Because of all I have learned and applied through FIE, I have developed strategies to think better, and I've realized the power of my own decision making abilities. As I've made better decisions, I've seen myself stepping out courageously to do things I never would have done before. It's taken me to a new level

Layers of Healing

of confidence, and I'm so thankful God introduced me to this program. Have you ever heard the statement "All wisdom is God's wisdom"? It's basically saying humans can come up with some great ideas, but if you look carefully, you'll see it was actually God's idea, and His wisdom can be seen as the basis for the idea. The foundation of FIE is the practice of learning to change your thinking patterns in order to change your behavioral patterns. If you're familiar with Romans 12:2, all of this should sound a little familiar to you. That verse says, "Be transformed by the renewal of your mind." (ESV) Or as the New Living Translation puts it, "Let God transform you into a new person by changing the way you think." FIE is based on wisdom which actually originated with God. But, like the statement says, ALL wisdom is His in the first place.

God's wisdom and grace have been all over my healing journey.

Adventure Therapy

Have you ever heard of "Adventure Therapy"? It involves taking someone out of their physical comfort zone and their natural environment, and into unfamiliar territory in order to change their perspective and to show them they are capable of changing their lives. It includes travel and outdoor activities specifically designed to reset the body, help you enjoy nature, and try new things. I only recently learned about this, but let me tell you, going on adventures was a big part of God's treatment plan for me. It played a part in the healing of my body and soul, but at the time, I had no idea how much I needed it.

But again . . . God did! He's the best therapist.

Road Tripping with Kristen

"Hey Mom! Wanna take a trip?"

These are some of Kristen's favorite words. This fiercely-courageous, adventure-loving second-born daughter of mine has talked me into some of the craziest trips I've ever taken. She's my kid who never sits still. It's always been that way.

My firstborn, Ashlyn, was a calm child, even in the womb. I remember thinking for sure I was going to have a boy when I was pregnant with Kristen because of the activity level of that baby. When I had been pregnant with Ashlyn, she sometimes got into a position which made me uncomfortable, and I could gently press on the elbow or knee or whatever body part she was using to poke me in the ribs. I would just press on that spot and she would freeze. No more movement. Like she actually understood what I was doing and wasn't going to argue about it. But with Kristen—whole different ball game. It was obvious from the get-go she wasn't going to be like Ashlyn. I tried the same tactic with her, to gently push her when she made me uncomfortable, and immediately she would hit back or kick back with a fierce little jab. *Not having it, Mom. I liked my knee right where I had it, thank you very much!* That literally happened so many times it became predictable, and I could tell people, "Hey, watch this!" She would kick so hard they could see it.

As soon as I saw her red hair when she was first born, and considering her behavior in utero, I figured she was going to be my feisty one, for sure. And I was right! She has a lot of the stereotypical traits of a redhead. She's outgoing, adventurous, passionate, empathic, hilarious, and so much fun. Her red hair caught me completely by surprise, though. I did have red hair when I was born, so I shouldn't have been so shocked. But mine was more like strawberry blonde and it quickly turned blonde. Mine had been red enough for my brothers to nickname me "Red," and the name stuck long after it had lost the red tint. But still, I never even imagined having a baby with red hair.

Kristen's activity level was so much higher than Ashlyn's had been, and I had a hard time keeping up with that child. I still do, actually. She's always on the go, and she has traveled more than all my other kids put together. When she was 24 years old, she and a friend decided they wanted to see Europe. So they planned a trip, and visited France,

Layers of Healing

Italy, Switzerland, Greece, and Poland. They often traveled by train, and after they got back I found out how risky it sometimes was. I don't think either of them were even worried, but the idea of two beautiful young women walking through alleys in the dark to get to the train station made me crazy! But God protected them, thankfully, and they had a great time seeing the world. Kristen's a big daredevil, so she made sure she found all the high risk activities while they were there. She went bungee jumping in the Swiss Alps, rode donkeys down steep, narrow paths in Santorini, and took a twelve hour boat ride to Athens. I think there were some go-cart rides down the side of a mountain too. She's a crazy girl!

At some point in her twenties, Kristen set a goal for herself to see all 48 contiguous states before she turned thirty. And she recently accomplished her goal. I actually benefited from her goal, because for several of those trips she asked me to be her travel buddy. I didn't realize it at the time, but those trips were actually part of my healing.

Remember how I said the road trip through Italy with Savannah gave me newfound courage? These trips did too. The first one we took was to New York and New England in 2019. The part which required courage was that we did this in January. Being from the South, we don't see much snow, and it isn't something we're used to driving in. But we drove through a whole lot of snow on that trip. A nor'easter actually hit while we were there, and we drove through the beginning of the storm before we got snowed in at my niece's house for a couple days. On the trip we visited all six of the beautiful New England states. We watched the sun set over Plymouth Rock, and we walked along the historic Freedom Trail in Boston. We sipped hot tea at the Boston Tea Party Museum, and we spent a day walking all over New York City. We also went over into Canada to see Niagara Falls which, by the way, is absolutely magical when it's covered in snow and sparkling crystals of ice.

Everywhere I Look

Kristen & me at Niagara Falls

I have to say the highlight of the trip was also the scariest thing we did. And maybe the dumbest. Kristen always looks up each state before her trips to find out what places are must-sees in that state, and what activities she wants to do. When she looked up New England she thought it'd be fun to go dog-sledding.

But here's the thing about traveling with Kristen. She doesn't like to plan everything out. My old fashioned Gen X version of traveling would involve hotel reservations and arrival and departure times for all the stops along the way. Nope, that's way too restrictive. She just drives until she feels like stopping and then decides along the way what she wants to do and where she wants to stop. When we were discussing our first trip, I remember saying we needed to decide where we'd stop and go ahead and get a hotel lined up. She looked at me like I had three heads. *Why in the world would we do that?* There are hotels on every exit, and AirBnB's in between. There's no shortage of places to stop. And in fact, when she went with a friend on a cross-country road trip to California they only had one time where they couldn't find a room. So they slept in the car. *Whew! Okay then.* I soon realized I'd need to get used to a whole new way of traveling.

The day we decided to go dog-sledding in New England, of course we didn't have a plan. I was actually Googling it and calling places to get a reservation while we were driving. I finally found someone with

Layers of Healing

an opening, and the guy gave me an address and time. So we headed that way, and eventually found ourselves out in the middle of nowhere. We were completely dependent on the GPS and it kept going in and out (remember Italy?!) so we weren't even sure if we were going the right way. But we finally made it to the destination, and it was literally just an empty gravel parking lot. Nothing else in sight. We felt a little weird about it, but my hesitation grew when a guy pulled up with a truck load of dogs, and he was all alone. He got the sled and the dogs all set up, then gave us directions about where to sit and how to hold on. And then off we went into the woods, with a complete stranger, and suddenly my hesitation turned into full blown fear. How did we get ourselves into THIS crazy mess? Riding off into nowhere with a total stranger and a bunch of wild dogs, and no other humans in sight. I kept trying to figure out if he was a serial killer, and I was hoping someone could track our phones to find our bodies if it turned out he was. It was total insanity!

But he was actually a really nice guy, thank God. And the dogs were sweet, and the ride was a lot of fun. He even let Kristen take the lead and taught her how to do a little mushing herself. It was a great little adventure, even if it was a really risky one.

I never would've done that on my own, but Kristen has no fear. As I've tagged along on her adventures, I've overcome my own fears little by little, and I've learned it's true—you only live once. So you might as well enjoy it to the fullest.

Seeing the States

Since the New England trip, we've taken several others. The next trip was in 2020 through Tennessee, Kentucky, Indiana, Illinois, and Wisconsin. Savannah joined us on that one. And again, it was in January. Don't ask me why I would sign up for another snow trip. I know it's crazy. But Kristen just decides she's ready to take a trip and it doesn't matter what the weather might be. I think in her mind it's even more fun if there is a risk involved, so snow just makes it even better.

Everywhere I Look

We only slid off the road once. And thankfully there was no damage to the car, so we all laughed at how loudly we had screamed, and then drove back onto the road.

With Kristen & Savannah in Chicago

We stopped in Chicago to see "The Bean" (Cloud Gate) in Millennium Park, then went up to Willis Tower's Skydeck. On the 103rd floor, with incredible views of four states, the Skydeck has clear observation boxes, and I had to take a few deep breaths and overcome my fear of heights to step out onto the glass platform for a picture with the girls. The next day we drove through a snowstorm to Wisconsin and visited a cheese factory. Then we went downtown and ate some of the best cheese curds I've ever had in my life.

In June of the same year, she and I took another road trip to see all the southern states. We drove a circuit from South Carolina up to North Carolina, then over through Tennessee to Arkansas, then down through Oklahoma and Texas. For the last leg of the trip back, we crossed Louisiana, Mississippi, Alabama, and Georgia. Ten states in five days. We moved quickly through the places, but stopped along the way to enjoy the sites, like Broadway in Nashville and Graceland in Memphis. I fell in love with Hot Springs, Arkansas—a gorgeous historic town with natural hot springs everywhere. The national park in the middle

Layers of Healing

of town is covered with lush, green grass and thick, green vines which grow abundantly due to the steam rising from all the hot springs. We ate dinner in Oklahoma City, next to a canal which winds through their beautiful downtown. The next day we walked through Dealey Plaza in Dallas, Texas, and met an interesting guy next to "the grassy knoll" who had witnessed John F. Kennedy's assassination when he was a little boy. He described in detail how he went to the plaza that fateful morning with both of his grandmothers, and saw the whole thing. Our trip was short, but filled with memorable moments like that one.

The following year in June of 2021, Ashlyn and my sister, Sara, joined us for a trip out West. What an incredible adventure! We flew that time, then got a rental car and drove through Wyoming, Montana, and Idaho. Oh my goodness, the beauty is indescribable. In Glacier National Park we saw breathtaking views of snow-capped mountains and crystal clear lakes lined with colorful rocks. We decided to rent a dune buggy to drive up the side of a mountain so we could get the best views possible. In Idaho we visited a potato museum and got our picture taken beside a giant baked potato. Then we hiked around Craters of the Moon, a national monument in Idaho with huge lava fields and interesting caves to explore. We stopped in Jackson Hole to ride a Cowboy Coaster and of course, we got a photo under the Elk Antler Arch. Then we visited Yellowstone National Park to watch Old Faithful erupt right on time, and to hike to the Grand Prismatic Spring—the gorgeous, rainbow-colored hot spring I have always wanted to see. Basking in all of the splendor and beauty is definitely good for the body, soul, and spirit.

Everywhere I Look

With Sara, Kristen, and Ashlyn in Glacier National Park

With each of these trips, I feel like my view of God and the world has expanded and my perspective on life itself has grown. And again, I can see that even though I didn't realize how much I needed all this, God knew how much good it would do me. He was pulling me out of my world and giving me a better vantage point again to help me see beyond my circumstances. Through all of this I have learned traveling can be very therapeutic, and adventures are good for the soul.

I'm so thankful God gave me an adventure-loving girl to lead the way and show me how to do it.

Into The Blue

How does someone who's not even a great swimmer end up taking boat trips across the wild, blue ocean? If you had told me a few years ago I'd be doing this, and loving every minute of it, I wouldn't have believed you. Remember how I mentioned a girl named Richelle Lawrence I knew back when I was in college? When I got in all that trouble, and they moved me into the new dorm, she lived across the hall from Andrea and me. We barely knew each other in college, but somehow we both ended up in Greenville, South Carolina along with Andrea and Val, so we literally have a college reunion going on in this town.

Charity, Val, & Andrea

Richelle and I reconnected a couple times through the years, but when she went through a divorce, our friendship took on new meaning. When you've been through that fire, you understand it better than others who haven't. So she and I started hanging out more, and we grew closer through the process. One of the things I love most about Richelle is she loves to have a good time. She's a planner too, so she enjoys getting fun things on the calendar and lining up all the details. We started planning all kinds of things to do together, and it kept us both busy and looking forward to the next adventure . . . which I've found has also been a part of my healing.

In 2020, Richelle invited Andrea and myself, along with two other college friends, Donna and Greg Crase, to join her on her company boat trip. Richelle's boss, Britt Goodson, is from Jacksonville, Florida, and he loves being on the water. He owns a beautiful boat, aptly named Into The Blue, and each year he enjoys taking his employees and some of his friends on a boat trip. Britt is incredibly generous and his guests pay very little on these trips. He loves to treat everyone, even though I can't imagine how expensive it is for him.

I couldn't believe this offer when Richelle invited me. Basically a free trip. Who could pass this up? I did tell her I wasn't a great swimmer, and I hoped we wouldn't be jumping into the middle of the ocean at some point. She laughed and assured me I didn't have to get in the water if I didn't want to. She also told me Britt is extremely prepared and has state of the art equipment on board in case of an emergency. So she put my mind at ease, and we started making our plans.

On a scorching hot day in June, we climbed aboard and boated along the Intracoastal Waterway from Jacksonville to Daytona Beach. Later we made our way to St. Augustine and walked around the beautiful old city, and then eventually we boated back to Jacksonville. The trip went beautifully, and we had an absolute blast. I had not known Greg and Donna well when we were back in school together, but we hit it off and became great friends. We've stayed in touch ever since. Turns out, it was one of the most relaxing vacations I've ever taken. Sitting on the boat, soaking in the sunshine, and having the wind cool us off while we stared in amazement at the beauty surrounding us—what a dream! We were all in awe of the grace of God being poured on us.

Charity, Richelle, Donna, & Andrea

Layers of Healing

The following year, she invited me again, and this time we boated along the Intracoastal from Jacksonville to Amelia Island, then up to Savannah, Georgia. I love the beautiful, historic city of Savannah. It's one of my favorite places on earth, and I've been there a million times, but never from a boat. It was so amazing to come around the bend in the Savannah River and see the riverwalk from the water. Such an incredible experience. On this trip, Richelle invited a friend of hers I had never met, Debbie Kimble. Even though I didn't know her, we had a lot in common and had both been through a painful divorce. It's a club you never want to be in, but there is an instantaneous camaraderie. Debbie is such a sweet, gentle soul and she loves Jesus deeply, so we also hit it off, and still keep in touch. Another beautiful trip, another gift from God.

The next year, in 2022, Richelle asked me to go on the annual boat trip again, and this time we boated along the Gulf coast instead of the Atlantic. We started in Tampa, Florida and boated to Fort Myers, stopped at Sanibel Island, then back to Tampa. Richelle invited a high school friend, Belinda Martin, on this trip. Belinda has also survived the nightmare of divorce, and also has a passionate love for God, so again—instant friendship. I don't know what it is about that, but it just keeps happening. Richelle is really great at picking friends, so that helps. And there's just a bond created when you've experienced similar pain. I guess there's an unspoken understanding that this person will "get me." They will know what I've been through, and they will have a mutual perspective on life. Belinda is also hilarious, so we laughed a lot on that trip, and the three of us had such a great time together.

Each time we go on these trips we stay in beautiful resorts at our destinations, and for this trip we stayed at a place called the Pink Shell Beach Resort. These places love to pamper their guests, and at this resort, when we walked into the lobby they gave us cold washcloths scented with eucalyptus oil. I put the cloth over my face and it felt absolutely heavenly. After being in the sun for hours, the cool cloth

Everywhere I Look

was so refreshing, and we all laughed at how easily we were impressed with this place all because of a simple washcloth. But really, it felt so strange to be treated like a queen, and I still remember thinking about the goodness of God, and how undeserving I was to be able to enjoy such an extravagant vacation. Mind blowing, and very humbling.

In 2023, I couldn't believe it when Richelle invited me again, and this time we were going to the Bahamas! Whaaaat?!! She said we would fly into Nassau and boat over to Eleuthera to our resort, then spend the week exploring the Exumas. Belinda was coming on this trip too, and so were Greg and Donna. I was completely beside myself with excitement!

Richelle & me on the boat trip

On our boat trip over to the resort from Nassau, a rogue storm arose out of nowhere. Apparently it's common for that area, but it's not something most of us had ever experienced, so we all hunkered down and prepared to hold on tight. At first we were taking selfies and laughing, but very soon, all cameras were put away and we were hanging on for dear life. A trip which should have taken an hour and a half, ended up taking twice that long, and we rode a roller coaster of waves 11

Layers of Healing

feet high! None of us could even talk to each other, but thankfully we had an incredibly capable captain at the helm. In spite of the intensity of the storm, Britt guided us safely to shore and afterwards, we compared what we had been thinking while we had been riding it out. We discovered all of us were wondering if we would make it off that boat alive. Several of us (myself included) were wondering if our kids knew where our life insurance policies were. It was a pretty terrifying boat ride, but it didn't stop a single one of us from getting back onto that boat the next day. I think this was probably because Britt had proven himself to us, and we knew we were in good hands. We also wanted to see the Exumas.

The rest of the trip was simply amazing. One day we boated out to a coral reef to snorkel, and I was way too afraid to try it. I've snorkeled before, but the current was crazy and we were in the middle of the ocean. Didn't any of these people know sharks live in oceans? After several people snorkeled and came back to the boat talking about the incredible things they saw, I tried to muster up my courage. One of the guys used to be a lifeguard, so I agreed to go only if he was in my group. We swam out and grabbed onto a huge black rock jutting up out of the water, then took turns diving to see the stunningly beautiful reef and all the brightly colored fish. It was an absolutely incredible sight, but I have to say I was terrified the whole time. It took every bit of my concentration just to breathe calmly and not panic. We swam back to the boat, against the current, and I fell onto the boat completely exhausted. But what I also felt was an incredible sense of accomplishment. I had faced my fears, once again, and had lived to tell about it.

It's a lesson I've learned over and over, especially since being divorced and on my own. I can't give myself the luxury of waiting until the fear is gone to get up and do something. I just have to do it afraid. If I wait until I feel courageous, I'll never do anything. I have to get out of the boat (figuratively, and in this case, literally) in spite of my fear. It's the only way to actually overcome it. Giving in to it only leads

Everywhere I Look

to more fear. Courage grows as you look fear in the face and refuse to back down.

In 2024, as I was working on this book, Richelle invited me to go on another annual boat trip. This was my fifth trip with them, and this time we were going to the Florida Keys. I'd never been before, and I'm always excited to do something new. Belinda was coming again, so I knew we would have a blast. And we did. We flew into Miami, boated to Key Largo for lunch, then on to Duck Key where we stayed at Hawks Cay Resort. We visited Key West one day, and had fun laughing at the chickens roaming free all over the island. We got our picture taken in front of the Southernmost Point buoy, and toured the home of Ernest Hemingway with all of his cats, then drove around the quaint little town on a golf cart. Another picturesque vacation, another gift from God (through Britt's incredible generosity).

As Richelle and Belinda and I looked back together over the last few years, and these fantastic vacations we've enjoyed, I got a little emotional thinking about the grace of God. I told them, "This needs to be in the book. It just HAS to be! Look at all this GRACE!" It really is mind blowing to think about. Every one of these trips has made me feel like God was lavishing His love on us. We've all been through so much pain, so much heartache. And look what God has done for us. He gave us "Adventure Therapy" when we didn't even know what that was.

He's brought us safely through. He's healed our broken hearts. He's strengthened us in the process.

And He's poured His amazing grace all over us. It's everywhere we look!

Layers of Healing

Praising God in the Beautiful Bahamas!

Building Bridges

Do you recognize areas of your thinking where you need healing? Are your emotions out of whack like mine were? Our body, mind, and emotions are all closely intertwined and they influence each other. We are such magnificently designed creatures. God knows exactly what you need, and if you'll ask Him, He'll show you. I'm not discounting the need for an actual human therapist. He often works through godly counsel, and I've certainly benefited from it. But, ultimately, He is the One who knows you best, and He can guide you step by step through your own healing journey.

And are you letting fear hold you back? Can you identify an area of your life where you are letting fear keep you from something you know God wants for you? 2 Timothy 1:7 tells us very clearly fear is not from God.

"God has not given us a spirit of fear, but of power and of love and of a sound mind." (NKJV)

Maybe you need some Adventure Therapy too. We have to come

Everywhere I Look

out of agreement with fear and refuse to let it hold us hostage. It can keep us from enjoying some of God's best gifts. We need to align our hearts with the Spirit of God who gives us power, love, and a sound mind. There's really nothing to fear, actually. Not even death itself. Even in scary situations I need to constantly remind myself that if I truly believe my life is in God's sovereign hands, fear has no place in my heart or mind.

So push through those fears, and don't let them stop you. The Hands which created the universe are holding you right now.

"Don't be afraid, for I am with you. Don't be discouraged, for I am your God. I will strengthen you and help you. I will hold you up with My victorious right hand."

(Isaiah 41:10 NLT . . . My favorite verse!)

Chapter Twenty-Five
Last, But Definitely Not Least

Gratitude. This one single word is such a game changer. It has also been a huge part of my healing journey, because it can shift my mindset like nothing else. Several years ago I read Ann Voskamp's book *One Thousand Gifts*, and I started my own list of one thousand gifts. It was a lot easier to do than I expected. One thousand sounds like a lot, but it's a drop in the bucket when you start realizing that literally everywhere you look, there's something else to be thankful for.

I've learned to make these lists whenever I need to get my head on straight. And for every painful experience I've been through I can still make a gratitude list. There are always good things that come from it, and I can say this confidently because the concept is straight from God's Word. Romans 8:28 gets thrown around a lot, and we have to be careful not to misuse it. Remember the discussion in chapter 22 about staying in Q1 and Q2? Quoting Romans 8:28 is actually jumping ahead to Q3, and that probably won't be appropriate if you haven't first walked through Q1 and Q2 with someone in pain. That's why it gets on our nerves when someone we barely know throws this verse at us. But the truth still stands: "In all things, God works for the good of those who love Him, who have been called according to His purpose." (NIV) God IS working all things together for our good, so we can be confident that in every hard experience, good is buried in there somewhere. We just have to find it!

After my Sawubona friends helped me process the pain of my second divorce, I tried to turn my heart toward gratitude, and I was actually able to make a list of good things which came from that crazy marriage. I still have the list on my phone, and I pull it out when I need to remind myself.

Spirit-Empowered Living

By far, the best gift God gave me through that relationship was how He opened my mind to a new and deeper understanding of the Holy Spirit. I'm a Baptist preacher's daughter, remember? And as I've already mentioned, my second husband was charismatic. He had also been raised in a Baptist church which held to a cessationist theology, but as an adult he started reading about and studying the gifts of the Spirit, and he became convinced we had grown up missing out on some things God meant for us to have. My only exposure to the charismatic world was what I had seen on TV. And I didn't know if I believed any of what I saw. I had heard of pseudo-faith healers who were eventually exposed as frauds, so I lumped them all together and dismissed the whole lot of them. I didn't mind free and passionate worship. Remember, as a child I loved going with my daddy to revival meetings where the Spirit would move, and people were very demonstrative and emotional. So I didn't feel uncomfortable with that. In fact, I preferred it. But I just wasn't sure about the supernatural gifts like healing and prophecy. I knew nothing about those.

I had been intrigued by all this at first, especially when we were just dating. But after we were married, many personal issues in his life were exposed, and I started having serious reservations about his theological positions. How could someone speak so confidently about the power of the Spirit but show no evidence of that power in their life? So I gradually became resistant again to a continuationist position, and reverted back to just wanting to throw it all out.

But during our marriage he insisted we go to a charismatic church. Because I knew we desperately needed to be in a community of faith, I was willing to go along with it. I did love that kind of worship, and

Last, But Definitely Not Least

I felt like I had a solid theological foundation so I figured I would just sift carefully through the teaching and sermons, praying for discernment. I was surprised to find there really weren't huge differences between the charismatic churches we visited and the churches I had been used to. I think the enemy has exaggerated the differences and blown them way out of proportion to cause division. We agree on way more than we disagree on. And none of the differences affect core theological beliefs, in my opinion. I know there are churches on both sides which are out of line and even way off track. I'm speaking generally here.

The first church we attended welcomed us with open arms, and one of the pastors even counseled us for a while. I loved these people, and I found they did have a refreshing perspective of the Holy Spirit and of the gifts of the Spirit. They didn't pick and choose which gifts were still in operation. They wanted them all and they believed they could have them all. This actually sounded pretty Scriptural to me, and as I started studying it, I couldn't really find a good, solid Scriptural basis for my cessationist theology. Cessationists maintain that the supernatural gifts ceased to exist after the New Testament time period, and I had been a cessationist simply because it's all I ever knew. I figured if I hung out with these people long enough I'd find out if those gifts ceased or not. I asked God to show me the truth, and I decided to watch and see what He revealed.

The first thing God showed me was how I had ignored whole passages of Scripture. When I opened my Bible to read up on all of this, I was so ashamed at how little I had even read about it, much less studied it with an open mind. For example, most Christians are very familiar with 1 Corinthians 13, the "Love Chapter." But that's right smack in the middle of an entire explanation of the gifts of the Spirit which starts in chapter 12 and goes through chapter 14. Chapter 13 is just a piece of what He was getting at, just a side note for clarification, not His entire thought process. In my Bible, chapter 13 was highlighted, and I had written notes all over the place for that chapter. But chapters 12 and 14 .

.. completely bare. No highlights, no notes. I was immediately convicted. That is the definition of taking Scripture out of context right there. And I felt a strong pull from the Spirit to spend some time studying the entirety of what Paul was saying.

Another passage God brought to my attention was Ephesians 4, which describes five ministry roles God has called Christians to fill in the church: apostles, prophets, evangelists, shepherds, and teachers. The churches I had always been in had shepherds (pastors), teachers, and sometimes visiting evangelists. But their position on apostles and prophets was that those roles had only been temporary, and we didn't have any today. If you don't look up all the debates about this, but just take Scripture at its word, the passage actually tells us the purpose of these and how long they will be in operation, and also why they're given. It's all right there.

"And he gave the apostles, the prophets, the evangelists, the shepherds, and teachers, to equip the saints for the work of the ministry, for building up the body of Christ, until we all attain to the unity of the faith and of the knowledge of the Son of God, to mature manhood, to the measure of the stature of the fullness of Christ, so that we may no longer be children, tossed to and fro by the waves and carried about by every wind of doctrine, by human cunning, by craftiness in deceitful schemes." (Ephesians 4:11-14 ESV)

Did you catch that? The purpose of all five of those is to equip us all and build us up. And how long will this continue? Did Paul say it would just be through the New Testament period and then we would see a couple of them drop off the scene? No mention of that here. In fact, it clearly says the opposite—these are given to us until we all reach unity in our faith and reach maturity and the whole measure of the fullness of Christ. Are we there yet? Clearly not! We don't even have unity about this one particular topic. And I don't know about you, but I'm still a work in progress. I have definitely not reached the whole measure of the fullness of Christ. I also have a hard time seeing where

Last, But Definitely Not Least

we, in these crazy last days, don't still need all five roles and also all of the gifts, including the supernatural gifts. The only explanation I've heard is that some of these ceased because they were only needed to get the church off the ground. But doesn't the church have to get off the ground in every new generation? One church generation dies off and a new one is born. The new church doesn't need what the first church needed? I just couldn't find anywhere in Scripture that said all of this was only for New Testament believers.

The other argument I personally had held against all this, which is the weakest of all arguments, was I had no personal experience with any of this. I had not seen anyone miraculously healed, and I had no knowledge of modern day apostles or prophets. But this holds no weight whatsoever, and is actually a logical fallacy known as the "anecdotal fallacy." This occurs when people use their limited experience to try to prove something doesn't exist or to make some general conclusion. We as Christians hate this fallacy because people use it to defend their belief that there is no God. Just because I haven't experienced something does not mean it doesn't exist.

So again, I took all of this to God and asked Him to reveal the truth to me. I told Him if apostles and prophets are still walking this earth, I'd love to meet them. And if He's still giving supernatural gifts, I'd love to see them in operation.

And guess what! He took me up on it.

Honduras

Several years had passed since I went on the trips to Slovenia, and mission trips were not on my mind. But one morning when I was getting ready to go to church I distinctly felt the Spirit of God bring missions to my mind, and it felt like He was telling me it was time to think about this again.

I had barely started going to this new church, and didn't really know many people. I didn't even know if they took mission trips, but

Everywhere I Look

I told God that morning I would try to find out. Later in the morning at church during the announcements, someone got up and said they were planning a mission trip. I almost fell over because God had clearly prepared me for this a couple hours before I heard those words. I knew I was supposed to go ask about it after church. So I did.

The guy explained to me how they were planning to go to Colombia, South America, and they would love for me to join them. I started to get excited about it, but a couple weeks later he told me the dates. It was right around the same time Savannah was getting married. Ugh! That wouldn't work. I started wondering why God had led me down this dead-end path. The guy also told me they had a sister church which also took trips, and he thought they might be looking for some people to go with them to Honduras. I nodded and said I'd think that over, but I really didn't want to do it. I wouldn't know anyone on the team, and one of the great things about going is the relationship-building. I was counting on making some new friends through this experience since I was new to the church and didn't really know anyone.

But I decided to go home and pray about it. For some reason, I kept feeling like God wanted me to go. Every time I prayed about it, the pull kept getting stronger, but I kept resisting. I kept telling God I didn't know anyone who was going or even in the other church. It would be so weird. But I still felt like He kept telling me He wanted me to go, so I finally got the names of the people leading the team, and gave them a call.

Sonny and Sheila Horton had led missions trips for more than twenty years. They had it down to a science. When I first spoke with Sheila, she gave me all the details and said this trip to Honduras would be a combination of construction and medical missions. I didn't say it, but I immediately thought, "Ohhhh okay. No thanks." I knew my skill set included working with kids and teaching, but not medicine—I hate the sight of blood, and I'm actually puke-phobic, so sick people aren't generally my thing. My sister is the nurse in the family, not me! And

Last, But Definitely Not Least

construction definitely wasn't in my skill set.

But again, when I told all this to God, He STILL kept pressing me to go. Now I was completely baffled. Why would He want me to go with a bunch of people I don't know to do something I know nothing about? I actually hated the thought of being with a bunch of people who had all gone on trips together, who went to church together and were all friends, and there I'd be without one single person to hang out with. I laid all of this out to God, but immediately felt like He was saying, "I'll be with you. Is that enough?"

So I talked to Sheila again and told her I had hesitated about going on a medical mission trip since I'm a teacher and not a nurse, but I was wondering if I could still be of help. She assured me there would be plenty I could do. She explained how after the people came through the medical clinic, some of our team would share the Gospel and pray with them. Now THAT I could do! So I finally agreed to go.

When we arrived in Honduras, a medical doctor from Guatemala joined our team, and he led us in devotions and prayer each day. I loved the things he taught us. He encouraged us each day to remember a six-fold prayer during this trip. He said we should pray for:

1. Unity among our team
2. Supernatural love from God for the people we were serving
3. Protection from spiritual warfare
4. Gratitude for our supporters and prayer partners
5. Forgiveness for quenching the Spirit
6. Power from the Spirit of God

The "quenching the Spirit" point intrigued me and convicted me, so I asked God for clarity. I started realizing my arrogance and cynical attitude toward the things of the Spirit were actually quenching His work in my life. I prayed for an open and willing heart to receive whatever He had for me.

Everywhere I Look

One day when we were riding our bus to the clinic we had set up, a lady on our team mentioned her carpal tunnel syndrome was acting up and her wrist was really hurting. Now, this is where I would normally start digging through my purse to find some Tylenol. Not that there's anything wrong with that . . . it's just all I knew how to do. I'm sad to admit prayer was not my first go-to unless the situation was more serious. I'm trying to change that. But these people clearly ran to God first. The doctor turned around and took her wrist in his hands and started praying out loud. Anyone who was close enough also laid their hands on her and joined him in praying out loud. I was watching this unfold and thinking this was a refreshingly faith-filled response. When they finished praying, she shook her wrist around a little, clenched and unclenched her fist, then just calmly said "Thanks. That's much better." And everyone turned and went back to their conversation like nothing had happened. I tried not to look as shocked as I was, but I began to wonder if this was why God wanted me on this trip. I had asked him to show me if all of this was real. And this looked pretty real!

But an even more amazing thing happened a couple days later. A preteen girl who lived nearby had come to help us each day. One morning I came out of the building to see several people gathered around her. She was seated in a chair, crying, and she looked terrified. Everyone around her looked very concerned. Another worker told me she had lost all feeling in her left arm. It was completely numb and she couldn't move it. Weird! The doctor came over and knelt beside her and put his hands on her arm. They all started praying over her, and she sat there, quietly sobbing with tears streaming down her face. I was standing several feet away, still so unfamiliar with this whole scene, and just trying to take it all in. When they stopped praying, I heard him ask her about her arm, and she shook her head and said she still couldn't move it. He hesitated and looked down for a few seconds, then he started praying again. This time he wasn't asking God to heal her arm, but he was speaking with authority in Jesus' name and rebuking any demonic activity which

Last, But Definitely Not Least

might be causing this. Even as he was speaking she started moving her arm! Her face lit up and she started waving her arm in the air, saying, "I can feel it!" Everyone praised God for a few minutes, then they all went back to work, like this was something they see every day.

But I could not believe my eyes. I stood there staring at them, totally amazed and trying to process what just happened. As it started to sink in, I literally wanted to fall on my face and worship God for the rest of the day. It absolutely blew my mind, and I felt so humbled and also so ashamed at my unbelief. Why wouldn't God still heal people? He told us in His Word that He does not change. But why had I never seen this? Why doesn't He heal everyone? And why didn't He heal her the first time they prayed, for that matter? I was full of questions.

On the bus ride back later the same afternoon, I made sure I got a seat beside the doctor. I needed to ask him about all this. We had a fascinating conversation the whole way back, and I wish I had a recording of it, but I wrote down everything I could remember. He said when her arm was still numb after the first time he prayed, he sensed the Spirit of God was alerting him to demonic activity. So he knew he needed to take authority over it and tell it to leave, in Jesus' name. Wow! Okay, how did he sense that? He explained to me how discerning spirits is a spiritual gift, and we are given gifts randomly as the Spirit decides to give them when we need them. It's not in our control, and we can't dictate them or question them. We just submit ourselves to be tools in His hands and we leave the results to Him. He said he just prays in faith and trusts the Spirit with the rest.

Oh my goodness! This was *really* starting to look like New Testament faith, and I felt like such a Pharisee for the way I had always been so cynical. I immediately started praying for God to change my heart and increase my faith. I wanted the kind of faith I saw in these people and I see in Scripture.

I started reading, studying, and praying for eyes to see more of what the Spirit was doing, and ears to hear Him teach me about all of this.

It would take a whole other book to tell you everything He has done in response to that prayer, but I will just say this . . . I will never doubt again. God is actively working in this world and He's still a supernatural, all-powerful God. We are the ones who try to put Him in a box with our small-minded limitations, but He will not be contained. And if you ask Him to prove all this to you, guess what . . .

He will.

Serving on the prayer team in Honduras

A New Church Family

A few years after this, God very clearly guided me to the church I'm currently a part of. After the pandemic, I had to make myself go back to church. I hate to admit that, especially as a preacher's kid, but it's true. Mainly because I wasn't firmly planted in a church when the pandemic hit. Ever since my second divorce, I felt sad when I was at the church we had attended together. Too many painful memories. So I had started visiting other churches, but I just couldn't get settled. Then came the pandemic, and like a lot of people, I got used to having church on my living room couch. I have to say, there was something very healthy about stepping away from everything during the lockdowns. It was a chance for us all to re-evaluate what we were doing and decide what

Last, But Definitely Not Least

we wanted to jump back into. As much as I love going to church, I also hate being a visitor. By this point my mom had come to live with me. She was getting older and frail, so getting out and going to church was quite an ordeal. Since we would have to go to all that work just to be a visitor and deal with all of the awkwardness, I just kept avoiding it. For several months, I "sabbathed" on Sundays and just let my heart and soul heal.

But after a while, I started really longing to be back in a community of faith. It's not like I didn't have Christian fellowship. I still had my Sawubona sisters, but we only met once a month. And I have lots of wonderful, godly friends, and we have great conversations about our faith and what God's teaching us. But still, there's just something very unique about being a part of a community of faith that serves each other, and serves the community and the world, and meets together every single week. There's also nothing like corporate worship to light my soul on fire!

So when Savannah invited me to go with her to a church she was visiting, I was happy to go. By this time, my kids were all aware of how I loved charismatic churches, and she told me she thought I'd like this place. She was right. Legacy Church was right up my alley! She had actually seen video clips of the pastor, Mark Wagnon, on TikTok and had started following him. She loved him so much, but for some reason assumed he wasn't a local pastor. When she found out his church was right here in Greenville, she visited it and loved it. We went for several weeks, and I really enjoyed the sweet Spirit there and the anointed worship and sermons. I decided to keep going and eventually started bringing Mom with me, and she loved it too. I think it reminded her of Tabernacle with the clapping and shouting they used to enjoy there. When I was growing up, I never remember her raising her hands in church. My dad did all the time, and he would shout and praise God freely with such joy. But Mom was always very reserved and quiet. Well, let me just say—not anymore! I couldn't believe my eyes, but she was actually raising her hands and saying, "Amen!" She still does, every Sunday.

I wasn't sure what denomination this church was or if it was non-denominational. It didn't specify anything in the name of the church, so I kept wondering about it. I could tell it was charismatic, and there was an emphasis on the prophetic, but I wondered what it actually was. One Sunday, a man wearing a suit was called to the stage. Dress is generally casual in my church, so that was strange. He was introduced as a superintendent, and then they said the words "Church of God of Prophecy," and I almost fell over! I also almost burst out laughing! I could not believe my mom and I were sitting here in a Church of God of Prophecy and actually loving it. I'm not sure what I thought one would be like, but it wasn't this. I think I probably imagined old-school Pentecostal with maybe just a piano on the stage, and a few snake handlers. But this church was so similar to what I was used to, even the non-charismatic churches I'd been to. I'm telling you, there really is very little difference between all of them, and it's just so sad to me how we have walled ourselves off from each other. I am pretty sure this is exactly what the enemy wants.

Semantics

I have to admit I was a little weirded out when I first heard someone called "Apostle." But the more I've learned about this, the more I laugh at the fear I had. "Apostle" literally means "sent one," and we have these in every church I know of, charismatic or not. They may be called missionaries, church planters, or vision pastors. I just wasn't used to hearing them called "apostles." Again, I had always heard the only apostles were the disciples plus Paul. To get that title someone had to actually see Jesus. But I can't find this in Scripture, and since the word means "sent ones" I'm not sure why we would think we don't have "sent ones" today or why the Spirit would stop sending people. But it does make sense the enemy might convince us that the Church

Last, But Definitely Not Least

doesn't need prophets or apostles anymore so we don't focus on them. If the five-fold ministry Paul mentioned in Ephesians 4 was established and gifted to 'believers' for us to become equipped and strengthened to maturity, then removing or minimizing some of them seems like a pretty good strategy for the enemy.

In non-charismatic churches, we also have people who are gifted prophetically but again we don't use that terminology and sadly, we discourage people from leaning into that gifting. I know the word "prophecy" might freak some people out, so let me just clarify this—I'm not talking about fortune-telling or declaring the date of the second coming of Christ. That's what I thought of modern day prophecy. But it's nothing like that. Speaking prophetically just means you're saying what God wants you to say, and most of the non-charismatic Christians I know do this frequently. They just don't call it "prophecy." When a pastor stands in the pulpit, he's telling us what God has given him to say. He's sharing God's heart with us, and if it's truly a message from God, then there's a good chance he's being "prophetic." When you send a note to a friend, and you ask God what to say, then feel led to write out a specific verse for them, it might be considered prophetic. Learning to listen for the leading of the Spirit, then saying what He tells you to say—that's what being prophetic is all about. And now that I'm aware of all this, I can clearly discern when someone is preaching, but it's NOT necessarily prophetic.

I'll tell you what I mean. The best way I know to describe non-prophetic preaching is it's heavily cerebral and very knowledge-based. It's basically good teaching, and there is a place for that (remember "teachers" are listed in Ephesians 4). It's taking the Word of God and breaking it down into bite-sized pieces, and then adding some life-lessons or good illustrations. Some teachers are highly gifted at this, and I love sitting under their teaching. But that's exactly what it is . . . it's teaching, but it isn't necessarily prophetic. The danger in this is it often isn't enough. Man's interpretations of Scripture are just his thoughts, and those can fall flat. It also carries a potential danger, in that, the more knowledge we get, the prouder we become. "Knowledge puffs up" (1 Corinthians 8:1, ESV). We've all been in churches where it was clear everyone had been under good teaching for a long time. The levels of knowledge were impressive, but the level of love was lacking, and the anointing of God was altogether absent.

On the other hand, when someone has the Spirit's anointing on them, and the Spirit is guiding their words, something supernatural happens in the heart of the hearer. A hundred people can be hearing the same guy, but the Spirit is speaking to hearts and applying it specifically to each individual's life. There's not a human on this planet who can do that! It only comes from the Spirit's anointing. The charismatic churches I've been in have a strong emphasis on being led by the Spirit of God and anointed by Him to speak words which go straight to a person's heart.

I was surprised to learn many famous preachers I had always respected were actually firm continuationists, and some spoke boldly about it. One of my favorite authors is Andrew Murray. My dad once gave me a set of Murray's "pocket books" on the secrets of the Christian life, and told me to dig deep into their treasures. I did, and I still cherish those little books. I was happy to find out Andrew Murray was a bold voice for continuationist theology and taught extensively on the fullness of the Spirit. John and Charles Wesley were also strong voices on the subject, but my biggest surprise was when I read about Charles Spurgeon. A well-known Baptist preacher from England, Spurgeon told stories in his autobiography that would shock many who love him. Although he didn't consider himself prophetic, he was actually given words of knowledge by the Holy Spirit on many occasions, exposing the secrets of people's hearts even while he was preaching. Once he suddenly stopped in the middle of a sermon, pointed to a man and said, "Young man, those gloves you are wearing have not been paid for. You have stolen them from your employer." And later the young

Last, But Definitely Not Least

man told Spurgeon he had indeed stolen them, and was going to make things right. Spurgeon told other similar stories and stated that these supernatural revelations happened many times while he was preaching and were given by the Spirit to move people to repentance.[19] That is definitely operating in a prophetic gift of the Spirit.

In 1 Corinthians 14, Paul describes how this experience of having "secret thoughts exposed" will put a person on their knees. It's so true. I've experienced it myself, and I've witnessed it now many times. And speaking of 1 Corinthians 14, I have to say it is now fully highlighted in my Bible! The very first verse of the chapter following the famous love chapter actually tells us very clearly to "earnestly desire the spiritual gifts, especially prophecy." (I Corinthians 14:1, ESV). Isn't that interesting? How earnestly do you desire that gift? Has anyone ever even told you that you should? Well, Paul did, but if you're like me, you may have overlooked the little instruction.

Another powerful passage I discovered was 1 Thessalonians 5:20 (ESV) where Paul, under the inspiration of the Holy Spirit tells us, "Do not despise prophecies." And yet how many Christians do you know who definitely despise anything considered 'prophetic'? Also interesting to note is the verse preceding that one. 1 Thessalonians 5:19 (ESV) says, "Do not quench the Spirit." I'm pretty sure the two concepts go hand in hand, and multitudes of Christians, sadly, are guilty of both quenching the Spirit and despising prophecy.

I've actually learned to appreciate all things prophetic, and I have to say my mom does too. The little Baptist preacher's wife is not one bit concerned about being in a charismatic church or about it being a Church of God of Prophecy. She loves it, and I love seeing her worship with freedom and joy. It's absolutely precious. And I know my dad would love it too. He was a highly anointed preacher, and what I saw in him is what I recognize in the anointed messages I hear at my church. We just used different words to describe it.

Everywhere I Look

Leaning into the Prophetic

"You need to make sure you sign up for the Prophetic Encounter we're having!"

When one of my pastors told me this last year, I was immediately curious and you better believe I signed up for it. Remember I had told God that if prophets were walking this earth, I'd love to meet one, so I was ready to see what this was all about.

Ed Traut is a born-again Jew from South Africa, and he pastored for several years before he founded Prophetic Life Ministries. He's very local-church oriented and works through the church to train and equip believers in the prophetic. His ministry hosts these encounters, which are two-day discipleship training events. They travel to churches around the world, and they also have an academy for further teaching and training.

I came the first night, praying for an open heart and mind to receive all God wanted for me. Still battling cynicism, I really wanted to reject any Pharisaical arrogance, and fully lean into the Spirit's leading. But as soon as he started talking, I had questions. He had encouraged us to stop him and ask if we had questions, so it wasn't long before I raised my hand. He had just mentioned getting a word of knowledge, so I asked, "When you're getting 'a word' for someone, how does that feel in your mind? Is it a random thought just out of the blue, or does it go along with something you're discussing or you perceive about a situation?" His answer blew me away.

He paused, and walked close to me with an intrigued look on his face, and said, "Your problem is you're relying on your intellect. This isn't from your mind, it's from your spirit, where the Spirit speaks to you. But you tend to overthink and it's very difficult for people like you to empty your mind of your thoughts so God's thoughts can come in. You lay in bed at night trying to figure all this out, and you want to get it right."

At this point it's hard to describe what I was feeling, but I knew he

Last, But Definitely Not Least

was speaking under the power of the Spirit because his words were hitting me with an intensity I had never experienced. But then he went on to say, "You want to get it right because you've always gotten it right. You're a Daddy's girl, and he always thought you were perfect so perfection has always been your goal. You're afraid to say anything for fear that it's not perfect. But you have to get past the fear and just start stepping out. Just say it. Don't overthink."

I sat there in tears, trying to process what he had just said. This guy knew NOTHING about me. This word came straight from the Spirit of God, and it pierced my heart because it was so personal and so accurate. Later in the evening I asked the Spirit to help me remember it all, and I can tell you his answer today word for word because I wrote it down. Even now as I type this it brings me to tears again, which has always been a confirmation to me that I'm hearing from God. His voice makes my heart so sensitive and so tender toward Him. I think that's pretty common because, as we went through the prophetic encounter, it happened to everyone in the room. When Ed spoke a word from the Lord to someone it made them cry. I watched it over and over, and I was absolutely amazed.

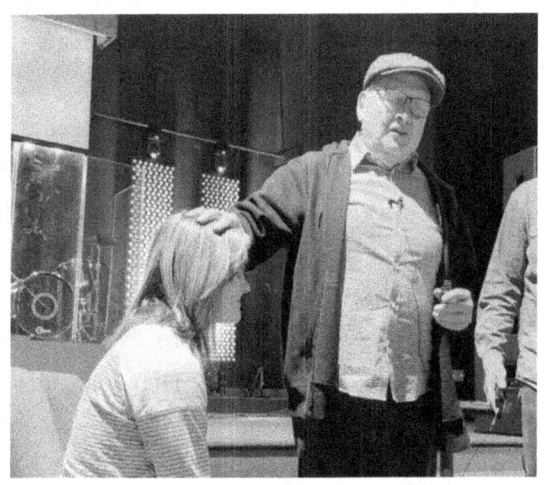

Prophetic Encounter with Ed Traut

Everywhere I Look

I could go on and on about that experience, because what I just described to you was only the first time God spoke to me during the encounter. It happened many times, and through that experience God confirmed to me several things I had been personally praying about. One of those involved an intercessory ministry I felt called to establish before the event, and God clarified the details of it during and after the event. I'm leaning into that calling in several ways now, and it's happening because I attended the event and truly encountered the Spirit of God during those sessions. By the end of those two days I was fully convinced this was completely for real. No more doubting. No more cynicism. No more quenching the Spirit. Those days are over for this girl.

And it's a good thing, actually, because do you know what God said would happen in the last days when He poured out His Spirit on all mankind?

He said our sons and daughters will prophesy! God told us this through the prophet Joel in the Old Testament (Joel 2:28), and He repeated it again to us through Peter in the New Testament (Acts 2:17). Peter was explaining to everyone that what Joel had prophesied was happening right there before their eyes. But the actual time frame of the prophecy was "the last days." And I'm pretty sure we are still in what's considered to be "the last days."

When God showed me this, I felt so convicted because I suddenly realized that in my stubbornness and resistance toward all of this, I was actually resisting the move of God in the last days. That's a very sobering thought.

New Wine, New Oil

The word "gethsemane" comes from the Hebrew word which means "oil press." The Garden of Gethsemane, where Jesus prayed on the night He was betrayed, is actually a grove of olive trees. Because of the meaning of that word, most people believe there was an olive press

Last, But Definitely Not Least

there, where olive oil was made. There is such beautiful symbolism in this. Just think of the pressure He felt that night. Just think of the "oil" which was produced. Olives are valuable, but when they are crushed, the oil that's produced holds even more value. In the same way, when we are "pressed"—when God allows us to experience the intense pressures of life—He also loves to produce new, valuable oil in the process.

Another word picture the Scriptures gives us is the stretching of the wineskins to hold new wine. Old wineskins become brittle and can't handle the fermentation process, but new, flexible wineskins can hold new wine.

God has used the "pressing" and the "stretching" in my life, to produce new oil and to hold new wine. This new alignment with the Spirit of God has rocked my entire world and has brought more healing than everything else put together. I've learned not only how to lean into the Spirit's words and guidance, but I can stand confidently now in His power and authority. We are called by God to be the hands and feet of Jesus in this world. This means we carry the resurrection power of the living Son of God in us, and we carry the authority of the Most High God. Not only does that enable us to live in victory, but we also bring His victory into every situation and to every person God brings along our path. The Spirit breathes life and power into our words and actions.

You actually wouldn't be holding this book in your hands if the Spirit hadn't taken me on this journey. God is the One who called me to write this book, but being my hard-headed self, I resisted Him for a very long time. I had every excuse lined up, and I told Him those excuses constantly. But He wouldn't let it go, so here we are!

And guess what God has brought to me through the writing of this book—even more healing! As I have looked back over my life and even looked back to the time before I was born, the 3D pictures of grace keep jumping out at me, and I've even connected dots where I had no idea I even needed to. God knew how good this whole process would be for me, and His Spirit convinced me to do it. He truly is the best therapist, and He has taken me through the most amazing journey of healing.

Building Bridges

I'm sure this is a lot to process, but I want to ask you to do something. If you are still questioning what I've said about the Spirit of God, please take time to sit with Him for a while and humbly ask Him about all of this. God wants all of us to walk in victory and experience the fullness of His Spirit. If there is more He wants to show you, I hope you'll be open to that.

Here's what I would encourage you to do: hold out both of your hands, open them up, and keep them open. Now try to have this posture about what I've said. Don't close your hands, fold your arms, and say, "Nope. She's got it all wrong." Ask God. Ask with open hands and an open heart and mind. Be willing to lean into what He says. Be teachable. And most of all, be humble, because God resists the proud, but guess what He promises to give to the humble . . .

GRACE.

Back to that 3D Image

During our monthly meeting, I recently discussed with my Sawubona sisters this strange phenomenon of having eyes to see what God's doing in our lives, and I gave them the analogy of the stereogram I mentioned in the introduction of this book. We looked at a couple of stereograms, and everyone stared intently at them, trying to see the 3D image. It was interesting to watch everyone's responses. Some people looked for a minute or two then excitedly shouted, "I see it!" Others kept trying and trying but they just couldn't see it. Some became really

Last, But Definitely Not Least

frustrated and said they had never been able to see these stupid things. Then I listened to them as they tried to help each other. They said things like, "Get it really close to your face, then slowly pull it away." Or "Try to look THROUGH it." Or "Let your eyes make it really blurry."

I told them to listen to what they were saying to each other and pay attention to the spiritual parallels. I heard one girl say to the person beside her, "If it starts to come into view, don't blink, it might go away." Another one said, "Sometimes you can see it, but then all of the sudden you can't see it." As one girl tried to help someone see it, another one said, "Don't you wish you could just make her see it?"

And I said, "Do you hear what we're all saying? We can give each other tips, and we can tell people what we see and what's working for us, but no matter how badly we want to, we just can't see it for them."

Then one of the girls named Lawanna spoke up and gave us a profound insight. She said, "I can't see this thing, and it's so frustrating. But I hear you all say you can see it and I believe you. I have to believe it's there, even though right now I can't see it." And we all sat there pondering the spiritual application of her words for a few minutes. Whew, that is powerful!

Just like we all wanted to help each other see the image, I want so badly to help you see the 3D image of God that has come into view for me. That's why I wrote this book. I want more than anything for the 3D image of God's grace to come clearly into your vision through the stories I've shared about my heritage and home, our highlands and heartaches, and our healing. I can see so clearly, the beautiful grace, as I look back on my parent's lives and their marriage, how God brought together two people from completely different worlds to create a family that would bring Him glory. I see it in the story of my dad's legacy as a minister and a father. I see it in the redemption of my brothers, from rebels to saints. I see it in the way God took me from brokenness to wholeness in Christ, and how He took my kids from painful places into realms of restoration and beauty. I wrote this so you could see all of this with me.

But I also wrote it so you can see the 3D image of God in your own story of grace. His goodness and mercy have been pursuing you too, and I hope it's coming into focus.

I wish I could see it for you, but I can't. You have to take it from here. When you start to see it, don't blink . . . Try to stay focused! When you desperately want to make someone see it, remember you can't, but the Spirit can. And when you're frustrated because you can't see a thing, trust those who are seeing clearly, and hold on to the truth that it's there. HE is there. Even when you can't see Him.

I'm praying for you. I'm cheering you on! And I'm asking God to help you see His beautiful grace in the story of your life . . .

Everywhere you look.

Epilogue

"So, I think this book is actually gonna have five parts instead of three."

I was verbally processing with Amber Olafsson, my cousin and editor for this book, and we were both watching it take shape. I had not written an initial outline, but I did have three big ideas I wanted to cover: my heritage, my family of origin, and my own faith journey. But as I started writing, it literally took on a life of its own. It just started coming into focus, much like the stereogram I described at the beginning.

I started realizing after writing several chapters, that I needed to break up the section about my family of origin into separate sections, our home and then our good times and our bad. So I did, and then I started working on titles for the different parts. The theme of looking and seeing started to emerge, and then I started also realizing I had some alliteration going with my "H words" . . . Seeing God in my heritage, home, and heartache. " A nod to my sweet daddy and his love for alliteration.

I didn't have a good H word for the good times, though. "Happy Times" didn't really convey it well. It wasn't about our happiness, but more like being on an upward trajectory, or an ascent. But that didn't give me an H word!

One morning during my coffee time with Jesus, I was studying and reading, with worship music playing in the background. I suddenly felt distracted from my reading by the song that was playing. It was very familiar, but I'd never stopped to listen to the lyrics. I turned back to my Bible reading, but felt like the Spirit wanted me to stop and listen to the lyrics. So I did. I actually looked them up on my phone so I could follow along.

And WOW! Those lyrics were amazing and I was completely undone. I got caught up for a few minutes in worship, and afterwards, I looked again at the title of the song. It was like the Spirit kept drawing my attention to it, and then suddenly it hit me. The name of the song is Highlands by Hillsong United. The subtitle is Song of Ascent, and the message of the song is that we can praise God in the highlands and in the heartaches. It may feel like we're descending in the natural world, but that's not the reality in the spirit realm. In the highlands and the heartaches, we are always gradually ascending if God is the treasure of our heart. I was so busy praising God for this truth it took a second for me to realize that right there was my H word! Highlands. Upward trajectory . . . song of ascent. If you don't know this song, please look it up. It's powerful.

I told Amber all of this in our conversation, and then I also told her it looked like there would be five parts to the book. She stopped me and said, "Charity, do you know the Biblical significance of the number five?"

I didn't. I knew seven was the number of perfection or completion and other numbers did have significance, but I couldn't remember what the number five symbolized. So she reminded me.

Grace. The number five represents GRACE! I wanted to scream and shout, "Look at You, God!"

I looked it up and read this about it:

"The number five symbolizes God's grace, goodness, and favor toward humans and is mentioned 318 times in Scripture. Five is the number of grace, and multiplied by itself, which is 25, is 'grace upon grace' (John 1:16)."

As I was finishing up Part 5, I kept having to add chapters. I felt like the book might end up having 20 chapters, and that actually shocked me. I couldn't believe there was that much to say. But then I needed a couple more chapters, and a couple more. Eventually it was clear I was going to finish up with 25 chapters. Completely unplanned. All of this was completely unplanned, but did you see what the number 25 signifies?

Grace Upon Grace!

This phrase actually means "a constant overflowing gift." It means that "as believers, we are constantly being inundated with the grace of God because of Jesus Christ."[21]

A constant overflowing gift. We are constantly inundated by it. In other words . . . the grace of God is EVERYWHERE.

It's very literally . . .
Everywhere We Look!

With my kids and grandchildren

Acknowledgements

This part overwhelms me. There are just too many to name. I have been blessed with some of the best family members, friends, mentors, and ministry partners on this planet. And I'm grateful for every single one of you! If I have already named you in this book, I won't do it again here. But please know I count you among my highest treasures.

A big, huge thank you to my kids and their spouses, my extended family members, and all of my friends who encouraged me to write down these stories of grace. I'm not sure if I would've had the courage to take on this project if you hadn't been cheering me on.

My co-workers at The Pearl Center surround me with grace every day. Lisa Clark, Suzanne Ringger, Linda Driscoll, Tiffany Hangen, Theresa Mettee, Lauren Kirk, Rosemary Houston, Noelle Knutson, Mary Ellen DeGarmo, and Karen O'Neal—you all are some of the 2D images revealing the goodness of God to me on a daily basis. You make going to work a joy, even on our hardest days. Your love and support have seen me through some of my most challenging seasons, and from the bottom of my heart, I thank you.

To all of the Renewal Ladies of Miracle Hill Ministries who have taken our cognitive development classes (lovingly referred to as "Dot to Dot"), I want you to know you have taught me way more than I ever taught you. I'm in awe of your courage, perseverance, and determination. And I'm especially amazed by your infectious love for God. Thank you for showing me how to do hard things for the glory of God!

To my Sawubona Sisters, God has used you all to teach me what it looks like to live authentically in community. Traci Newkirk, Michelle Alvarez, Sheila Hardin, Amy Baron, Karen Boyd, Michelle Brown, Christy Burke, Tiffney Davidson-Parker, Tracey Brown, Lawanna Dendy, Meredith Fossing, Suzanne Hayes, Jane Habich, Vicki Webb, Tracey MacDonald, Jill McNamara, Sherry Marks, and Renee Stovall—thank you for your love, your wisdom, and your grace. And for a million great memories!

Special thanks to some of the ministries that have poured into my story of grace. Legacy Church, Pastor Mark & Jennifer Wagnon and Pastor Dillon Mantooth—thank you for welcoming me and my gang into your church family.

Metka & Goran Macura, Zvonko & Dubravka Turinski, and Randy & Joan Bell, your love for Slovenia and your ministries there changed my life. Thank you for the privilege of serving with you in that beautiful country and in your amazing kids' camp in Croatia.

Sonny & Sheila Horton, the Beech Springs Mission Team, and Enrique & Jackie Valdez—thank you for giving me the opportunities of serving with you in Roatan, Honduras. They were life-changing experiences for me. Hermann Alb and the Medical Missions Ministries in Guatemala, your teaching and influence were powerfully used by God in my life. Thank you for serving Him so faithfully and for demonstrating to me the power of the Holy Spirit.

Gary and Sherry Williams, thank you for opening your home to me, for sharing sweet stories of my brothers and my family, and for cheering me on in this project. Your help and encouragement were invaluable, and I'm very grateful. Phyllis and James, thank you for taking the trip with me to their home. That experience was sweet on so many levels, and it boosted my excitement for this book.

Amber Olafsson and Jessica Russell, you guys have been the best editors ever! You've gone way beyond editing, to give me wisdom and guidance and to cover me with prayer. The writing retreat you provided for April Knopp and myself helped us both navigate the tricky waters of becoming an author and gave us courage and joy in the process. A million thanks to both of you. Amber, it has been especially sweet to have you, as my cousin, review our family's history and help me write about it. All glory to God!

Thank You, Jesus, for Your unconditional love and for Your amazing grace. Thank You for bringing all of this into focus and revealing Yourself to me. This is for You.

"Now to Him who is able to do far more abundantly than all that we ask or think, according to the power at work within us, to Him be glory in the church and in Christ Jesus throughout all generations, forever and ever. Amen" (Ephesians 3:20-21 ESV).

Notes

1. Lewis, C.S. Preface. The Screwtape Letters, Fleming H. Revell Company, 1976, p. 17

2. Piper, Barnabas. *The Pastor's Kid: Finding Your Own Faith and Identity*. David C. Cook Publishing, 2014

3. Carmichael, Amy. "In Acceptance Lieth Peace." New Things, 2013. https://newthingspringingforth.wordpress.com/2013/05/07/in-acceptance-lieth-peace.

4. Oswald Chambers, *My Utmost for His Highest, Updated Edition*, "The Secret of the Lord." June 3 Entry (Grand Rapids, MI: Discover House Publishers,1992)

5. Tan, Author Calvin. "Only One Life: By C.T. Studd." Inspire To Pray, August 13, 2021. https://inspiretopray.com/2021/08/13/only-one-life-by-c-t-studd/.

6. Vernick, Leslie. *The Emotionally Destructive Marriage: How to Find Your Voice and Reclaim Your Hope* . Colorado Springs, Colorado: Waterbrook Press, 2013.

7. "Power and Control." The Hotline, July 4, 2023. https://www.thehotline.org/identify-abuse/power-and-control/.

8. Flint, Annie. "The Red Sea Place." Poetry Nook. Accessed September 7, 2024. https://www.poetrynook.com/poem/place-sea.

9. Young, Sarah, and Katya Longhi. *Jesus calling*. Nashville, TN: Tommy Nelson, 2023.

10. Muller, George. "Trials Are the Very Food of Faith." George-Muller.org, 2015. https://www.georgemuller.org/quotes/trials-are-the-very-food-of-faith.

11. Furman, Gloria. "Kissing the Wave." Web log. *Desiring God* (blog), September 10, 2013. https://www.desiringgod.org/articles/kissing-the-wave.

12. Church, Harmony. "Fan or Follower." Harmony Community Church, 2024. https://www.harmonycc.org/podcast/fan-or-follower/.

13. *rope illustration*. Accessed 2024. https://youtu.be/86dsfBbZf-Ws?si=API8qpDYOqvvrW8A.

14. Cook, Christopher. *Healing what you can't erase: Transform your mental, emotional, and spiritual health from the inside out*. Colorado Springs: WaterBrook, 2024.

15. Kelley, Lee. "4 Phases of Healing after a Divorce." OMG Law Firm, September 14, 2022. https://www.omglawfirm.com/4-phases-of-healing-after-a-divorce/.

16. Levi, Allen. *Theo of golden: A novel*. Hamilton, GA: Allen Levi, 2023.

17. Staff, Loom. "Sawubona!" Loom International, August 14, 2020. https://www.loominternational.org/sawubona/#:~:text=It%20literally%20means%20%E2%80%9CI%20see,and%20weaknesses%2C%20and%20your%20future.

18. Townsend, John Sims. *People fuel: Fill your tank for life, love, and leadership*. Grand Rapids: Zondervan, 2019.

19. Deere, Jack S. *Why I am still surprised by the voice of God: How God speaks today through prophecies, dreams, and Visions.* Grand Rapids: Zondervan, 2022.

20. Watchman-Scribe, Posted by The. "Grace upon Grace." Scribe, August 22, 2017. https://watchmanscribe.wordpress.com/2017/04/10/grace-upon-grace/#:~:text=The%20number%205%20symbolizes%20God's,two%20sets%20of%205%20commandments.

21. "John 1:16." BibleRef.com. Accessed July 3, 2024. https://www.bibleref.com/John/1/John-1-16.html#:~:text=The%20Greek%20phrasing%20could%20be,to%20us%20to%20provide%20salvation.

About the Author

Charity has been an educator for over thirty years, serving in various capacities with a deep commitment to helping students thrive and become successful, independent learners. She is a Professionally Certified Educational Therapist, a Licensed FIE Practitioner, and a Structured Literacy/Dyslexia Specialist. Charity currently serves as the Program Director for The Pearl Center for Learning in Mauldin, South Carolina.

In addition to her professional work, Charity is deeply passionate about powerful and prophetic intercessory prayer and considers it a great honor to serve in the prayer ministry of her local community of faith, Legacy Church. She finds great joy in mentoring and discipling women, especially those who have come out of destructive relationships, helping them discover healing and hope through Christ. Along with several co-workers, Charity enjoys teaching cognitive development classes at a local center for women recovering from substance abuse. Charity also loves going on mission trips, where she gets to combine her heart for service, prayer, and encouragement. Whether through her work with students, mentoring women, or global missions, Charity has a special place in her heart for the hurting and a deep desire to see them find joy and purpose through a growing relationship with Jesus.

Some of Charity's favorite things are traveling, spending time with friends, eating Mexican food, and enjoying her favorite time of the day- mornings with Jesus, sipping a good cup of coffee! Above all, she loves making memories with her family and playing with her grandkids. Charity's greatest desire is to make a difference for the Kingdom and to share her passion for seeing God *everywhere we look*.

www.ingramcontent.com/pod-product-compliance
Lightning Source LLC
Chambersburg PA
CBHW070127080526
44586CB00015B/1595